3 4028 08003 7543
HARRIS COUNTY PUBLIC LIBRARY

D1226419

Bloom's Modern Critical Interpretations

The Adventures of Huckleberry Finn
The Age of Innocence
Alice's Adventures in Wonderland
All Quiet on the Western Front
Animal Farm
Antony and Cleopatra
The Awakening
The Ballad of the Sad Café
Beloved
Beowulf
Black Boy
The Bluest Eye
The Canterbury Tales
Cat on a Hot Tin Roof
Catch-22
The Catcher in the Rye
The Chronicles of Narnia
The Color Purple
Crime and Punishment
The Crucible
Cry, the Beloved Country
Darkness at Noon
Death of a Salesman
The Death of Artemio Cruz
The Diary of Anne Frank
Don Quixote
Emerson's Essays
Emma
Fahrenheit 451
A Farewell to Arms
Frankenstein
The Glass Menagerie
The Grapes of Wrath
Great Expectations
The Great Gatsby
Gulliver's Travels
Hamlet
Heart of Darkness
The House on Mango Street
I Know Why the Caged Bird Sings
The Iliad
Invisible Man
Jane Eyre
John Steinbeck's Short Stories
The Joy Luck Club
Julius Caesar
The Jungle
King Lear
Long Day's Journey into Night
Lord of the Flies
The Lord of the Rings
Love in the Time of Cholera
Macbeth
The Man Without Qualities
The Merchant of Venice
The Metamorphosis
A Midsummer Night's Dream
Miss Lonelyhearts
Moby-Dick
My Ántonia
Native Son
Night
1984
The Odyssey
Oedipus Rex
The Old Man and the Sea
On the Road
One Flew over the Cuckoo's Nest
One Hundred Years of Solitude
Othello
Persuasion
Portnoy's Complaint
Pride and Prejudice
Ragtime
The Red Badge of Courage
Romeo and Juliet
The Rubáiyát of Omar Khayyám
The Scarlet Letter
A Separate Peace
Silas Marner
Slaughterhouse-Five
Song of Solomon
The Sound and the Fury
The Stranger
A Streetcar Named Desire
Sula
The Sun Also Rises
The Tale of Genji
A Tale of Two Cities
The Tempest
"The Tell-Tale Heart" and Other Stories
Their Eyes Were Watching God
Things Fall Apart
The Things They Carried
To Kill a Mockingbird
Ulysses
Waiting for Godot
The Waste Land
Wuthering Heights
Young Goodman Brown

Bloom's Modern Critical Interpretations

William Shakespeare's

Antony and Cleopatra

New Edition

Edited and with an introduction by

Harold Bloom

Sterling Professor of the Humanities

Yale University

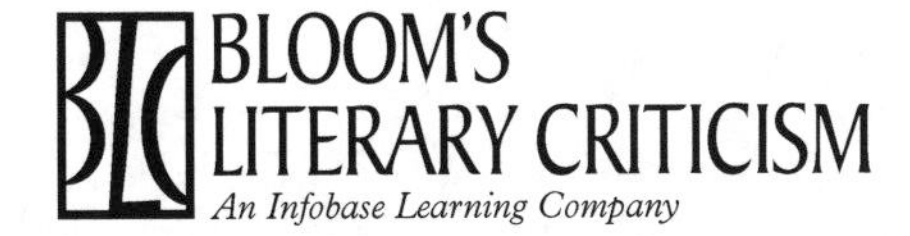

Bloom's Modern Critical Interpretations: Antony and Cleopatra—New Edition

Bloom's Literary Criticism
An imprint of Infobase Publishing
132 West 31st Street
New York NY 10001

Library of Congress Cataloging-in-Publication Data
William Shakespeare's Antony and Cleopatra / edited and with an introduction by Harold Bloom. — New ed.
p. cm. — (Bloom's modern critical interpretations)
Includes bibliographical references and index.
ISBN 978-1-60413-359-2
1. Shakespeare, William, 1564–1616. Antony and Cleopatra. 2. Cleopatra, Queen of Egypt, d. 30 B.C.—In literature. 3. Antonius, Marcus, 83?–30 B.C.—In literature. 4. Egypt—In literature. 5. Rome—In literature. I. Bloom, Harold.
PR2802.W55 2011
822.3'3—dc22
2010047664

Bloom's Literary Criticism books are available at special discounts when purchased in bulk quantities for businesses, associations, institutions, or sales promotions. Please call our Special Sales Department in New York at (212)967-8800 or (800)322-8755.

You can find Bloom's Literary Criticism on the World Wide Web at http://www.chelseahouse.com

Contributing editor: Pamela Loos
Cover design by Takeshi Takahashi
Composition by IBT Global, Troy NY
Cover printed by Yurchak Printing, Landisville, Pa.
Book printed and bound by Yurchak Printing, Landisville, Pa.
Date printed: April 2011
Printed in the United States of America

10 9 8 7 6 5 4 3 2 1

This book is printed on acid-free paper.

Contents

Editor's Note

My introduction centers on Shakespeare's mastery of the heterocosm he created in the play, perhaps his final tragedy to display such intensity of invention. J. Leeds Barroll concedes that the partial setting of the play is a hypothesis, a Rome of the mind reflecting the realities of Shakespeare's world. Michael Goldman then addresses the way notions of greatness are generated in the play and represented by its title characters.

Northrop Frye ascribes the play's increasing relevance to the fact that it conjures a world more like our own than Shakespeare's. Jonathan Gil Harris then notes the ways *Antony and Cleopatra* takes up Elizabethan notions of narcissism and desire.

Susan Snyder examines the intersection of metaphor and motion in the play and in *Macbeth*, after which Thomas M. Greene revisits the pressure Shakespeare's Plutarchan source exerts on the play.

Patricia Parker returns to the contemporary resonances contained in Shakespeare's Roman representations. Alan Stewart concludes the volume by looking at the interrelations of history, narrative, and documentation in the play.

HAROLD BLOOM

Introduction

Cleopatra is endless in her variety, as Enobarbus rightly says. Her personality is as richly expressive as Falstaff's, and hers is the most challenging role for an actress in all of Western drama. So dazzling is she that she eclipses Antony, who in most Shakespearean plays would be the dominant characterization. It is the perpetually changing glory of *Antony and Cleopatra* that the public world, from Rome to the Parthian border, constitutes a third prevailing presence in this overwhelming play. That may be why Shakespeare gives us so major an ellipsis: We never see Cleopatra and Antony alone onstage together, free of their entourages. There is one moment only in the wings, when Antony is rightly furious at her pragmatic treachery, but it tells us nothing about their intimacy.

Treachery is quite mutual between Cleopatra and Antony, since their relationship is as much political as it is erotic. Each is aging, though Antony's tendency to decline is sharper in its way down and out than Cleopatra's, since she shares with Falstaff a gallant denial of time. Bewildered by his own falling fortunes, Antony at last doubts his own identity. Cleopatra's inner self, for all her outward metamorphoses, keeps her vision of herself constant.

Shakespeare, from *Romeo and Juliet* onward, covertly invents a new meaning of eros, which is that it comes into being when desire is death. At the drama's close we have to understand that their authentic mutual love has destroyed both the protagonists. Cleopatra's self-staged death has a sublimity denied to Antony's since his bungled suicide repeats his developing ineptitude throughout. The impression that Cleopatra has been sustaining Antony hardly can be avoided. His end crosses tragedy with pathos; hers is wonderfully stylized and goes beyond tragedy.

Shakespeare's mastery of the heterocosm he creates in this play is astonishing, even for him. Something vital in the dramatist is lavished here, and he will not again write tragedy with this intensity of invention. The contrast between *Antony and Cleopatra* and *Coriolanus* is startling. Exuberance of being, the wonder of Cleopatra and of Antony, is wholly absent from the great killing machine and mother's boy Coriolanus. Personality makes a last stand in *Antony and Cleopatra* and expands until it bursts. Even Prospero, the magus of *The Tempest*, lacks the energetic overflow that goes from Falstaff through Cleopatra.

Huge as *Antony and Cleopatra* is, nothing in it can be spared. Rammed with life, for me it competes with *Henry IV, Part 1* as Shakespeare's most comprehensive work. I cannot judge which drama is wealthier, since both cover a cosmos, mixing politics, warfare, and the personal into an amalgam that baffles our analytical powers. Only Hamlet is worthy to stand with Falstaff and Cleopatra as a total consciousness. Iago is veiled, even from himself, and Lear transcends our apprehension, as do his Fool and the enemy brothers, Edmund and Edgar.

Shakespeare's supremacy over all other writers, even Dante, Cervantes, and Tolstoy, is evidenced in virtually every scene of this vast play. Every production I have attended has travestied it. Is there no director who will allow Shakespeare to be Shakespeare? High-concept directors have no hope of attaining Shakespeare's conceptual abundance, and the consequences are dismal. Since Cleopatra is a self-dramatizer, hers is as difficult a part to play well as any in Shakespeare. Antony's role is scarcely simpler. His personality is not as infinite, but the aesthetic beauty of his descent from grandeur into pathos demands an artistry very rare even in major actors. And the third protagonist, the struggle between East and West, has a prophetic quality that is disturbing for us at this time when Islam and the West move toward a disaster of confrontation.

As with *Henry IV, Part 1*, this play is supremely comic, depending on the reader's own perspective. If you want to regard Falstaff as only a rancid old roisterer, the loss is entirely yours. Should you behold Cleopatra as a royal whore and Antony as her decadent gull, the splendor squandered is again your own. Shakespeare offers his audience everything, on many levels, as do his peers Dante and Cervantes or, in another mode, Montaigne. No creator ever has been less tendentious; he has no design on you. He holds the mirror up not only to what is natural in you but to your occult or secret self, you own genius or daemon. *Antony and Cleopatra* may be the largest of those mirrors and the most salutary in this bad time.

J. LEEDS BARROLL

The View from out of Rome

I

Form is a hard master and, in some ways, dramatic form may be the hardest of all—at least for imparting those values by which we are asked to judge the lives we have witnessed on stage. The means available are limited: only the actors speaking lines. They can, it is true, enact vignettes which make ethical points—we have seen these—but if an *Antony and Cleopatra* holds many such moments making many different and even contradictory points, where are we then? Or if the small lives of the background figures ruefully show us only how to trip ourselves up, what can we learn that is affirmative? "This is not the way to live," to be sure. But then, how to live instead?

Bringing out an actor to recite a sermon signed by Shakespeare is not allowed in this kind of drama, and although some of his forebears and contemporaries may have been driven to something approaching this, Shakespeare himself seems to have stayed within his form. He avoided formal chorus or the obviously preaching figure and instead wove "statement" into the very structure of his make-believe. And nothing more clearly suggests this weaving in *Antony and Cleopatra* than the constant reminder of a specific refrain.

It is a tone recalling those resonances we feel at the repeated sounds of "fool" and "folly" in the world of *King Lear*, of "heaven" and "hell" in *Hamlet*, of "blood" and "sleep" in *Macbeth*. Truly the remarks of small and large figures alike in those three tragedies project us into *topos*, into echoes of traditional

---

From *Shakespearean Tragedy: Genre, Tradition, and Change in* Antony and Cleopatra, pp. 243–78.

aphorisms. But if "fool," "hell," and "blood" are obvious ethical and cultural clues to *Lear*, *Hamlet*, and *Macbeth*, the *topos* expressed, developed, and shared by the people of *Antony and Cleopatra* is more evasive. The sentiment lacks, at least, an immediate and gripping application to the urgent businesses in hand.

Antony reacts to his wife Fulvia's death early in the play.

> There's a great spirit gone! Thus did I desire it.
> What our contempts doth often hurl from us,
> We wish it ours again, The present pleasure,
> By revolution low'ring, does become
> The opposite of itself. She's good, being gone.
> (1.2.122–26)

So Antony in Egypt. Several scenes later Sextus Pompeius arrives to tell us of his hopes for defeating the triumvirate, and his scene begins with this conversation between himself and the pirate Menecrates:

> *Pom.* If the great gods be just, they shall assist
> The deeds of justest men.
> [*Mene.* F1] Know, worthy Pompey,
> That what they do delay, they not deny.
> *Pom.* Whiles we are suitors to their thrones, decays
> The thing we sue for.
> *Mene.* We, ignorant of ourselves,
> Beg often our own harms, which the wise pow'rs
> Deny us for our good; so find we profit
> By losing of our prayers.
> (2.1.1–8)

The motif surfaces yet again in that scene when Rome learns of the death of Antony:

> *Caes.* The gods rebuke me but it is tidings
> To wash the eyes of kings.
> [*Agr.*] And strange it is
> That nature must compel us to lament
> Our most persisted deeds.
> (5.1.27–30)

The appearance of this ancient motif—the vanity of human wishes—presents a viewpoint which seems to melt together in the heat of relativity the strong beliefs and desires animating the conflicts of Shakespeare's Roman tragedy.[1] If regret always does attend upon the fulfilling of our wishes, then wanting in itself must become suspect. The hints are a dilemma. If we never know what we should want, and if, indeed, to get is merely to grasp a handful of ashes, then what should we desire in life if we wish "to do the right thing"?

But we cannot say that Shakespeare's drama, in its moral cast, is really a variation on this theme of vanity in human wishing—this and nothing else. Those remarks, shared as they are by various persons in the play, do remind us, it is true, that we never quite know, we fallible humans, why we want what we want, and it is certainly important to be aware of the existential futility of all the highly cherished contests we have observed in *Antony and Cleopatra.* But judging what arises through the authorial use of still other techniques in this drama, it appears that we are not to be allowed the luxury of some soft, general, world-weary, and perhaps ignorant, cynicism. For Shakespeare cuts through the mimetic surface of the tragedy with a traditional technique from earlier drama.[2]

This was a way often employed rather woodenly. A morality play would show quasi-biblical activity on stage; then a character would cite the relevant verses from Scripture, words and stage action both pointing to a biblical locus whose doctrinal relevance was well known. Later, especially in Shakespeare, such allusions were more elliptical, less heavy-handed. Claudius, a brother, speaks of the "primal eldest curse" surrounding his act of fratricide in *Hamlet* and thus reminds, us of the various scriptural significances of Cain's crime beyond that of literal murder. "Fratricide," perhaps, as a symbol of man's murderous aggression against his own kind, as illustrated by the slaying of Remus by Romulus to found the greatest earthly power in history.

But often such references to cultural or scriptural *idées reçues* were presented in language which, to be understandable, could not be taken so literally. Rather, metaphor and paradox, literally incomprehensible but figuratively suggestive, seemed to give signals. So Shakespeare's porter in *Macbeth* is either insane as he talks of hell while he is tending the gate of Macbeth's castle, or he is to be understood figuratively and tangentially. And it is in a similar fashion that Shakespeare takes another, porter-like figure, a "simple countryman" suggested by Plutarch as the carrier of death to Cleopatra, to make him into a weaver of figures and tropes which are often the same kind of nonsense if conceived literally.

> *Cleo.* Hast thou the pretty worm of Nilus there
> That kills and pains not?
> *Clow.* Truly I have him but I would not be the party that should desire you to touch him, for his biting is immortal; those that do die of it do seldom or never recover.

Cleo. Remember'st thou any that have died on't?
Clow. Very many, men and women too. I heard of one of them no longer than yesterday, a very honest woman—but something given to lie, as a woman should not do but in the way of honesty—how she died of the biting of it, what pain she felt. Truly, she makes a very good report o'th'worm; but he that will believe all that they say, shall never be sav'd by half that they do. But this is most falliable, the worm's an odd worm.
Cleo. Get thee hence, farewell.
Clow. I wish you all joy of the worm.
[*Setting down his basket.*]
Cleo. Farewell.
Clow. You must think this, look you, that the worm will do his kind.
Cleo. Ay, ay, farewell.
Clow. Look you, the worm is not to be trusted but in the keeping of wise people; for indeed there is no goodness in the worm.
Cleo. Take thou no care, it shall be heeded.
Clow. Very good. Give it nothing, I pray you, for it is not worth the feeding.
Cleo. Will it eat me?
Clow. You must not think I am so simple but I know the devil himself will not eat a woman. I know that a woman is a dish for the gods, if the devil dress her not. But truly, these same whoreson devils do the gods great harm in their women; for in every ten that they make, the devils mar five.
Cleo. Well, get thee gone, farewell.
Clow. Yes, forsooth. I wish you joy o'th'worm.[3] *Exit.*
(5.2.243–79)

The clown's talk is thus a tissue of seeming contradiction. People sometimes recover after they have "died." A woman who died can still speak. Women should only "lie" in an honest fashion. But by anachronistically mentioning the Devil, the "clown" does point for us a way. The devil was, by hoary tradition, a serpent. As Arthur Golding, translator of Shakespeare's Ovid, phrased matters:

> Yet have we one thing in ourselves and of ourselves,—even original sin, concupiscence, or lust—which never ceaseth to egg us and allure us from God and to stain us with all kind of uncleanness according

> as St. James sayeth. "Every man is tempted of his own lust." This is the breath of the venomous cockatrice which hath infected the whole offspring of Adam. This is the sting of that old Serpent.[4]

The bite of that old Serpent could "kill" in a sense which we often meet in discourses differentiating the death of the body from the "death" of the soul.[5] Isabella voiced this distinction in *Measure for Measure* when she refused Angelo's proposition of sexual intercourse as a way of saving her brother from execution.

> Better it were a brother died at once,
> Than that a sister, by redeeming him
> Should die for ever.
> (2.4.106–8)

So when Cleopatra asks the clown to specify the kind of people who "die" from such an "immortal" bite, he describes an appropriate type. Using various shadings of the Elizabethan term "honest"—respectable, truthful, or chaste—he alludes to one woman who, apparently, is "something given to lie."[6] She makes "a very good report o'th'worm," but, because she is a liar—or because of other kinds of "lying"—the reports of such as she should not be taken too seriously. In fact, "he that will believe all that they say shall never be saved by half that they do."

Despite Cleopatra's vain attempt to dismiss him here so that she can get on with her own theatrics, Shakespeare allows his clown to persist in telling the queen about "worms." The "worm" cannot act otherwise than is his nature: he is one "not to be trusted," for there is no "goodness" in him. It takes wisdom even to deal with him, and if Cleopatra is not one of those "wise people," she deals with him at her peril. "Will it eat me?" she asks as the imagery changes, suggesting the Devil when spoken of by Shakespeare's contemporaries as a predator of souls.[7] You must not think I am so simple, jokes the clown, "but that I know the devil himself will not eat a woman." But, he continues, when she is not a "dish" prepared by the "Devil," a woman is worthy of the gods.

When the simple countryman concludes that the devils, however, do manage to "mar" five out of every ten women created,[8] I think he alludes to the popular understanding of the parable of the Wise and Foolish Virgins who were, by tradition, supposed to be ten in number. The story itself, and its symbolism, are provocative because of the echoing metaphors in Cleopatra's own final speeches with her waiting women. Their "lamp is spent," they are for the dark, and death is to be a marriage. But of course the general significance of the parable itself moved in the direction opposite to that intended by the queen. For the biblical story in *Matthew* 25 of the virgins who awaited the coming of the Bridegroom with their lamps trimmed with oil was taken to suggest the state of the soul on Judgment Day. The five Foolish Virgins (the *fatues*) fell asleep while waiting, ran out of oil for their lamps, and were shut out of the marriage festival. In the tradition of biblical exegesis, all this activity was taken to refer to the idea of souls "asleep" in sin. The *fatues* had not reinforced their faith (the lamps) with works (the oil) or vice versa. They were thus denied the Bridegroom which was Christ.[9]

To follow the "simple" countryman there is, however, hardly need for such detail. It is enough to know that the parable of the Virgins was almost universally understood merely as a reference to Judgment Day. Christopher Sutton's *Disce Mori*, first published in 1600 and reprinted four times by 1609, discussed the art of dying well in these terms.

> It is time to arise from sleep. Our spring is fading, our lamp is wasting, and the tide of our life is drawing up little and little unto a low ebb. Whatsoever we do, our wheel whirls about apace.

Thus, later: "Foolish virgins think that their oil will never be spent." Why do we expect to live forever? The moisture in our lamps will last just so long "until at last the light goeth out, the lamp is spent, and so an end" (from the 1601 edition: sigs. Q2–R6^{v}).

Should Cleopatra convert, then, to Christianity? It does seem unlikely that this is the ethical emphasis of the tragedy. Rather, the remarks of the Egyptian peasant focus on the idea that there are other approaches to death and dying than those presented first by Antony and his Elysian Fields and then by Cleopatra with her upper-world of giants and gloaters speaking glorious blank verse. The simple countryman, as it were, broadens the discussion of the tragedy to go beyond the universe structured by Cleopatra and by Antony. The Clown recalls to us what snakes represent in other countries of the mind. Judgment Day parables, one gathers, might even be vaguely relevant, as well as the whole problem of all those who, like Dr. Faustus perhaps, give a good report of the worm. For "worms" and being "saved" in certain cases do not go together. The protagonists' anticipations about existential affairs—or perhaps their attitudes causing them so to anticipate—might need, according to the Egyptian countryman, to be compared to other versions of knowledge available perhaps not to Cleopatra but to Shakespeare's audience. The porter of Macbeth has become an Egyptian.

There are, perhaps, disadvantages in relying only upon cryptic speakers such as the Clown or the Porter to inculcate in an audience a particular moral attitude. In any event, Shakespeare used other "moral" techniques, if

I may be permitted the term. Such techniques do not point us to specifically biblical loci, however. Indeed, dramas written before Shakespeare was born show the use of what could be called "dramatic allusion" to remind an audience of well known moral or at least gnomic statements not in the Bible at all. A drama written in 1562 depicts the results of parting a kingdom between two rulers, deploring the deed. To this effect the audience is offered an initial dumb show enacting the elements of an Aesopic fable on the subject of strength-in-unity. Here are the stage directions for the beginning of this well-known tragedy.

> *The Order of the Dumb Show Before the First Act,*
> *and the Signification Thereof.*
>
> First, the music of violins began to play, during which came in upon the stage six wild men clothed in leaves. Of whom the first bare on his neck a fagot of small sticks, which they all, both severally and together, assayed with all their strengths to break; but it could not be broken by them. At the length, one of them plucked out one of the sticks, and brake it; and the rest plucking out all the other sticks one after another, did easily break them, the same being severed; which being conjoined, they had before attempted in vain. After they had done this, they departed the stage, and the music ceased. Hereby was signified that a state knit in unity doth continue strong against all force, but being divided, is easily destroyed.[10]

Dumb shows were not always necessary. A well-known *topos* with its illustration could emerge as part of the story activity. This seems strange but, in the end, it was dissimilar only in degree to some sequence which, in a modern film, might position the dead hero in some "accidentally" hanging position with his arms out, recalling crucifixion. Macduff, fresh from the atrocities of the malign king Macbeth, converses in England with Malcolm about Edward the Confessor's power not to harm but to heal. And what has that to do with the play? What indeed!

In *Antony and Cleopatra* similar sequences are articulated into the tragedy through episodes fashioned from the intellectual idiom of Shakespeare's own cultural milieu. They comment on one of the important obsessions of the play: war and empire. Thus, early in the play, when the triumvirate have come to terms with Sextus Pompeius, Enobarbus holds the stage alone with one of the two chief pirates who follow Sextus. "You and I have known, sir," the pirate Menas ventures to Enobarbus. "At sea, I think," he responds. And Menas: "We have, sir."

Eno. You have done well by water.
Men. And you by land.
Eno. I will praise any man that will praise me, though it cannot be denied what I have done by land.
Men. Nor what I have done by water.
Eno. Yes, something you can deny for your own safety: you have been a great thief by sea.
Men. And you by land.
Eno. There I deny my land service. But give me your hand, Menas; if our eyes had authority, here they might take two thieves kissing.
Men. All men's faces are true, whatsome'er their hands are. (2.6.86–97)

It was not especially vindictive for Enobarbus to call Menas a "thief." Shakespeare's was a pirate-conscious age which rarely romanticized raiders.[11] But what is interesting is Menas's rejoinder. And though Enobarbus, a soldier, denies his own thievish status humorously—for his own "safety" as he suggests Menas ought to—the soldier's metaphor confirms Menas. If their eyes were police, observes Enobarbus, they might now be able to arrest their clasped hands as thieves in the act of conniving. (Hamlet called hands "pickers and stealers," after the Bible.)

Enobarbus's is a very damaging admission, but not for him only. His role in the play has principally been defined by his association with Antony, and if Enobarbus's soldiering is to be regarded as thievery, one must remember for whom he works. More importantly this small episode—which is not drawn from Plutarch—strikingly resembles a popular anecdote concerning Alexander the Great. It was an anecdote illustrating the well-known argument in Saint Augustine's *City of God* which also appeared in Cicero's *De Republica* (lost to the Elizabethans, however, and preserved only in the *Somnium Scipionis* sequence, through Macrobius).

The argument had to do with the concept of Rome, its system of building an empire, and whether "Justice" could describe what Rome stood for. Augustine observes, in John Healey's translation of 1610:

> Set justice aside then, and what are kingdoms but fair thievish purchases? Because what are thieves' purchases but little kingdoms? For in thefts the hands of the underlings are directed by the commander, the confederacy of them is sworn together, and the pillage is shared by the law amongst them. And if these ragamuffins grow but up to be able to keep forts, build habitations, possess

> cities, and conquer adjoining nations, then their government is no longer called thievish, but graced with the eminent name of a kingdom, given and gotten not because they have left their practices, but because that now they may use them without danger of the law. For elegant and excellent was that pirate's answer to the great Macedonian Alexander who had taken him. The king asking him how he durst molest the seas so, he replied with a free spirit: "how darest thou molest the whole world? But because I do it with a little ship only, I am called a thief. Thou doing it with a great navy art called an emperor."

The similarity of this account to the incident created by Shakespeare is highly suggestive. The juxtaposition of soldier to pirate, together with the accusation by soldier and rejoinder by pirate are obvious echoes. Furthermore, no knowledge of Augustine was required of Shakespeare's audience, for this pirate anecdote had a wide circulation—through Gower, through Chaucer, through the *Gesta Romanorum*, and through other sources.[12] Its ubiquity derived from a general line of discussion in English writing from John of Salisbury through Sidney and Sir Walter Raleigh for which the Alexander episode was one of a number of traditional illustrations. And whether or not Augustine (with Cicero) was an ultimate source—Plato's *Republic* or Cicero's *De Officiis* being equally valid possibilities—the anecdote was part of the common and traditional argumentation in contemporary discussions on the philosophy of governing. Unless society be bound by the order of justice and benign rule, the argument went, the mode of governance becomes tantamount to the behavior of lawless thieves.

Fair names might well be used in such situations, went the argument, but these names are only masks attempting to hide the fact that it is avarice and ambition which are the true forces at work. Pierre de La Primaudaye, the French writer whose works were so popular in England, wrote typically in a chapter entitled "Of Ambition." As he discussed the societal ramifications of greed and ambition he mentioned, among others, the triumvirate of Octavius, Lepidus, and Antony. He went on to observe:

> And, in truth, howsoever they dissemble, they [ambitious princes] purposely war one with another, watching continually for means to surprise and overreach each other. But in outward show they use these two words of peace and war as a piece of money, according as it shall make best for their purpose, not for duty's sake, or upon reason and justice, but for their own profit and advantage, wickedly disguising in that manner the intermission and surceasing from

> the execution of their ill will and purpose with the holy name of justice and amity. Princes therefore must not think it strange if sometime private men (howbeit that doth not excuse them) find the like dealing profitable unto them, according as it falleth out for their purpose. For in so doing, they do but imitate and follow them that are their masters in all disloyalty, treason, and infidelity, thinking that he bestirreth himself who least of all observeth that which equity and justice require. Thus did Dionides the pirate fitly give Alexander the Great to understand when he asked of him why he troubled the whole sea and robbed every one. (sig. Q3)

The usual anecdote follows as La Primaudaye echoes Enobarbus that "All men's faces are true, whatsome'er their hands are."

The conversation between Enobarbus and the pirate was perhaps anticipated by Sextus Pompeius a few lines earlier as he quarreled with Antony.

> *Ant.* Thou canst not fear us, Pompey, with thy sails;
> We'll speak with thee at sea. At land, thou know'st
> How much we do o'ercount thee.
> *Pom.* At land indeed
> Thou doest o'er-count me of my father's house;
> But since the cuckoo builds not for himself,
> Remain in't as thou mayst.
> (2.6.26–31)

We are not likely to see Antony as a "thief," even though his soldier Enobarbus has agreed with the pirate Menas about the thievery inherent in his own "land service." What is happening, I think, is that the drama is setting the kind of activity that goes with being "Roman" in a particular and traditional ethical framework. And when Antony sees fit to participate in this "Romanness," he becomes tarred with that brush. Caesar's career in this drama has indicated in some detail what that means—and sometimes Antony is indeed like Caesar.

When "in Rome," Antony, for example, seems to have no qualms about doing such a thing as marrying Octavia for his "peace," even though he intends to desert her. Nor is it Caesar alone who pushes war between the two. Antony wants part of Caesar's conquests. Thus when, early in the play, Enobarbus is seeing things rather clearly, his clear seeing aligns him—at least for the brief moment—not with but opposite Antony. Maecenas is speaking conciliatory words to draw Caesar and Antony together from their estrangement.

Maec. If it might please you, to enforce no further
The griefs between ye: to forget them quite
Were to remember that the present need
Speaks to atone you.
Lep. Worthily spoken, Maecenas.
Eno. Or, if you borrow one another's love for the instant, you may, when you hear no more words of Pompey, return it again. You shall have time to wrangle in when you have nothing else to do.
Ant. Thou art a soldier only, speak no more.
Eno. That truth should be silent I had almost forgot.
Ant. You wrong this presence, therefore speak no more.
Eno. Go to, then—Your considerate stone.
(2.2.99–110)

The situation in which Antony is now involving himself in this return to Romanness is one which Ulysses described in *Troilus and Cressida* when he warned on what follows the ignoring of what he sees as "degree."

Force should be right, or rather, right and wrong
(Between whose endless jar justice resides)
Should lose their names, and so should justice too!
Then every thing include itself in power,
Power into will, will into appetite,
And appetite, an universal wolf,
(So doubly seconded with will and power),
Must make perforce an universal prey,
And last eat up himself.
(1.3.116–24)

Enobarbus thinks in these terms as he thinks of the fall of Lepidus.

Then, [world,] thou [hast] a pair of chaps—no more,
And throw between them all the food thou hast,
They'll grind [th'one] the other.
(3.5.13–14)

This concept is expressed in another way—again by activity whose prototype is the dumb show preceding *Gorboduc*. In Shakespeare's play it is the banquet of the triumvirate with Pompey. Attending are the pirates, as well as the "great fellows"—Enobarbus's term—and it is Enobarbus with Menas who devises the metaphor from the feast as we see the drunken Lepidus helped away by attendants.

> *Eno.* There's a strong fellow, Menas.
> *Men.* Why?
> *Eno.* 'A bears the third part of the world, man; seest not?
> *Men.* The third part then is drunk. Would it were all,
> That it might go on wheels![13]
> (2.7.88–93)

To speak of a world as drunk is to create wider matter for metaphor, as we are reminded not of chemical inebriation but of that spiritual "drunkenness" alluded to by such writers as Sir Thomas More, La Primaudaye, and others of Shakespeare's age who saw inebriation as a symbol of a psychological state.[14] It was that condition in which man was dazzled and unbalanced not with alcohol but with his own greeds and urgings.

The drunk begin a dance, usually a familiar paradigm of order, a *locus classicus* for Shakespeare's time on this point being John Davies's symbolic poem *Orchestra*.[15] But Ben Jonson's masques introduced the contrasting metaphor, the wilder dance which beat to disorder. And this is appropriate to Shakespeare's play where now pirates and kings join in antic dance. It suggests not the rhythms of justice and order which move to the music of the spheres described by Lorenzo in *The Merchant of Venice* but the drunken brokenness of the disharmony and disorder which is the Roman world.

> *Ant.* Come, let's all take hands,
> Till that the conquering wine hath steep'd our sense
> In soft and delicate Lethe.
> *Eno.* All take hands.
> Make battery to our ears with the loud music;
> The while I'll place you, then the boy shall sing.
> The holding every man shall [bear] as loud
> As his strong sides can volley.
>
> *Music plays. Enobarbus places them hand in hand.*
>
> THE SONG.
> Come, thou monarch of the vine,
> Plumpy Bacchus with pink eyne!
> In thy fats our cares be drown'd,

With thy grapes our hairs be crown'd!
Cup us till the world go round,
Cup us till the world go round!
(2.7.106–18)

Such is the glamour of "empire," and well may Menas the pirate tell Pompey that he has it in his power to become the earthly Jove. In the ambition and greed which is the drunkenness of this world, the prize appropriately belongs to the one who has no trouble slitting three throats. The audience is merely reminded here of what had always been said of the morality that was Rome.[16]

Are these instances subjectively imagined? It is so easy to make any dramatic sequence symbolic of anything. But in this kind of allusion, our hint is, I think, the busyness of the figures in the scene to call its archetypal quality to our attention. Parallels come to mind from another Shakespearean play. There is Gloucester's suicide attempt and his "miraculous" preservation. Here Edgar acts as our guide, insisting to Gloucester that his life is a "miracle" and that a devil stood next to the old man at the top of the "cliff." The Renaissance spectator would inevitably think of Christ's temptation in the wilderness to cast himself from the temple. God's angels, said Satan, would be quick to keep Christ from being injured, but Christ, we recall (as Milton recalled in his *Paradise Regained*), answered Satan that God must not be tempted to miracles. Presumably this background has some bearing on Gloucester's experience. Elsewhere, Edgar himself, naked and a fugitive, becomes through the words of Gloucester and other bystanders an archetype of all beggars, all fugitives. In *Macbeth* it is the physician who, watching Lady Macbeth's vain hand washing, indicates to us that she needs more the divine than the physician, thus placing her hand washing—if it ever needed to be placed—within the Christian context of sin and "absolution," or of Pilate's memorable moral evasion.

When he moves to such allusiveness, Shakespeare does not require our critical improvisations. There are always bystanders to alert us. The allusions themselves, however, we must, as twentieth-century readers, work to reconstruct from what we can learn of the everyday understandings of Shakespeare's contemporaries.

II

And so there is nothing? We have seen what passed for passion between famous lovers: in the end this was not a pattern of inspiration. Rome we also know. Is this then the sum of all: no truth but despair for the way humans are, no reassurance beyond the pessimism of the dreadful cheerfulness attending so many of the events we watch? Is there lacking here the reassurance that is the role of tragedy, leaving only placid cynicism, the shruggings of a Menas and an Enobarbus?

> *Eno.* Menas, I'll not on shore.
> *Men.* No, to my cabin.
> These drums, these trumpets, flutes! what!
> Let Neptune hear we bid a loud farewell
> To these great fellows. Sound and be hang'd, sound out!
> *Sound a flourish, with drums.*
> *Eno.* Hoo! says 'a. There's my cap.
> *Men.* Hoo! Noble captain, come. *Exeunt.*
> (2.7.130–35)

There is more than this, I think. Shakespeare moves to surmount the complex *disputatio* of his tragedy by invoking the fiat of the supernatural. Indeed, a superhuman being, when not involved in the dubieties clustered around the ghost of Hamlet's father, can have an ultimate authority. The supernatural can issue the flat imperatives denied the subtler and self-contradicting persons who inhabit the tragedies. Thus the audience of *The Winter's Tale* is convinced, even if Leontes is not, that the king is wrong to be jealous: no less an authority than the Oracle of Delphi has said so. Similarly, *Cymbeline* presents us Jupiter with a thunderbolt explaining matters to the lesser ghosts. A soothsayer interprets the "label" found on Posthumus's bosom after his dream. There are similar devices in *Antony and Cleopatra*. Typically, such speakers in the tragedy are never so definite as in these other instances, according, perhaps, with the relativistic sense which seems to permeate the drama. And, as with Cleopatra's "simple countryman," views are conveyed again elliptically, sometimes mysteriously.

> *They place themselves in every corner of the stage*
>
> *2 Soldier.* Here we. And if to-morrow
> Our navy thrive, I have an absolute hope
> Our landmen will stand up.
> *1 Soldier.* 'Tis a brave army,
> And full of purpose.
> *Music of the hoboys is under the stage*
> *2 Sold.* Peace, what noise?
> *1 Sold.* List, list!
> *2 Sold.* Hark!

1 Sold. Music i'th'air.
3 Sold. Under the earth.
4 Sold. It signs well, does it not?
3 Sold. No.
1 Sold. Peace, I say.
What should this mean?
2 Sold. 'Tis the god Hercules, whom Antony lov'd,
Now leaves him.
1 Sold. Walk; let's see if other watchmen
Do hear what we do.
How now, masters?
Omnes. (*speak together*) How now?
How now? Do you hear this?
1 Sold. Ay. Is't not strange?
3 Sold. Do you hear, masters? Do you hear?
1 Sold. Follow the noise so far as we have quarter;
Let's see how it will give off.
Omnes. Content. 'Tis strange. *Exeunt.*
(4.3.9–22)

Plutarch, in his rendering of this episode, did not give the name of the god who, in his account, was most probably Bacchus. That the spirit in this drama turns out to be Hercules is thus important.[17] But why? Leaving before one of Antony's battles, Hercules might seem to foreshadow military defeat, but, oddly, this was not the case. Hercules was here departing from the only one of the three battles Antony ever won! These are other than military foreshadowings. Indeed, Renaissance tradition established that Hercules was not a figure of combat but a symbol of other values.

He was a contradictory symbol. In one mode Hercules was that famous hero at the crossroads—celebrated later in Bach's cantata, *Hercules am Scheideweg*—who when faced with the temptation of choosing one of two roads pointed out by Voluptas and by Virtue, chose the latter. But this chooser of the road of Virtue had, as in Ben Jonson's *Pleasure Reconciled to Virtue*, made his own great error. This was in his subjugation to Omphale. Thus in English (and Continental) Renaissance literature and art Hercules was simultaneously the archetype of the "effeminate" thralldom to "incontinence" and also the hero who resisted these temptations of mind and body to follow a higher path. Thus Holbein's portrait of Erasmus shows him resting his hand on a book entitled in Greek "the labors of Hercules."[18] And so when Edmund Spenser wrote of Artegal and of the Aristotelian virtue of justice in Book 5 of the *Faerie Queene*, he celebrated Hercules in his opening stanza as the wielder of the club of justice. Yet when Artegal is enslaved by the Amazon Radegund, Spenser again invokes Hercules: but this time as the prototype of disgraceful bondage.[19]

Antony himself recalls this ambivalent Renaissance Hercules, and, I think, by Shakespeare's design.[20] At the beginning of the play Antony is with Cleopatra. This is not necessarily, by the standards of the drama itself, bad. But when there in Egypt he is also idle, self-indulgent. And when he is drawn from this activity back to Rome, his is not necessarily a return to honor, to justice, or to other virtues. He returns to the theft, hypocrisy, and greed that characterize the Roman world, the injustice against which Pompey so ineptly inveighs. Antony again departs, but again he does not leave Rome in pursuit of virtue. "I'th'East my pleasure lies," he tells us. And though he returns to Cleopatra he also returns to things which do not necessarily have much to do with her: self-indulgence, physical self-glorification, egoism: all nearer the *Voluptas* road than the road of Virtue which Hercules himself chose. Indeed, if Antony was ever "Herculean" in Egypt in any specific sense, it was according to Cleopatra's memory, when he wore her "tires and mantles" while she girded herself with his "sword Philippan." What could better recall Hercules's service to Omphale, when he wore women's clothes while she wore his lion's skin?

After his military defeat, Antony lapsed into mere irascibility, which led to the whipping of Thidias, a messenger, and to his offer of his own hostage in Caesar's hands to the same treatment. In this process he began to lose more than he had lost at Actium. Deluded, boastful, empty, he was not Hercules but, to Cleopatra, an Ajax—that traditional symbol of bloody loss of self-control. Blaming the unpleasant consequence of his delirious military thrashings—the last two battles—on Cleopatra, he moves from whipper to would-be murderer, flogged forward to a rage he compared to the burning of the poisoned robe of Nessus, urging by this his resemblance to Hercules. Hercules was journeying home from his amorous dalliance with Iole when he received this poisonous robe from his wife, Deianeira, who hoped it would act as a love charm. The resemblance fits ironically. Cleopatra hopes that word of her suicide will act as the love potion, for she is terrified by Antony's self-indulgent and blame-shifting rage. Hercules and Antony are similar in having caused their own mortal burnings.

It was prior to these events, on the night before the second battle, wherein Antony hoped to be "born again," to regain what he termed his "honor," that the Hercules of this play left Antony. And this Herculean departure was cosmic definition of the ethics of the battle Antony anticipated.

> I will be trebel-sinew'd, hearted, breath'd,
> And fight maliciously; for when mine hours
> Were nice and lucky, men did ransom lives

> Of me for jests; but now I'll set my teeth
> And send to darkness all that stop me.
> (3.13.177–81)

This was the boasting and merciless mood not of a Hercules, but of a *miles gloriosus* who is not very funny, of a Hercules gone mad, of a suicidal Ajax killing innocent sheep in spite.

If the supernatural Hercules, by his departure, reminds us of those concerns in human life which Antony forgets as he drives himself through tragedy, the Herculean avatar, leaving in night and mystery, is companioned in the drama with other mystery, with other manifestations. This is not merely one figure, such as Hercules, but nothing less than the whole order of events in the world. And perhaps this is appropriate. For Antony was living in a significant time for mankind, as Shakespeare's contemporaries saw it. The years were drawing near to an end of the ancient pagan world. The time of Christendom was at hand and the tragedy knows it. Cleopatra refers to Herod whose name we so often hear in the drama, and Caesar reminds us that

> The time of universal peace is near
> (4.6.4)

while, at the early beginnings of the tragedy, Charmian daringly hopes for a future such as this:

> Let me have a child at fifty, to whom Herod of Jewry may do homage.
> (1.2.28–29)

Throughout the drama we also hear much about what is called "fortune," of what, we remember from Boethius, was traditionally a mere aspect of the workings of Providence, itself the writer of history. In fact, Shakespeare also introduces an authority to tell the figures in the play about what men often call "fortune" and "chance." It is the soothsayer who, in the reality presented by this drama, assumes supernatural authority for us through the mysterious accuracy of his grave predictions.

> *Ant.* Say to me, whose fortunes shall rise higher,
> Caesar's or mine?
> *Sooth.* Caesar's.

He further specifies:

If thou dost play with him at any game,
Thou art sure to lose; and of that natural luck,
He beats thee 'gainst the odds. Thy lustre thickens
When he shines by.

Antony is quite irritated, but after he has dismissed the soothsayer and remains alone, he acknowledges:

Be it art or hap,
He hath spoken true. The very dice obey him,
And in our sports my better cunning faints
Under his chance. If we draw lots, he speeds;
His cocks do win the battle still of mine,
When it is all to naught; and his quails ever
Beat mine, inhoop'd, at odds.
(2.3.16–39)

Perhaps this "chance" was even applied by Shakespeare to the Battle of Actium. Scarrus, describing the circumstances of Cleopatra's flight, notes that it happened

i'th'midst o'th'fight,
When vantage like a pair of twins appear'd,
Both as the same, or rather ours the elder. . . .
(3.10.11–13)

Going beyond his Plutarchan source, it is as if Shakespeare made Actium conform to the kind of situation—equal "chance"—in which the soothsayer told Antony his opponent reigned supreme.

This general ideological context is also importantly pertinent to the soothsayer's words about Antony's and Octavius's games.[21] Curiously, some notions about God's Providence underlay many Renaissance English condemnations of dueling, of dice-play, and of certain kinds of ceremonial dependence on the use of "lots." For example, ceremonial dueling to prove the justice of a cause, as in *Richard II*, was viewed as an appeal to God's Providence. Consequently the fighter who had right on his side would triumph, despite, or because of, the accidents inherent in armed conflict.[22] On the other hand, dice-play and lot drawing were regarded as an abuse, because the participants were making games based on the principle of chance, thus prostituting God's Providence by playing, as it were, with destiny.[23]

Furthermore, it was just this way of thinking that underlay the Act to Restrain Abuses, a regulation well known to scholars of the Jacobean dramatic milieu. Promulgated in 1606, less than two years before *Antony and Cleopatra* was entered in the Stationers' Register, the act forbade the naming of the deity in stage-plays. Based on the same one of the Ten Commandments as was used to prohibit games of chance—the commandment against taking the Lord's name in vain—the statute stipulated

> If at any time or times, after the end of this present session of Parliament, any person or persons do or shall in any stage play, interlude, show, May-game, or pageant jestingly or profanely speak or use the holy name of God or of Christ Jesus, or of the Holy Ghost, or of the Trinity, which are not to be spoken but with fear and reverence, [such persons] shall forfeit for every such offense by him or them committed, ten pounds.[24]

Ten pounds was the average receipt for one play in an afternoon.

Although Elizabethan and Jacobean gamesters probably did not lose much sleep over the peril of playing with Providence in dice-games, the dice-play mentioned in *Antony and Cleopatra* seems significant. Everyone in Shakespeare's time understood from centuries of religious commentary that Augustus had been "destined" to unify the world, to order it for the birth of Christ; thus the idea of Providence being on Caesar's side was hardly absurd. And if Caesar, in Shakespeare's play, is not presented as the most virtuous of figures, there is no inconsistency here. Caesar could be extremely "fortunate," just as was, say, Tamburlaine, but in neither case was this fortune any guarantee of moral probity. If the dice games and cockfights could tell Antony—or a Jacobean audience—anything, they would warn that Caesar, whom "the very dice obey," had merely been marked out to be supreme in the gifts of Fortune. Indeed, what more could Fortune give than the whole world, which Caesar literally possesses at the end of the play? But though Joseph, the Virgin Mary, and Christ were to be Caesar's legal subjects, their lesser "Fortune" in the sublunary world was obviously no indication of their status.[25]

A particular sequence in Shakespeare's drama, finally, is quite interesting for its supernatural implications about dice and lots. Obscured for readers by the absence of a stage direction, the incident occurs when Pompey is meeting with the triumvirate in Sicily.

> *Pom.* We'll feast each other ere we part, and let's
> Draw lots who shall begin.
> *Ant.* That will I, Pompey.

> *Pom.* No, Antony, take the lot; but first
> Or last, your fine Egyptian cookery, etc.
> (2.6.60–63)

That Mark Antony, after the conversation with the soothsayer, wants no part of anything like lot drawing is understandable, but here the outcome is surprising. In the text the talk drifts away from lots to Egypt, but then, later, Pompey says to Enobarbus:

> Enjoy thy plainness,
> It nothing ill becomes thee.
> Aboard my galley I invite you all.
> Will you lead, lords?
> *All.* [*Caes., Ant., Lep.*]. Show's the way, sir.
> *Pom.* Come.
> (2.6.78–81)

It would be odd for Pompey here to seize a precedence he has just denied Mark Antony, so it would seem that lots have indeed been drawn—Plutarch and other historical sources available to Shakespeare certainly said so. But if the lottery was held, the results are strange. Caesar, who always wins games of chance against Antony, loses one to Sextus Pompeius!

It is difficult to tell how we should take all this except to note that Pompey indeed does get his fortunate chance—by virtue of the very lottery, if it indeed took place on stage. The chance, we remember, comes in the form of the situation of the banquet. They are all on Pompey's own ship—the three world leaders—surrounded by Pompey's pirate crew: only a cable-length from world power. For Pompey and Menas can slice this cable, sail out, and then cut throats. So Pompey has indeed come nearest of all to the big prize.

Events would seem to indicate, then, that Pompey is potentially the most "fortunate" of them all—but what does this mean? Clearly, nothing much, morally. Certainly Shakespeare does not seem to have been impressed with Octavius who so many Renaissance and medieval historians had said was "destined" to rule the world in which Christ was to be born. And if Pompey had indeed seized his own "fortune," by slitting throats, any moral distinction between him and Octavius would have been slight. Fortune, it seems, implies nothing about morality: Lady Philosophy had said this long ago to Boethius.

An authority on Fortune, and on what there is in the world of this play besides Fortune, seems to be Shakespeare's soothsayer, as we have seen. Indeed, he began by telling Charmian and Iras that the fortune they would be experiencing in the future would not be as "fair" as it had been before, but that they themselves would yet be fairer than they had been, and more beloving than beloved. The accuracy of this prediction again establishes the seer's authority, and, if so, then it is crucial and extremely interesting that Shakespeare returns to this supernatural authority again for a defining moral view. It comes to us in the form of a paradoxical statement about one of the tragic protagonists, Antony himself.

The seer has suggested a profoundly cautious and humble view of knowing. In impressive humility he has not purported to speak for the gods but describes his knowledge as a vast ignorance cleared momentarily by flashes of intuition. "Is't you that know things?" Charmian asked him gaily, and he:

> In nature's infinite book of secrecy
> A little I can read.
> (1.2.10–11)

Antony accosted this soothsayer, we remember, when he inquired about his and Caesar's fortunes, but I did not note the way in which this conversation began.

> *Ant.* Now, sirrah; you do wish yourself in Egypt?
> *Sooth.* Would I have never come from thence, nor you thither.
> *Ant.* If you can, your reason?
> *Sooth.* I see it in my motion, have it not in my tongue.
> But yet hie you to Egypt again.[26]
> (2.3.11–15)

But why?

> Thy daemon, that thy spirit which keeps thee, is
> Noble, courageous, high unmatchable,
> Where Caesar's is not; but near him, thy angel
> Becomes a fear, as being o'erpow'r'd: therefore
> Make space enough between you.[27]
> (2.3.19–23)

Surely Hercules is the "angel" or "daemon" to which the seer refers. But when Antony returns to Egypt, Hercules eventually leaves him! For very good reasons too, as we remember. It is also true that Antony cannot win games of chance or even battles around Caesar, as the soothsayer predicted. But why then is the alternative for the hero, from the soothsayer's viewpoint, to be Egypt? This is the place of Antony's destruction.

It is important to remember, however, that neither Cleopatra nor Egypt is necessarily a malevolent force. Egypt is morally no more threatening in its temptations—what there are of them that we see in the play than is Italy. The greatest feasting and drinking—if even that is to be considered evil in this tragedy—occurs scores of miles from Egypt, on the ship of Sextus Pompeius in Italy. And, as for Cleopatra—presumably one of Egypt's unique temptations—it is Antony's response to her, and to Egypt, that is concerned with his tragic destruction. Yet it is true that to place Antony in Egypt is to risk Antony's self-destructive response. Why then does the soothsayer, teller of truths, counsel Antony to go there?

The tragedy is enigmatic on the point, but it does provide some indications. Most important, I think, is the fact that Egypt is a place which is not Rome, for we have come to know what Rome stands for. Within its influence Antony comports himself in specific and unusual ways. He becomes a thief and a hypocrite: in many ways a moral twin of Caesar. Elsewhere, away from Rome, the audience likes Antony, but it is not for such behavior as his belittling of Octavia with his cynical response to their marriage, or for his relationship with Caesar which, according to a servant to the banquet, allows them both constantly to "pinch one another by the disposition."

In Rome Antony is someone who must be informed very carefully of a victory by one of his generals. In the scene immediately following the banquet on Pompey's ship Silius urges his general, Ventidius, speedily to follow up his victory over the Parthians so that Antony will place a garland on Ventidius's head and give him a triumph. But Ventidius:

> O Silius, Silius,
> I have done enough; a lower place, note well,
> May make too great an act. For learn this, Silius:
> Better to leave undone, than by our deed
> Acquire too high a fame when him we serve's away.
> Caesar and Antony have ever won
> More in their officer than person. Sossius,
> One of my place in Syria, his lieutenant,
> For quick accumulation of renown,
> Which he achiev'd by th'minute, lost his favor.
>
> . . . .
>
> I could do more to do Antonius good,
> But 'twould offend him; and in his offense
> Should my performance perish.
> (3.1.11–27)

This is a Rome too where Antony was a Caesarian hypocrite long before he entered into his marriage with Octavia. So say the "asides" between Enobarbus and Agrippa as Caesar bids his sister farewell.

> *Eno.* [*Aside to Agrippa.*] Will Caesar weep?
> *Agr.* [*Aside to Enobarbus.*] He has a cloud in's face.
> *Eno.* [*Aside to Agrippa.*] He were the worse for that, were he a horse;
> So is he, being a man.[28]
> *Agr.* [*Aside to Enobarbus.*] Why, Enobarbus?
> When Antony found Julius Caesar dead,
> He cried almost to roaring; and he wept
> When at Philippi he found Brutus slain.
> *Eno.* [*Aside to Agrippa.*] That year, indeed, he was troubled with a rheum;
> What willingly he did confound he wail'd,
> Believe't—till I weep too.
> (3.2.51–59)

So it is in *Rome*, to disagree with the early opinions of Demetrius and Philo, that Antony

> comes too short of that great property
> Which still should go with Antony.
> (1.1.58–59)

Then, insofar as there is some geography for virtue in this tragedy, Egypt, as the soothsayer tells Antony, is this place. For in Rome we find only the struggle for loot. Egypt promises something more, if Antony will only see it. For the promise does not lie in Acrasian bowers infected by Roman greeds, or in the early strident egoism associated with Cleopatra. The promise lies in the idea of an Egypt for which the Cleopatran interval has been inadequate historical expression. For there is another Egypt, inhabited perhaps by Hercules, and certainly by the deeply seeing soothsayer who has urged Antony south again from Rome.

This ancient Egypt was most eloquently alluded to in Shakespeare's time in that sequence of Edmund Spenser's *Faerie Queene* where Britomart spends the night in the temple of the Egyptian goddess Isis, whom Charmian playfully mentioned as a potential grantor of her sexual prayers. But as Britomart sleeps, Spenser observes (5.7):

> Naught is on earth more sacred or divine,
> That gods and men do equally adore,

Than this same virtue that does right define:
For th'heavens themselves, whence mortal men implore
Right in their wrongs, are rul'd by righteous lore
Of highest Jove who doth true justice deal
To his inferior gods, and evermore
Therewith contains his heavenly commonweale:
The skill whereof to princes' hearts he doth reveal.

Well therefore did the antique world invent
That justice was a god of sovereign grace,
And altars unto him, and temples, lent,
And heavenly honors in the highest place,
Calling him great Osiris, of the race
Of th'old Egyptian kings that whilom were;
With fained colors shading a true case.
For that Osiris, whilst he lived here,
The justest man alive, and truest did appear.

Spenser had drawn upon the *Moralia* of Plutarch wherein the long essay on Isis and Osiris offered interesting and detailed observations about Egyptian piety, emphasizing the highly moral character of the priests of Isis whose religion tied them to chastity and mortification of the flesh. Depicting the early Egyptians too as sincere and devout followers of a mysterious divinity which they consciously described through the symbolism of their mythologies, Plutarch promulgated a view of ancient Egypt which had come to Shakespeare and his contemporaries through other sources. This view is best described in the playful words of D. C. Allen.

> Much of the history, moral doctrine, natural science, and theology concealed by Homer in the lines of the *Iliad* and the *Odyssey* had been learned during his student years in Egypt. But he was not the only Greek to owe matter and method to the Egyptians. Solon, Thales, Plato, Eudoxus, and Pythagoras had travelled to the Nile to hear the lectures of Chonuphis of Memphis, Sonchis of Sais, and Oenuphis of Heliopolis; in fact, if Plutarch is right, Pythagoras, whose precepts are "not unlike the writings called hieroglyphs," was particularly admired by his teachers and imitated "their symbolism and occult teachings." But for Christians Moses was more important and ancient than Homer; he, depending on the authority consulted, was instructed by the Egyptians or instructed them. . . .

> Knowledge of the history and religious philosophies of Egypt, which were undoubtedly extensively concealed in the unfathomable hieroglyphic, increased as men of the Renaissance read the allusive passages in Herodotus, Pliny, Lucian, Plutarch, Diodorus Siculus, and Strabo and picked up crumbs of information from Latin men of letters like Tibullus, Propertius, Ovid, Claudian, and Apuleius. [Sir Walter] Raleigh's chapters on the history, religion, and customs of Egypt . . . seem practically fictional when compared with the early eighteenth-century *Origines Mundi* of Nicolas Gurtler. . . . But Raleigh lived far away from Rome, the center of the new excitement.[29]

The great pseudohistorical figure of the Egyptian, Hermes Trismegistus, was at once symptom and cause of this reverent curiosity. He lived, it was believed, before Plato, and was discussed at length by Saint Augustine in the *City of God*, and by Lactantius, as one of the most important wise men and seers of the ancient world. He prophesied, in fact, the coming of Christ, although Augustine thought that this was only through Hermes' concourse with knowledgeable demons. Thus, when one of Cosimo de Medici's men was able to find a Greek manuscript containing the *Corpus Hermeticum*—the works of Hermes—this was important enough to have Cosimo interrupt the labors of Ficino. He was to temporarily abandon his work on his important translation of the manuscripts of Plato to translate this great Egyptian whose writings were, after all, the great source of early wisdom from which Plato and the Greeks had themselves drawn their own currents.[30]

For readers of popular works, there was *The Golden Ass* of Lucius Apuleius, translated by Richard Adlington in 1566. Much read in Shakespeare's time, this work of a second-century Greek was much discussed too by Augustine and presented an attractive and moving picture of Egyptian piety.[31]

The attitudes of the English dramatists toward the authority of Egyptian soothsayers stemmed from this same view of Egyptian antiquities, and certainly we can observe intimations of this in the play *Mysogonus*. The vice, Cacurgus, pretends to be an Egyptian soothsayer and pretends to be a skillful prophet, a magician, and a reader of palms. He claims thus to be a true Egyptian and observes that "I must neds be very cuninge. I have it be kinde." In a rather different vein, the Egyptian soothsayer of Lyly's *Endymion* enters the stage in the company of Pythagoras. Although both are told that they are welcome to Cynthia's court if they shed their vain opinions, we understand that they were specifically sent for to diagnose Endymion's mysterious condition.[32]

It is this kind of Egypt, then, that we must see looming silently behind the presence of Mark Antony's Egyptian soothsayer, humble intuiter of Nature's secrecies, when we consider why the seer feels that Antony should leave Rome. For the seer comes from a place infinitely better than first-century Rome, from a place which the poet and dramatist Samuel Daniel also bore in mind when he wrote his *Tragedy of Cleopatra*, a closet drama whose chorus of elders mourns the coming of Rome, and the coming of Cleopatra too.

Mysterious Egypt, wonder breeder,
strict religions strange observer
State-orderer zeal, the best rule-keeper
fostring still in temp'rate fervor:
O how cam'st thou to lose so wholly
all religion, law, and order?
And thus become the most unholy
of all lands that Nylus border?
How could confus'd disorder enter
where stern law sate so severely?
How durst weak lust and riot venture
th'eye of Justice looking nearly?
Could not those means that made thee great
Be still the means to keep thy state?[33]

This is the Egypt of the soothsayer, I think, and it is to this ancient land near ancient truth that we may, with the seer, wish Antony back again. For though we know what he can and cannot do, and though we have seen how he will inevitably deal with a woman such as Cleopatra, we are allowed in Egypt by Shakespeare other glimpses of an Antony. This is of a hero whose special and important qualities have, as the soothsayer himself feels, greater scope and play in the land to the south.

We do not find this Antony in that soldiership so constantly praised by the scars of Scarrus and the respect of Caesar and Pompey. We find him elsewhere. For there is a special quality in Antony which transcends that militarism which in him never seems glorious. There is, instead, Antony's sense of the community of human beings and his own desire to envelope it. To his servitors in farewell he can say:

I wish I could be made so many men,
And all of you clapp'd up together in
An Antony, that I might do you service
So good as you have done.
(4.2.16–19)

It is to something like this, even when his "greatness" is going, that he continually returns. At the last battle he sees his men making friends with Caesar's troops and he laments

> All come to this? The hearts
> That spannell'd me at heels, to whom I gave
> Their wishes, do discandy, melt their sweets
> On blossoming Caesar.
> (4.12.20–23)

A little later than this, more quietly, very wrong, but very Antony, he tells Eros:

> I made these wars for Egypt, and the Queen,
> Whose heart I thought I had, for she had mine—
> Which whilst it was mine had annex'd unto't
> A million moe (now lost).
> (4.14.15–18)

This was, we remember, to have been his suicide speech before he "learned" that Cleopatra had killed herself.

> Nay, weep not, gentle Eros, there is left us
> Ourselves to end ourselves.
> (4.14.21–22)

All this, the sense of deep grief and of finality, is not the grief of an Alexander bested in war. It is the sorrow of a man who, inside of him, feels fellowship with a community of human beings.

It is this Antony who, in the tragedy, has not the fear but the love of his hard soldiers. They weep as did Enobarbus, on what they think is his last evening with them, and, indeed, throughout the drama, messengers, soldiers, and servitors love Antony with their silences, their, tears, and their scars, even to the end.

> *Ant.* Bear me, good friends, where Cleopatra bides,
> 'Tis the last service that I shall command you.
> *1 Guard.* Woe, woe are we, sir, you may not live to wear
> All your true followers out.
> *All.* Most heavy day!
> *Ant.* Nay, good my fellows, do not please sharp fate
> To grace it with your sorrows. Bid that welcome

Which comes to punish us, and we punish it
Seeming to bear it lightly. Take me up.
I have led you oft, carry me now, good friends,
And have my thanks for all.
(4.14.131–40)

This is an Antony whose death makes even Caesar's followers weep, and that at the moment of Octavius's arrival into earthly splendor far greater than what Antony once had. So when Decretas enters to them with the bloody sword:

This is his sword,
I robb'd his wound of it; behold it stain'd
With his most noble blood.
Caes. Look you sad, friends?
The gods rebuke me, but it is tidings
To wash the eyes of kings.
[*Dol.*] And strange it is
That nature must compel us to lament
Our most persisted deeds.
Maec. His taints and honors
Wag'd equal with him.
[*Dol.*] A rarer spirit never
Did steer humanity; but you gods will give us
Some faults to make us men.
(5.1.24–33)

It is, finally, an Antony who, in the middle of his tragedy, shows that he can reach out to cherish others—an extremely rare quality in this play. He hears Cleopatra's admission of guilt, after she has sought to evade responsibility for the consequences of her fleeing ship at Actium:

Cleo. O, my pardon!
Ant. Now I must
To the young man send humble treaties, dodge
And palter in the shifts of lowness, who
With half the bulk o'th'world play'd as I pleas'd,
Making and marring fortunes. You did know
How much you were my conqueror, and that
My sword, made weak by my affection, would
Obey it on all cause.

Cleo. Pardon, pardon!
Ant. Fall not a tear, I say, one of them rates
All that is won and lost. Give me a kiss.
Even this repays me. We sent our schoolmaster,
Is 'a come back? Love, I am full of lead.
Some wine within there, and our viands! Fortune knows
We scorn her most when most she offers blows.
(3.11.61–74)

In his statement of values, Antony hardly speaks for the play we know, of course, but he does speak as himself. And this "self" is not simply a deluded and comic lover maundering in a euphoria that leaves the world well lost. These final lines in the scene show that Antony understands his calamity and that he feels it. Swept up in it as he is, however, he can still attain a selflessness of forgiveness and comfort.

He does this more than once. Enobarbus deserts him and, in response, Antony sends him treasure and apologies. Caesar's soldier, standing there comments

Your emperor continues still a Jove.
(4.6.27–28)

And it is in such sequences that Antony seems to become arbiter and paragon for the play, honored not only by Eros in that figure's sorrowful death, but also in the broken-hearted expiring of Enobarbus, and finally, though of course ambiguously, in the suicide of Cleopatra. Love is always around Antony.

The departure of Hercules, in this context, is, I think, reinforcement. Until the "death" of Cleopatra sobers him from the drunkenness of his rationalizing rage, impelling him back into the nature of his deepest character, Antony has lost those qualities which we associate with his true greatness. Indeed, the whole tragedy has witnessed the struggle of these deepest values to assert themselves in an Antony who constantly wanders elsewhere. Caesar's Rome, Cleopatra's heaven, Ajax's battlefield are all uniquely Renaissance countries of the mind to which this chameleon figure has lent passing allegiance. And though there is much truth in Cleopatra's vision of Antony the giant, the departure of Hercules seems to say that here was a figure, the ideal Antony, whose Herculean nature, no longer stifled by the self-loving mystique of a Caesar or of a medieval knight, could have held something of hope for the wretched world in which all the people of the play live. It is Antony alone, for a moment and between delusions, who most nearly approaches something which has not been imagined by the others. And his failure is the ethical tragedy of Shakespeare's drama.

III

Shakespeare's Rome is not a guidebook to antiquities: it is a theory. Lacking firsthand or even archaeological knowledge of a civilization which existed more than sixteen hundred years before his time, the dramatist of such a scene inevitably offered hypothesis. Historical description was an integral part of the larger fiction of the drama itself. The ancient setting of the tragedy was a moral proposition about the world as it might be imagined to have existed in a story called "history," a tale, perhaps, that might even be true.

Shakespeare's story tells us that once upon a time there was a system of robbery and it was called Rome. Those who lived there spent time in ways they themselves disguised with names. Some people lent allegiance to rapine on such a scale that it engaged their intellects in what they saw as "concerns of empire." Others, only pretending a passion for theft, chased the sensuality of long knives, butchering the bodies of others to know the reality of their own. They called this assertion "war" and themselves "soldiers." And still others in this world scorned realms and wars for dreams. They wanted to be gods and to sense the sweetness of transcendence over the plunderers and the great killers. This dream they called by many names. Such was the intoxication men call history.

But because this drunkenness was from themselves, the dwellers in this world knew continual confusion. They did not think their desirings were a dream and that the tipsiness of their vagrant wishings was the intoxicated misunderstanding of the possibilities of themselves. Indeed, the revolving self-satisfaction and despairs of two of the dwellers in this world—Cleopatra and Antony—are so inebriatedly magnificent as to make us wonder whether, in fact, anything "tragic" occurred in them at all. But the intricate historical world made by Shakespeare's drama is also there to say something about these things.

Caesar, avatar of the quality of "Rome," teaches us by example. To attain A, employ Method A, not Method B: especially when Method B happens merely to be congenial. Living in Egypt; Antony's way; being the greatest soldier in the world; owning Rome: these are not the same things at all, nor are they to be gained by the same ways. And further—for Caesar has more to teach—a "king" does not constitute godhood, nor are men intrinsically "kings." Indeed, those who achieve royalty need its fiction the least, for sheer power is curiously humdrum in its methods and not to be confused with Cleopatra's huge assertions and colorful personal pantheons.

These realities offered us by "Rome" and its agents can move in us, the viewers, cruel judgments about those lovers who try to master Rome. For if the issue is the control of the world, it is not to be resolved in one's favor by that subjective and narcissistic vanity which Antony sees as his "soldiership." Nor are the harsh bricks and marbles which build world domination in this tragedy to be structured through quasi-psychotic and self-flattering redefinitions of the surrounding reality. In Rome, the nursing of asps is spectacular, but not effective; worth study, perhaps, but not definitive.

King Lear, close in time to Shakespeare's *Antony and Cleopatra*, presents a king who shares much with the royal lovers. Like them, Lear does not really want the iron rule of his world—to kill and seize like Macbeth, to administer justice, like Hamlet, or, like Coriolanus, to drown in war forever. Lear wants only to stand about being happy: it is his daughters who must be the Caesars. And when this escapist arrangement is denied him harshly, he weathers the storm but looks forward again to coming out of the storm again to stand about being happy. Denied again, he looks forward to being happy in jail with Cordelia "like birds in a cage."

Such stillness holds vast appeal for Antony. "Here is my space." "Kingdoms are clay." "The nobleness of life is to do thus." But if these noble lines resound for us with the happiness to be gained from cultivating satisfactions, Cleopatra's idlenesses are equally eloquent. Her games and dreams seek to freeze Antony, her world, and time into that stasis to be achieved only in some well-wrought urn: "Forever shalt thou rule and he be fair."

Shakespeare, creator of the lovers and of Lear, has them all killed. *King Lear*'s savagely post-Arthurian world requires that attention be paid at all times; otherwise Cordelia may be found hanging in the birdcage. Mark Antony thinks to swim through the bloody waters of piracy and carnage, even to show his back above the element he lives in. Cleopatra believes her glamorous game, in which life is a play arranged for her greedy need of transfiguration. Thus the two lovers, like Lear, seek to live like birds in an Egyptian cage where the pastime is not gossip but self-glorification.

As in *King Lear*, however, there is the world outside. It belongs to the Caesars and it tends to liquidate un-Roman problems. For if, to some, Rome is a trifle, it is a huge trifle, and to achieve something like it takes at least a furious energy which the lovers, if they would out-caesar Caesar—or even survive—must strive for in every waking minute. And that they misunderstand this fact shows their vanity, and their ignorance too. To stay above Rome they think merely to trifle with its spiritual debasement, but it rots their own souls. Antony dies proudly speaking of being a "Roman" and Cleopatra drifts to sleep with the image of a vanquished Caesar part of her last waking dream.

If, to the last, both lovers think to be transcendent, they die merely seeing themselves as transcendent Romans.

So in this story Rome stands supreme over the world. Even Christ would seem to acquiesce in this fact through his incarnation as a citizen enrolled in Caesar's census.[34] But still, Rome is merely Rome—an inevitable overripening of that postlapsarian world which man alone created and which is now reaching through time toward what Caesar himself calls "the time of universal peace." The marketing of Octavia, the hideous scars of the soldiers, the bloody whipping of Thidias, and the murder of Pompey suggest the nature of Rome's ripening and suggest too its rottenness. For this world does not enchant all in the tragedy with its final allure.

If, in *King Lear*, Edgar has asked, "Is this the promised end?" Enobarbus asks something similar, dying alone, true in his mind to Rome but bewildered by the strong feelings that now drive him beyond the pale of the eternal city. In Enobarbus's confusion, and in the deaths of Eros, Charmian, and Iras—in supernatural suggestion too—we find the responses of the tragedian to the paralyzing questions he has raised.

The poet answers by showing how once there lived a man called Antony who made men think of love. He had an ardor so strong that it drew his enemies, enfolded his servants, embraced his soldiers, held Cleopatra. He insisted upon love—as did Lear—but he himself demanded objects for it, wished for self-sacrifice and self-sacrificing. And so he was loved by others, from Caesar's great companions, Maecenas and Agrippa who mourn his death; to the messenger too full to speak of Antony's mounting troubles; to Sextus Pompeius who merely wants to be Antony's friend; to Eros who kills himself rather than outlive the man whom he serves.

This astounding quality is unique to Antony among all Shakespeare's tragic heroes. And in the worlds of Egypt and Rome, this quality, not "soldiery," is Antony's huge force. It breaks Enobarbus from the stiffness of his Roman bent to emotion, and it renders one of the world's great egoists, Cleopatra, into a queen almost able to envision, as the greater and more profound egoism, service to someone else. This lesson, which Cordelia and the Fool almost taught to Lear, is almost taught to Cleopatra too as, in the end, she has the vision to be Antony's spokesman, celebrating not his heroism but his bounty.

Therefore, the tragedy of Antony becomes the tragedy of his world too. The greed that is Rome infects him and, in the end, he cannot escape it. His one great truth he abandons for two lies. The one is Rome, the other, himself as hero and soldier. His one great truth is his loving and the love he causes in others. His tragedy and the tragedy of his world is that he does not hold this truth any more strongly than he finally holds his sword. In the end, he is too much of Rome.

But Antony's truth exists, in the drama. That it is more appropriately acted out in Egypt than in Rome is suggested by the silent, modest, and profound seer who walks in the oneness of those eternal mysteries linking the most ancient past with the modernities of the English Renaissance. Antony's soothsayer shadows that ancient land where man first began to revere moral ideas. If these ideas now lie hidden, paled in the glitter of Romanized Egypt, they are fitfully alive in Cleopatra. A child of Egypt whose spirit constantly muses on absolute things which other men call "God," she, though trapped in her mind and world, wants transcendence. Like Egypt, she becomes lost in trivialities no more nor less tempting than those which snare Antony and all the other inhabitants of her time. The iron steadfastness of her vision of some other world is too crucial to be wasted as it is, but for both the lovers, the idea of "Egypt" is haunting and futile evocation.

But it is something to know enough finally to despise the mechanical operations of the world which to Iras, Charmian, and Eros too seems well lost without love. That Cleopatra and Antony know only imperfectly is, of course, their tragedy, evolved through modes and wide events to the complex clarity of Shakespeare's dreaming on what we are not and what we are.

Notes

1. The previous speech of Menecrates, as Highet suggested, reads as if it had been adapted from Juvenal's famous Tenth Satire whose theme is "what should we pray for?" (Hamlet presumably read this satire and shared it with Polonius, as it tells of the evils of old age.) For a survey of the tradition embodied by Satire 10—often entitled, after Johnson, "The Vanity of Human Wishes"—see Gilbert Highet, *Juvenal the Satirist* (Oxford: Clarendon Press, 1954), pp. 27–77 (n. 1 to chap. 19).

2. In the *Castle of Perseverance*, to take quite an obvious example, the three scaffolds of the World, the Flesh, and the Devil allude to the New Testament triplicity of sins presented by Saint John.

3. For "worm" see *OED*: worm 1.1.a: the word was used to refer to any serpent; 1.6.b: the word was also used to refer to the pains of Hell, as well as the agency of the pain.

4. See the dedicatory epistle to *The Psalms of David* (London, 1571), sig. *4. The asp was specifically associated with evil serpentine activity. See Florence McCulloch, "The Metamorphoses of the Asp in Latin and French Bestiaries," *Studies in Philology* 56 (1959): 7–13. Thomas Wilson, *A Christian Dictionary* (London, 1612) refers to the well-known locus in Romans to describe types of asp: "Another [kills] by sleep; thus doth the slothful slay their own souls. . . . The wicked are said to have *the gall of asps within them*, Job 20:14; *to suck the poison of asps*, ibid. 16; to have the poison of asps under their lips, Rom. 3:13. Whereby may be perceived they are malicious dangers." When Charmian dies after the queen has kissed her, Cleopatra plays on this idea: "Have I the aspic in my lips?" The context to Wilson's definition is rather more general than he suggests. See the Geneva Bible (Rom. 3:10 ff.): "There is none righteous, no, not one. 11. There is none that understandeth: there is

none that seeketh God. 12. They have all gone out of the way: they have been made altogether unprofitable: there is none that doeth good, no, not one. 13. Their throat is an open sepulchre: they have used their tongues to deceit: the poison of asps is under their lips. 14. Whose mouth is full of cursing and a bitterness. . . . The fear of God is not before their eyes."

5. Among the many loci in the Bible for this motif, see Rom. 8:1 ff.

6. In the Elizabethan play *Laugh and Lie Down*, the woman says to her ardent betrothed: "Be merry and take no thought, for I am for thee at an hour's warning, in the way of honesty, when thou wilt, and therefore, since you are so earnest on the matter, ask the banns." I have modernized the spelling of Nicoll's edition. See Cyril Tourneur, *Works*, ed. A. Nicoll (London: Fanfrolico Press, 1930), p. 291. Othello, of course, asks Desdemona if she is "honest."

7. See Francis Quarles, *Emblems* (London, 1639), Emblem 7, which alludes to 1 Pet. 5:7. Cf. Ralph Walker, *A Learned and Profitable Treatise of God's Providence* (London, 1608), sig. O^{v}: "Satan that ravenous beast swallows not up the godly," and reference is made to 2 Cor. 11:22. *The Glass of Vainglory* (London, 1605), sig. E3^{v} (attributed to St. Augustine: four eds. between 1585 and 1605) presents another example as does Henry Peacham's *Minerva Britanna* (London, 1612), sig. Y3, where the emblem is that of the ravenous crocodile. See also John Day, *A Book of Christian Prayers* (London, 1578), sigs. 213^{v}–2K.

8. There seems to be a play on some traditional expression whose meaning I have not been able to ascertain. In *RJ* Romeo describes himself in his first meeting with the nurse as one "that God hath made [for: Q1] himself to mar." Answers the nurse: "By my troth it is well said. For himself to mar, quoth 'a?"

9. For the Wise and Foolish Virgins generally, see *The Text of the New Testament*, ed. William Fulke (London, 1589), sigs. M2^{v}–M3. This is a Rheims New Testament comparing the text with the Bishops' translation. The parable occurs in Matt. 25. Fulke quotes Jerome, Augustine, and Gregory in a debate about whether the parable refers to grace or to merit, but the point here is their assumption that an interpretation of this general sort is indeed at issue. The basic premise is that the parable shows how, at Judgment Day, those excluded from Heaven will be the types whose lamps (protestations of faith) are not illumined with good works/Charity (depending upon the interpretation). For other treatment of the *fatues*, see the glosses of the various Bibles. The Coverdale Bible (1535) glosses according to Matt. 7:24, Mark 13, and Luke 6, 12, 21, whose consensus is that the parable indicates readiness is all. Matthew's Bible (1537) construes lamps without oil as works without faith. See also the "Great Bible" (1540) and the Geneva New Testament (1557). For comment, see also Thomas Gataker, *The Spiritual Watch* (London, 1619), passim; Robert Farley, *Light's Moral Emblems* (London, 1638), Emblem 55: "The Virgin's Lamp." For the ubiquity of the association of the parable with Judgment Day, see F. B. Deknatel, "The Thirteenth Century Gothic Sculpture of the Cathedrals of Burgos and Leon," in *Art Bulletin* 17 (1935): 243–89, esp. p. 342. "G.B.'s" sermon on the Last Judgment in *The Narrow Way* (London, 1607), sigs. H3–H3^{v}, preached at Paul's Cross shortly before *Antony and Cleopatra* appeared in the Stationers' Register, furnishes a context. "The five wise virgins who had oil in their lamps, that is, whose good works and godly lives did shine and give light unto others as a lamp gives light unto those that are in darkness . . . so the five foolish virgins who did slumber and sleep and had no care to expect the bridegroom coming, by a virtuous and godly life, those we see most justly to be shut out." John Day (n. 7 above) associates the *fatues*

text with the illustration and text of Rev. 12: "the great Dragon, that Old Serpent, was cast out," etc.

10. See T. Sackville and T. Norton, *Gorboduc*, ed. I. B. Cauthen, Jr. (Lincoln: University of Nebraska Press, 1970), p. 8.

11. See the diction of the anonymous *News from the Sea* (London, 1609), a sensationalist biography of Ward and Danseker the pirates. Enobarbus's term appears in Shakespeare's other plays where the Duke calls Antonio (*TN* 5.1.72): "Notable pirate! thou salt-water thief!" Leonine in *Per.* 4.1.97 refers to pirates as "roguing thieves."

12. For St. Augustine, see *City of God*, ed. L. Vives, trans. John Healey (London, 1614), sig. P2. Vives's note to the passage in Augustine alludes to Lucan's *Civil War* where Alexander the Great is roundly condemned at the beginning of Book 10, being called, among other things, *felix praedo*, but although a source of the general idea, Lucan does not have the pirate story. George Carey remarked in *The Medieval Alexander* ed. by D. J. A. Ross (Cambridge: Cambridge University Press, 1956), p. 356, that the story is to be found in Ranulph Higden's medieval *Polychronicon* (London, 1527), sig. P6, John Gower's *Confessio Amantis* (London, 1554), sig. K6v, the *Gesta Romanorum*, chap. 146, and alluded to in Chaucer's *Manciple's Tale*, ll. 226–34. With the exception of Higden, these are better than fair possibilities in Shakespeare's reading. Allusions to the story among Shakespeare's contemporaries can be found in those books of *The French Academy* translated and available in England before Shakespeare wrote *AC*. See La Primaudaye, *French Academy*, trans. T. B. (London, 1586), sig. Q3; Jean Bodin in the first chapter of his work *Six Books of a Commonweale*, trans. Richard Knolles (London, 1606), sig. Bv; Daniel Tuvill, *Essays Moral and Theological* (London, 1609), sig. C8.

13. "Going on wheels" has several contexts. Francis Quarles, *Emblems* 11 shows the globe of the world on a wheeled chariot drawn by a goat and a hog. The epigram of the emblem indicates that the Devil drives the conveyance and that God must pull on the reins to stop it in its fast course to destruction. John Taylor has a piece in *Works* (London, 1630) entitled "The World Runs on Wheels" where (sigs. 3A4v–3A5) an emblem is displayed in which a whore and a devil are pulling a coach on which there sits a globe. The poem below the emblem in part reads, as it tells us that the whore is really "the whorish flesh", "But for the World, as 'tis the World, you see /, It *runs on wheels*, and who the palfreys be / Which emblem to the reader doth display. / The *Devil* and *Flesh* run swift away. / The chain'd ensnared World doth follow fast, / Till all into perdition's pit be cast. / The picture topsy-turvy stands kewaw: / The world turn'd upside down, as all men know." Edward Sharpham in *Cupid's Whirligig* (1607), ed. A. Nicoll (Waltham Saint Lawrence, Berks.: Golden Cockerel Press, 1926), p. 47, has a character say: "Why they say the world is like a bias bowl, and it runs all on the rich men's sides. Others say 'tis like a tennis ball, and Fortune keeps such a racket with it as it tosses it into times hazard, and that devours all, and for my part they say 'twill shortly run upon wheels with me, for my master swears 'a will have me carted because 'a thinks I have lain with my lady." (I have modernized the spelling of Nicoll's text.) The response by Slack is: "Nay, then 'twill run upon wheels with thee indeed," thus suggesting two senses of the phrase. Cf. also Thomas Adams (1629) *Works*, ed. Joseph Angus (Edinburgh, 1861), 1: 87; John Foxe, *Actes and Monuments* (London, 1563), sigs. 2Wv–2W2, where it is stated that evil-willers of the realm will seize the occasion, if Lent is not properly enforced, to claim that "all goeth on wheels." Fernando Rojas, *Celestina*, trans. James Mabbe

in 1631 and ed. James Fitzmaurice-Kelly (London: Constable and Sons, 1884), p. 169, has a character reflecting on her past happiness, riches, and youth which are now gone. "But such is the world," she says, "it comes and goes upon wheels." This sense of backwardness is reaffirmed in Stephen Guazzo, *Civil Conversation*, trans. George Pettie and ed. Sir Edward Sullivan (London: David Nult, 1925) 2:117: "seeing the world to go on wheels, and backward in his course in exalting the wicked and oppressing the virtuous. . . ." The phrase, in another context, thus becomes associated with the concept of real or of spiritual drunkenness in a passage from Montaigne. See below.

14. For the concept of "spiritual drunkenness" see Thomas Wright, *Passions of the Mind*, sig. E3v; Thomas Adams, *A Divine Herbal* (London, 1616), sigs. Eff.; La Primaudaye, Bk. 2 (1618), sigs. 2S, 3F3v; Sir Thomas More's introduction to the Epistles of Pico della Mirandola in *Works* (London, 1557), sig. A5v. More also observes that the moral point of the Circe story uses drunkenness as a symbol of the spiritual state which changes Ulysses' followers into "animals." See also Davies, *Microcosmos* (Oxford, 1603), sig. G4v, and M. Y. Hughes, "Spenser's Acrasia and the Circe of the Renaissance," *Journal of the History of Ideas* 4 (1943): 381–99. Drunkenness becomes associated with the concept of "wheels" in Montaigne's essay "Of Repenting." The pertinent message, in the French, begins: "Le monde n'est qu'une branloire perenne. Toutes choses y branlent sans cesse." *Branloire*—see Edmond Huguet, *Dictionnaire de la langue française du seizième siècle* (Paris: Librarie Ancienne Edouard Champion, 1925–67)—means to "see-saw or to swing." R. Cotgrave, *Dictionary of the French and English Tongue* (London, 1611): *Bransler*: "move uncertainly or inconstantly." Florio translates these first two sentences of Montaigne: "The world runs all on wheels. All things therein move without intermission." The rest of Montaigne's passage (which yokes wheels and drunkenness) then continues: "Yea, the earth, the rocks of Caucasus, and the pyramids of Egypt both [move] with the public and their own motion. Constancy itself is nothing but a languishing and wavering dance. I cannot settle my object, it goeth so unquietly and staggering, with a natural drunkenness. I take it in this plight as it is at the instant I amuse myself about it. I describe not the essence but the passage . . . from day to day, from minute to minute. My history must be fitted to the present. I may soon change not only fortune but intention."

15. Dancing frequently symbolized both disorder and order. Elizabethan verses celebrating dancing as a symbol of order are cited by J. R. Brown, *Shakespeare and his Comedies* (London: Methuen, 1957), pp. 139 ff. In Jonson's *Hymenaei*, the four humors come out of a globe imagined as a microcosm. With them come the four affections to dance in disorder to a contentious music until Reason steps out of the same globe to put them all in order again. J. de Zettre, *Emblemes Nouveaux* (Frankfurt, 1617) has an emblem which presents the "dance of the world" or the Devil's dance (Emblem 85): presumably the "old dance" or "old measure" of Marston's *Dutch Courtesan* (2.3.75). The morris dance, a round dance like that of the triumvirate, was often associated with madness or with the Devil. See Thomas Adams, *Mystical Bedlam* (London, 1615), sig. G4v, who speaks of the "mad morisco" and Cyril Tourneur's *Laugh and Lie Down (Nicoll* ed., p. 290): "I thought if the devil had danced, there had been a morris for Hell." The witches in *Macbeth* continually hold hands to dance in the circle they term their "antic round" and Barnabe Barnes's *Devil's Charter* presents the devil's dance as an "antic" while Caesar says that the dance—or at least "the wild disguise"—has "antick'd us all." A dance to Bacchus was, as here,

a round dance according to Palingenius (sig. D2[v]) and an "antick of drunkards" is presented in the *Masque of the Four Seasons.* Enid Welsford, in *The Court Masque* (Cambridge: Cambridge University Press, 1927), gives passim a useful summary of the symbolic uses to which dances were put. See also the dedicatory epistle to *The Psalms of David* (London, 1571), sig. *4, and, finally, G. Whitney, *Emblems*, sig. Q[v]: *sine iustitia confusio*: the chaos of the elements is resolved by God, while the chaos of man is resolved by justice.

16. See Appian, *An Ancient History*, trans. H. Binniman (London, 1578), sig. B2[v]; Velleius Paterculus, *Compendium of Roman History*, trans. F. W. Shipley (London: Loeb Classical Library, 1924), pp. 237–39; Florus, *Epitome*, trans. E. S. Forster (London: Loeb Classical Library, 1929), pp. 265–69; Eutropius, *A Brief Chronicle*, trans. Nicholas Haward (London, 1564), sigs. L4[v] ff.; Sallust, p. 65; Lucan, 1:1–29. These for the tradition and, among Shakespeare's contemporaries: William Covell, *Polimanteia* (London, 1595), sigs. 2C4[v]–2D; A. Kelton, *A Chronicle with a Genealogy* (London, 1547), sig. D2; William Fulbeck, *Continual Factions* (London, 1601), sigs. A2–A2[v]; E. L., *Rome's Monarchy* (London, 1596), sig. A2[v]; Tacitus, *The End of Nero*, trans. Henry Savill (London, 1598), sig. *3[v].

17. As Plutarch observes, some thought "it was the god unto whom Antonius bare singular devotion to counterfeit and resemble him" but the music is described as "song as they use in Bacchus' feasts" (p. 78). Cf. p. 63: "It was said that Antonius came of the race of Hercules, as you have heard before, and in the manner of his life he followed Bacchus." Thus it seems to me that Shakespeare had an equal choice between Bacchus and Hercules when he assigned a god to leave his hero.

18. For the tradition, see E. Panofsky, *Hercules am Scheideweg* (Leipzig: B. G. Teubner, 1930), esp. pp. 37–83. Cf. J. Seznec, *The Survival of the Pagan* Gods, trans. B. F. Sessions (New York: Pantheon Books, 1953), passim, and Marcel Simon, *Hercule et le christianisme* (Paris: Publications de la Faculté des lettres de l'Université de Strasbourg, 1955), for the general medieval tradition here. For Renaissance commentary, see E. Tietze-Conrat, "Notes on 'Hercules at the Crossroads,'" *Journal of the Warburg and Courtauld Institutes* 14 (1951): 305–9; H. D. Smith, *Elizabethan Poetry* (Cambridge, Mass.: Harvard University Press, 1952), pp. 293ff.; Barroll, "Enobarbus' Description," *Texas Studies in English* 37 (1958): 61–78, and. Marc-René Jung, *Hercule dans la littérature du XVIe siècle* (Geneva: Librairie Droz, 1966). Important Renaissance loci were probably Cicero's *De Officiis*—(sigs. G3[v]–G4, Q2[v])—and, in the Countess of Pembroke's circle, probably Philippe de Mornay's *Discourse of Life and Death*, trans. Countess of Pembroke (London, 1592), sig. A3[v].

19. Hercules is a figure of lechery in Shakespeare's *Love's Labour's Lost* and *Much Ado.* The tradition behind this is discussed by Rosamund Tuve, "Spenser's Reading: the *De Claris Mulieribus,*" *Studies in Philology* 33 (1936): 147–65. There is satire using the motif in Thomas Tomkis, *Lingua* (London, 1607), 5.7.

20. The problem of this moral choice of Hercules between virtue and vice was often expressed by allusion to the capital Greek letter *ipsilon* (Pythagoras's letter—as it was known). See Panofsky, pp. 44, 65–68, and H. D. Smith, *loc. cit.* Ludovico Vives's commentary on *The City of God*, sig. I, refers to a poem on the subject supposedly by Virgil (later translated by the poet and dramatist George Chapman). See also Palingenius, sig. L8[v], and cf. W. Rankins, *A Mirror of Monsters* (London, 1587), sig. C4. Eugene Waith in *The Herculean Hero* (New York: Columbia University Press, 1962), p. 213 n. 3, took issue with my use of the Herculean analogy in a periodical publication of the present discussion ("Enobarbus' Description of Cleopatra": see n. 18 [previous]).

But the importance and complexity of the Herculean choice is, I think, central to the ethical framework of the tragedy. Yet see Adelman, who does not take this view (pp. 81–82) and *contra*, John Coates, "'The Choice of Hercules' in *Antony and Cleopatra*," in *Shakespeare Survey 31* (Cambridge: Cambridge University Press, 1978), pp. 45–52, who draws, however, a conclusion with which I would not agree.

21. Commentary on the "fortune" of the Romans was commonplace in Shakespeare's lifetime (see "Shakespeare and Roman History"). The understanding of his contemporaries was that God's providence had established this Roman empire for overriding historical and salvific purposes. Philemon Holland was vigorous on the point in his introduction to that essay in Plutarch's *Moralia* entitled "Of the Romans' Fortune"—see *The Morals*, trans. Philemon Holland (London, 1603), sigs. 3G2–3G2^{v}. For other such statements, see Quintus Curtius, *The Historie*, trans. John Brende (London, 1602), sig. A4, and Pompeius Trogus, *The Histories*, trans. Arthur Golding (London, 1564), sig. A3^{v}. This latter is from the Grynaeus preface also used (without the section on the fortune of the Romans) by Thomas Lodge in his 1602 translation of Josephus: for such use of Grynaeus see L. B. Campbell, *Shakespeare's "Histories"* (San Marino, Calif.: Henry E. Huntington Library, 1947), p. 38. See also Sir Walter Raleigh, *History of the World*, in *Works* (Oxford, 1829), 1:1.2ff.

22. See James I, *Basilikon Doron* (London, 1603), sig. F5. And thus Jean D'Espagne condemns those who defend the duel as "one kind of lot." See *Antiduello* (London, 1632), sigs. B3^{v}–F4.

23. Against lottery for these reasons were therefore such diverse writers as Samuel Byrd, *Paul and Demas* (London, 1580), sig. G8^{v} (and for the authorities he cites, see sigs. K2 ff.); Thomas Wilcox, *A Glass for Gamesters* (London, 1581), sigs. B8 ff.; John Northbrook. *A Treatise wherein Dicing, Dancing, etc. Are Reproved* (London, 1579), sigs. 04^{v} ff.; James Balmford, *A Short and Plain Dialogue concerning the Unlawfulness of Playing at Cards* (London, 1593); Pierre de La Primaudaye, *The French Academy* (1586), sig. 4K6; Thomas Beard, *The Theatre of God's Judgments* (London, 1612), sig. 2H8^{v}ff; J. Bastingius, *An Exposition or Commentary upon the Catechism* (Cambridge, 1595), sig. G5^{v}. King James, in *Basilikon Doron*, defends dice-play as not a casting of lots at all: for no one plays with any intention of acting to "clear any obscure truth" (sig. K6^{v}). So also John Downe argues that there is no immediate providence concerned with dicing at all: see *A Defense of the Lawfulness of Lots* in *Certain Treatises* (Oxford, 1633), sig. 2X3. Thomas Gataker writes *On the Nature and Use of Lots* (London, 1619) and also argues against the fact that there is a special providence in lots, and he defends this stand against subsequent attack in *A Just Defence* (London, 1623). In 1607–8 there was a lottery in London for silver and gold plate. Henry Parrot writes an epigram on it in *Epigrams* (London, 1608), no. 82, while the anonymous author of *The Great Frost* (London, 1608) notes that everyone is praying that God, "if it be his will," send him good fortune (sig. C3^{v}).

24. See E. K. Chambers, *The Elizabethan Stage*, 4 vols. (Oxford: Clarendon Press, 1923), 4:338–39. I have modernized the spelling.

25. This ancient tradition was first expounded by Orosius, *Historiarum Adversus Paganos Libri VII*, 6.23.

26. By "motion" the seer means something like Modern English "emotion." Cf. Florio's language in translating Montaigne, "when there is no person to induce us to prefer any one before others, they answer that this motion of the soul is extraordinary and inordinate, coming into us by a strange, accidental, and casual impulsion" (2.14). For Shakespeare and "motion," see *Artificial Persons*, pp. 36ff.

27. It would be a fruitless foray to attempt to rationalize among all the Neoplatonic references to "daemon," "angel," "spirit," (and "genius") throughout Shakespeare's lifetime. There are continual contradictions and overlaps so that one might most fruitfully consult Robert H. West, *The Invisible World* (Athens, Ga.: University of Georgia Press, 1939), chaps. 2, 5. In Shakespeare, since Macbeth speaks of his "genius" being rebuked by Banquo as was Antony's by Caesar, "genius" becomes synonymous with angel/daemon. This mixture occurs elsewhere. John Downe, *Polydoron* (London, 1630), sig. I 10v, observes that "there are some of opinion that each man hath a double *Genius*, a good Angel and a bad." John Bayley, one of the king's chaplains, observes in his sermon on "The Angel Guardian" (again in 1630) that Proclus describes a "*sacer daemon*" who has charge of the reasonable soul to incline the will to good, while there is a "Genius" who helps men's fortunes (*Two Sermons* [Oxford, 1630]), sigs. B2–B2v). A good, brief discussion of genius-daemon is in C. S. Lewis, *The Allegory of Love* (Oxford: Clarendon Press, 1936), Appendix 1, while traditional discussions about "daemons" may be found in Plutarch's *Moralia*, sigs. 5R ff., and in Augustine's *City of God* (trans. Healey), sigs. 2G6–2H. Plutarch's wording in the Antonius story is: "'For thy demon,' said he, (that is to say, the good angel and spirit that keepeth thee), is afraid of his." Shakespeare's own writing seems readily to assimilate the angel-daemon complex into the traditional notion of good and evil angels, the basis for the concept being *Matthew* 18:10. By this logic, the soothsayer senses that Antony's good angel is not operative when Caesar is by.

28. Steevens noted that a "cloud" is a black or dark-colored spot in the forehead of a horse between the eyes, this indicating bad temper—a blemish in a horse: see Case in his note to 3.2.52.

29. See D. C. Allen, *Mysteriously Meant* (Baltimore, Md.: Johns Hopkins University Press, 1970), pp. 107–111 and passim in chap. 5. For the wisdom and morality of ancient Egypt, see also La Primaudaye, sigs. 3G6–3G6v. For the dramatists on the subject, see E. H. Sugden, *A Topographical Dictionary to the Works of Shakespeare and his Fellow Dramatists* (Manchester: Manchester University Press, 1925), p. 168. Simultaneous was the tradition of Egypt in typology as representing the spiritual area of the Devil and his works. Rosemund Tuve reminded us of this awareness in the poets—*A Reading of George Herbert* (Chicago: University of Chicago Press, 1952), pp. 39, 51–52—and John Donne explains the Devil as "that great pharaoh" in *Essays in Divinity*, ed. E. M. Simpson (Oxford: Clarendon Press, 1952), pp. 72ff., following Benedictus Pererius's commentary on *Exodus*. The Tenebrae services of Holy Week, Tuve also reminded us, figured forth the "Egyptian darkness" of the ninth plague against which the light of the Paschal Candle on Easter was the reply. Various contemporary assumptions about this symbolism of Egypt as variously the Hell to which Christ descended or the sin in which mankind walked may be found in E. Hutchins, *David's Sling* (London, 1598), sig. 012; William Cowper, *A Conduit of Comfort* (London, 1606), sig. Dv–D2; G. B., *The Narrow Way*, sig. A3v; William Loe, *The Joy of Jerusalem* (London, 1609), sig. B7. Feste as pseudocleric commenting on the "Egyptians in their fog" in *TN* is presumably in this tradition.

30. See Frances A. Yates, *Giordano Bruno and the Hermetic Tradition* (Chicago: University of Chicago Press, 1964), chaps. 1, 2.

31. See L. Apuleius, *The Golden Ass*, trans. William Adlington (London, 1596), esp. chaps. 47–48 and sigs. A2v–A3 for Adlington's "allegorical" explanations. Augustine discusses Apuleius in *City of God* 8.14.

32. For *Mysogonus*, see *Early Plays from the Italian*, ed. R. Warwick Bond (Oxford: Clarendon Press, 1911), *Mysogonus* 3.3.36 and John Lyly, *Works*, ed. R. Warwick Bond (Oxford: Clarendon Press, 1902), 3: *Endymion*.

33. See Samuel Daniel, *Complete Works*, ed. A. B. Grosart, 5 vols. (London: Hazell, Watson, and Viney, 1885), 3:75.

34. This ancient tradition is first found in Orosius (*Historia Adversus Paganos* 6.23).

MICHAEL GOLDMAN

Antony and Cleopatra: *Action as Imaginative Command*

I

Most of Shakespeare's tragedies—*Romeo and Juliet* is perhaps the only arguable exception—are concerned, one way or another, with human greatness. Their heroes are larger than life and recognized as such by those around them. *Antony and Cleopatra*, however, differs from the rest of the tragedies in that it is centrally *about* greatness. The discussion of greatness is the activity to which the play's characters devote most of their time. In speech after speech, indeed scene after scene, they comment on each other's greatness—acknowledge it, praise it, measure it by various standards, are moved and changed by it, proclaim their own greatness, consider what greatness means. Love is also a subject of the play, of course. But the claim of the lovers—and even of their enemies—is that they are great lovers, no pair so famous, as Caesar says, and their language of love, particularly when quarreling and making up, is the language of fame, nobility, and superhuman comparison. They measure their passion against the scope and power of the universe and against all competitors, human, legendary, and divine. The competition knows no bounds, and there is no interest in second place, even in the hereafter.

Most critics of *Antony and Cleopatra* have recognized its concern with one aspect or another of greatness, but insufficient attention has been given to what the play conceives greatness to be. I would like to look into its

---

From *Acting and Action in Shakespearean Tragedy*, pp. 112–39, 178–79.

definition of greatness not simply as an abstraction, but as a way of experiencing life, a sense of process that critically affects our sense of action. What I have called a definition of greatness might more accurately, if more awkwardly, be described as a concern with a certain kind of greatness and its way of acting upon the world. It seems to me to offer a clue to the play's dramatic unity and to some of the problems it presents for performers and critics—to the way Shakespeare moves his actors on the stage, to the kinds of action we are shown and not shown, and to the difficulties and rewards of the main parts.

In *Antony and Cleopatra*, greatness is primarily a command over other people's imaginations. It depends on what people think of you and what you think of yourself. At the lowest level, it is style, effective self-dramatization; at the highest, it is a means of overcoming time, death, and the world. It is registered in the behavior of audiences, and a concern for greatness is reflected in a concern for audiences. The audience for greatness in *Antony and Cleopatra* is multiple: it is, first, the small group of people on stage at any time; second, the entire known world to whom Antony and Cleopatra constantly play and which seems always to regard them with fascination; it is also a timeless, superhuman audience, the heroes of history and legend and the gods themselves; finally, it is the audience of posterity, of whom we in the theater are a part. The play is very much aware that we have heard of its heroes before coming to the theater; their greatness, their ability to command imagination through time, has helped to draw us. When Cleopatra decides to stage her death—and it is a carefully planned spectacle—the immediate cause she cites is the prospect of an inadequate theatrical representation of her life, which will not do her justice but boy her greatness in the posture of a whore. And when Antony contemplates life after death with Cleopatra, he says that together they will make the "ghosts gaze" at them:

> Dido and her Aeneas shall want troops,
> And all the haunt be ours.
> (IV, xiv, 53–54)

Once more, it is the ability to command other imaginations that sets the seal on their greatness. Very closely associated with it, in this passage and throughout the play, is the ability to go beyond natural limit and thus to take on the transforming power of imagination itself.

Greatness, as Antony and Cleopatra possess it, is seen not as an aspect of one's deeds, nor even, primarily, as the potential for specific actions, but as a kind of emanation radiating from the two lovers across the civilized world and down through history. Even our first reference to Antony is not to his courage, strength, or martial skill, but to his eyes, "That o'er the files and musters of the war/Have glowed like plated Mars" (I, i, 3–4). And this sense of greatness as a radiant attribute is felt in the spectacle with which we are immediately presented. The stage directions for the entrance that immediately follows read:

> *Flourish. Enter* ANTONY, CLEOPATRA, *her* LADIES, *the* TRAIN, *with* EUNUCHS *fanning her.*
> (I, i, 10 s.d.)

One of the effects here, of course, is to place Antony amid the court of Egypt. There are no other Romans with him, so Antony is merely part of the entourage, part of the spectacle of Cleopatra's power which will add weight to Philo's description of him as a strumpet's fool. But the court is presented to us in its characteristic activity of *tending* Cleopatra, and this activity will catch our eye in the theater. Antony, Philo has said, has become the bellows and the fan to cool a gypsy's lust, and we immediately see Eunuchs fanning Cleopatra. The spectacle of the court of Egypt actively tending Cleopatra occurs repeatedly in the text and is repeatedly referred to, most notably in Enobarbus' speech and in the preparations surrounding Cleopatra's death. And there are many natural opportunities for it which go unmarked in the stage directions. Very likely, it should happen whenever the Queen appears attended. It will certainly form part of the audience's enduring picture of Cleopatra. What can all this tending and fanning mean?

Enobarbus' speech, in its elaboration of the picture, offers a clue. First of all, as Enobarbus makes clear, the tending of Cleopatra is an activity which expresses and contributes to her greatness, especially in the sense of imaginative command. It does so by a battery of transformations—in which all the objects and persons that tend her pass beyond natural limit, and in which nature itself is transformed as if by a desire to worship Cleopatra. The barge is a throne and its perfume makes the winds lovesick; the water seems controlled by the flute music which establishes a rhythm for the silver oars; it seems amorous of their strokes. Next, we come to the tending and fanning proper:

> On each side her
> Stood pretty dimpled boys, like smiling Cupids,
> With divers-colored fans, whose wind did seem
> To glow the delicate cheeks which they did cool,
> And what they undid did. . . .
> Her gentlewomen, like the Nereides,

> So many mermaids, tended her i' th' eyes,
> And made their bends adornings.
> (II, ii, 203–10)

There is constant renewal here; every gesture of Cleopatra's attendants adds to her beauty, and they in turn seem to grow more beautiful in her presence. Her attendants seem like mythological creatures or works of art, but their superhuman loveliness is controlled, as everything in the speech is, by Cleopatra herself. Her nature goes beyond art:

> O'erpicturing that Venus where we see
> The fancy outwork nature.
> (202–203)

But if her nature goes beyond art, her art—as we have seen—commands nature. Cleopatra may beggar all description, but Enobarbus' powers of description have certainly been regally expanded by his subject. The effect of the spectacle of Cleopatra attended in her barge is to command both nature and imagination. She draws the city's people to her, commands Antony himself, and the spectacle *we* see—three hard-bitten campaigners chatting on an empty stage, one of them moved to sudden eloquence, the others listening raptly, urging him to go on—demonstrates how, even in Rome, she commands Enobarbus' imagination, too.

The constant renewal, the suggestion that the fanning both relieves and excites, reflects a characteristic of Cleopatra herself, who makes hungry where most she satisfies. Summing it up then, the spectacle of her appearances attended, with their undulating movement, their splendor of dress, their warm focus on Cleopatra, heightens our sense of the specific character of her greatness—its commanding, sun-like radiance, its power to transform all it touches, its self-renewing fertility. We should note, too, if we wish to possess the design of the play, how the significances of this spectacle—not only as generally transforming, but transforming of Roman things—are enriched for us over the whole course of the action. We first see it, through Philo's eyes, as an example of a gypsy's lust—the gaudy, self-indulgent world that has trapped and unmanned Antony. That perspective is quickly challenged, however, and by the second act we see the spectacle from a different Roman point of view in the surprising relish and richness of Enobarbus' report. At the end of the play, the tending and adorning is part of the gallant, ecstatic preparation by Cleopatra and her maids for death, and it continues after she is dead—again a transformation, but an enhancing one, of something Roman, the high Roman fashion of suicide.[1]

II

Critics have occasionally complained that *Antony and Cleopatra* is actionless, but it is natural, given the play's notion of greatness, that so much of its on-stage activity is taken up, not with direct combat or intrigue, say, things we normally would think of as action, but with spectacle, praise—and reports. The play takes unusual interest in reports, particularly reports about the great, and especially the imaginative impact of reports both on the reporter and his audience. We think, of course, of Enobarbus' report of Cleopatra. But there are also the play's many messengers and the reports that come to Caesar and Pompey early in the play. Caesar is moved to an impassioned apostrophe to the absent Antony as news of Pompey's strength mounts, and shortly afterward Pompey, having delivered a nicely parallel invocation of Cleopatra's charms, turns from jaunty confidence to apprehension and foreboding when he learns that Antony is on his way to Rome. These reactions help to keep Antony in our thoughts while he is off-stage, and, more importantly, measure his greatness by showing how thought of him dominates and controls the mood of others.

The most dramatically notable report, however, occurs in the fifth act. It helps to provide what little suspense and surprise the plot holds after Antony's death, a main line of intrigue leading up to Cleopatra's suicide. Since it may easily be missed in reading, let me take a moment to sketch its dramatic force. Shortly after Caesar has left the monument, Dolabella reappears, in haste, with news of Caesar's true intentions. His language to Cleopatra is very interesting:

> Madam, as thereto sworn, by your command
> (Which my love makes religion to obey)
> I tell you this.
> (V, ii, 198–200)

And he tells her, concluding:

> I have performed
> Your pleasure, and my promise.
> (203–204)

"As thereto sworn, by your command," he says, and "my promise." But what is he talking about? He has sworn to nothing; he has made no promise. No explicit order has been given. Nevertheless, something has commanded him.

On his previous appearance, Cleopatra has won Dolabella to her purposes, and the full extent of her conquest appears only here. But it is *how* she has won him that is of interest to us. She has succeeded by commanding his mood, impressing him with her greatness and the greatness of her grief. "Your loss is as yourself, great," he says. More specifically, she has won him by a report of Antony's greatness, an immense speech of praise which, even more than Enobarbus' report, has been a work of the imagination, an elaborate hyperbolic portrait, measuring Antony by the world and, finally, by the limits not only of nature but of imagination itself. It is couched in and carries to an extreme the play's language of praise for Antony:

> His legs bestrid the ocean: his reared arm
> Crested the world: his voice was propertied
> As all the tunèd spheres, and that to friends;
> But when he meant to quail and shake the orb,
> He was as rattling thunder. For his bounty,
> There was no winter in't: an autumn 'twas
> That grew the more by reaping. His delights
> Were dolphinlike, they showed his back above
> The element they lived in. In his livery
> Walked crowns and crownets: realms and islands were
> As plates dropped from his pocket.
> (V, ii, 82–92)

Cleopatra's praise of Antony as both equalling nature in superhuman power and going beyond associates Antony with imagination, and is in fact presented as a dream. At this point, Dolabella gently denies that there can have been such a man. But Cleopatra is ready for him. Antony is more than the stuff dreams are made on. He, too, is greater than any fancy that can outwork nature:

> But if there be nor ever were one such,
> It's past the size of dreaming; nature wants stuff
> To vie strange forms with fancy, yet t' imagine
> An Antony were nature's piece 'gainst fancy,
> Condemning shadows quite.
> (96–100)

It is Cleopatra's portrait of Antony that converts her audience. Again, it is no anecdote of what Antony has said or done, but simply a fantastic projection of his greatness that controls the action, transforming Dolabella from a ready tool of Caesar into Cleopatra's devoted servant, a man who imagines he has sworn an oath and made a promise.

III

The play's emphasis on greatness as imaginative command has a radical effect not only on its treatment of action but on the acting it requires of its two heroes. The actors who play Antony and Cleopatra have to convince us from the start that they are great. They have to do this not by their actions—much of the time they are allowed action that does not show greatness but at best asserts it—but by their direct command over our imagination. We must always be aware of Antony and Cleopatra's greatness as a genuine issue. Without the audience's immediate assent that this man, Antony, looks like someone we feel willing, on faith, to measure by superhuman comparisons, without this the play will be tedious, empty at the center. It will be truly actionless, for whatever unifying sense of movement we get from the play depends on our sense that from these two lovers there springs a power that can dominate memory, compel extravagant loyalty, and exact the fascinated attention of the entire world.

We might compare other tragedies in which the heroes are considered great according to one definition or another, but in which they are given early opportunities to exhibit that greatness in action. Othello illustrates his nobility, courage, composure, authority, in the first act through conflict, by challenging Brabantio and Brabantio's men, by overcoming the doubts of his fellow Senators. But Antony and Cleopatra must establish themselves in an atmosphere that comments constantly upon their greatness yet does not test it in action.[2] If anything, what they do early in the play—and indeed throughout most of it—works against their greatness, or against the ordinary measures of greatness in their world. The drama comes from their giving to all things, even the worst, a touch of majesty, making vilest things "become" their greatness.

Consider the problems of an actor who must enter on the lines:

> You shall see in him
> The triple pillar of the world transformed
> Into a strumpet's fool.
> (I, i, 11–13)

The strumpet's fool might not be that hard to manage but the triple pillar of the world—who even as a strumpet's fool remains the triple pillar of the world! "Stand up, Mr. Jones, and try to look like the triple pillar of the world." It has the rawness, the unsupported nakedness of the initial awful moment in an actor's audition, which in most cases is the crucial moment—when you step out and the producer, not waiting to see you tap-dance or do your James Cagney imitation, says, "He'll do," or far more likely, "He won't do"—and doing, in fact, depends not on what you do but what you are, on something in you—that, as they say, you either have or you don't. It is raw presence that is wanted. And the play makes use of, draws its meanings out of, that raw appeal, the claim pure presence in an actor makes on an audience's minds and lives.

In the case of Antony, what the actor must have is the presence of the greatest man in the world. Caesar, by contrast, doesn't need it. If on his first entrance we discover that he looks unimposing, why that can fit into a characterization well enough. His greatness may lie in cunning, or policy, or self-discipline, or realism, or the material power behind him. But the actor of Antony must radiate a magnetism that justifies the admiration he receives.

Shakespeare has written a part that will reward and exhibit this power in the actor who possesses it. When he embraces Cleopatra on their first appearance, the convincing ease with which he requires "On pain of punishment, the world to weet / We stand up peerless" (I, i, 39–40) gives an exciting resonance to their passion, which is essential to the play and which depends on our belief that this is a man who can make the world take notice by sheer charisma. When he makes his followers weep, we watch him deliberately using it. When in the third or fourth act he pulls back repeatedly from dejection, we respond to the radiance that returns.

Antony's dejection is worth further consideration here, because it helps us understand the distinctive accomplishment required of both the play's leading actors. It points not only to a side of Antony's character, but to the essential quality of his relation with Cleopatra. Antony's dejection is deep, and any production will fail that fails to stress it. It consists in his feeling that his greatness has been demolished. The land, he says, is ashamed to bear him. When he can feel a way back to asserting his imaginative command, his spirits invariably revive. Sometimes he fumbles about in his effort to reassert his greatness, as in the pathetic messages to Caesar, but he is utterly renewed even by winning a skirmish we know to be meaningless—not because he expects to win back his material power, but because his greatness is shining forth once more on all around him.

The revival of his spirits at his deepest moments of dejection depends, of course, on Cleopatra. The actor and actress who play Antony and Cleopatra not only must exercise a convincing magnetism, they must convincingly respond to its presence in each other. I know of no comparable investigation, before the nineteenth century, of the way two people in love act upon and change each other, and we must be sure to get the dynamic of their relation right. Now, some critics have taken "the expense of spirit in a waste of shame" as the emblem of Antony and Cleopatra's connection, and seen it as an example of a lust that periodically gives way to remorse.[3] This constitutes, in fact, a fair statement of the typical Roman view of sex in the play, and Antony himself seems to have it in mind early on when he says:

> The present pleasure,
> By revolution low'ring, does become
> The opposite of itself.
> (I, ii, 125–27)

But this is not what happens between Antony and Cleopatra.

Instead of attraction giving way to disgust, we find that whenever Antony reaches a peak of self-revulsion and anger at Cleopatra (never the result of sexual fulfillment, by the way), it is her sexual appeal, even, presumably, from beyond the grave, that enables him to recover. Significantly, the position he comes round to as a result is always one we recognize as more noble than the one he has taken in disgust, more appealing, more in keeping with that great property which should be Antony's. After Actium, after the whipping of Thidias, after the final defeat, Cleopatra brings Antony back from a moment in which he feels his greatness is gone to one in which we—and his audiences on stage—feel that he is exercising it again, whether it be in revelry, battle, or suicide. After he vents his wrath on her, she wins him back to her and to himself. Their mutual attraction, their sexually charged admiration for each other, though it drives them to folly and defeat, likewise stirs them both to greatness—to renewed vitality, indifference to material fortune, and splendid self-presentation.

The sexual magnetism which Antony and Cleopatra exert on each other is very similar to the magnetism of great leaders and great actors, perhaps indistinguishable from it. What binds Cleopatra and Antony sexually is not unlike what binds the world to them and binds us to the attractive presences of the actor and actress who impersonate them. The power of presence in an actor is perilously close to glamour, but it can be taken beyond the limits of glamour by art. This is what the actors of Antony and Cleopatra are required to do, and the process works as a metaphor for the type of problematic splendor their characters manifest. For Antony and Cleopatra are most actor-like in that they exhibit a magnetism that is culturally suspect. Paramount among the vile things they make becoming to the audience are the particular vices of glamorous actors. Cheapness and self-indulgence, narcissism and whoredom, hover about all their gestures.

The challenge here is to skate as close to shoddiness, to the disreputable side of glamor, as possible, to invite demeaning comparisons, both as characters and actors. Antony strikes poses, tries to make his followers weep, takes out his frustrations on the powerless. Cleopatra bitches and camps. Yet they never entirely lose their hold on their on-stage audience, nor should they on us. Shakespeare frequently invites us to judge them harshly, but any interesting performance of the play must keep the higher valuation always before us at least as a possibility, the sense that we are in the presence of some remarkable kind of human richness. They must be, as the text demands, showy, self-regarding, manipulative, concerned with "image"—all the familiar trappings of the glamorous "star." But while showing the seams of their talent, all the glitz of their art, they must show its irresistible power, too.[4]

IV

Once we think of the action of *Antony and Cleopatra* as flowing from the glitzy/charismatic presences of the leading actors, we become aware of a larger process that is everywhere at work in the play. To describe it in the most general terms, it is the process by which things that are attractive but of questionable substance or significance exert a transforming force on the apparently more substantial and valuable world. In so doing, they transform *themselves* into valuable and enduring entities. More concretely, the process is felt in the way Antony and Cleopatra seem to make things happen by sheer magnetism, in the way Cleopatra can make defect perfection, in the way her art can transform nature and her nature outdo art, in the way imagination can alter and enhance reality.

An excellent way of appreciating the depth at which Shakespeare pursues this process is to look closely at one of the play's central terms, a word that occurs in some of its most familiar quotations:

> Vilest things
> Become themselves in her.
> (II, ii, 240–41)

> Fie, wrangling queen!
> Whom everything becomes.
> (I, i, 48–49)

"Become," in this sense of adornment or making attractive, occurs at least eleven times in the play, and is important not so much by virtue of its relative frequency as by the poetic effects to which it contributes. Shakespeare uses it to produce odd knots of meaning, where the general sense or emotion is more or less clear but an additional bend of suggestion is felt.

Let me give some examples:

But, sir, forgive me,
Since my becomings kill me when they do not
Eye well to you.
(I, iii, 95–97)

or

Vilest things
Become themselves in her, that the holy priests
Bless her when she is riggish.
(II, ii, 240–42)

At such moments we may be uncertain as to what is becoming to what or feel that the expected verb–object sequence has been suppressed or reversed. We would expect, for example, that attributes would become their possessors, as in *Mourning Becomes Electra*, but in some passages we feel that the relation has perhaps been altered and in others we are specifically told that the relation is reversed, that the possessors become their attributes. "Observe how Antony becomes his flaw," Caesar says, (III, xii, 34), and Cleopatra remarks:

Look, prithee, Charmian,
How this Herculean Roman does become
The carriage of his chafe.
(I, iii, 83–85)

This last quotation illustrates, in very few words, the complexities the use of *becoming* introduces, and, more importantly, the response to life it stands for. The general sense, I suppose, is: behold how attractively Antony carries his anger. But the words say the opposite. The chafe makes the carriage, and Antony adorns it. The same process is at work in Antony's exclamation, "How every passion strives, in thee, to make itself fair and admired." It is not that someone's management of an unpleasant emotion is attractive. In both cases, the vile thing transforms itself into attractiveness.

Here we see a further complexity. There is, of course, another meaning to *become*—to turn or change into, to develop. The word is used several times in this second sense in *Antony and Cleopatra*, but, more importantly, whenever it is used in the first sense it also takes on suggestions of the second. A sense of transformation always flickers around its edges. *Vilest things become themselves*: the overwhelming primary meaning is that *vile things seem attractive*, but how easy it would be to say *vile things become attractive*. And the additional complication of the passage, the problem of how something can become *itself*, adds to our sense of development, of becoming as contrasted to being. More strongly still, the context of the passage firmly establishes the sense of continuing process, improvement, endless renewal:

> Age cannot wither her, nor custom stale
> Her infinite variety: other women cloy
> The appetites they feed, but she makes hungry
> Where most she satisfies; for vilest things
> Become themselves in her.
> (II, ii, 237–41)

At this point we can conveniently relate these verbal effects to the action of the play. What *becomes* of Antony and Cleopatra flows from their *becomingness*. We feel their attractiveness not only as a source of static pleasure but as a transforming force, changing lives, shaping the course of history, making things happen in the theater. It is through their charismatic appeal that Antony and Cleopatra act on each other and on their audiences. They act on and act out their becomingness, striving even in death to *become themselves*, in both senses of the phrase. Their becomings kill them, as Cleopatra says, but they eye well to us.

One of the play's great emblems of transformation, of insubstantial attractiveness making substantial change, is to be found in the speech Antony delivers in his last moment of dejection. It operates in two ways: first, by suggesting Antony's transforming power over imagination even while claiming he has lost command; second, by a description of natural objects that are at once evanescent and solid, lacking in substance yet powerfully generative of significance:

> Sometime we see a cloud that's dragonish,
> A vapor sometime like a bear or lion,
> A towered citadel, a pendant rock,
> A forked mountain, or blue promontory
> With trees upon't that nod unto the world
> And mock our eyes with air. Thou hast seen these signs:
> They are black vesper's pageants.
> (IV, xiv, 2–8)

On the face of it, Antony is describing the insubstantial, shifting texture of clouds. His point will be that he himself is now of no more weight or account than they. But the feeling of the passage runs quite contrary to its argument. Not weightlessness but solidity dominates our most immediate impression. The stately progress of examples suggests, not watery evanescence, but large, heavy entities, each definite and strong, and all with varying degrees of strangeness that have in common a quality of attacking and commanding power. The dragon's fire passes over into the fork of the mountain; the rock hangs pendent over us. Our sense of the clouds comes from the progression of objects. So does our sense of Antony's emotion and our emotion toward Antony. Each image is one which we can easily associate with him, with his authority, his elevation, his extraordinary capacity to fight, to rage, to brood, to inspire awe. We are not meant to feel an insubstantial Antony here, but a weighty one.

Each of us will likely differ in interpreting the individual details of this immense piece of language, and differ as well in isolating the source of its effect—but if we step back, as it were, to look at the whole passage again, we can agree that what Eros and the audience have before them at this moment is *what happens in the* sky and not its emptiness, not the insubstantiality of clouds but the sweep and scope of their transformations, a huge, strange, heavy, flowing process on the great stage of nature, nodding to the world like the trees on the blue promontory, as great as the world, for all the world to see.

Even at this low point for Antony, then, there is about him a vivid aura of imaginative command, perhaps even a shade of the old self-conscious artistry—he makes Eros weep. His imagery asserts the claims of the imagination even while reminding us of the traditional case against it. Clouds are a familiar symbol both for the imagination's vagaries and for its influence. Antony's description, while ostensibly giving a negative value to the clouds, actually awakens for us all the clouds' grand power over mood and the power of mood to spread and to infect other imaginations. Antony tells us that he is nothing, but he has not lost command over our thoughts. He rules them, like black vesper's pageants. His very loss of power is a great work of dramatic art, a pageant in which Nature and fancy outvie each other, to which we and Eros listen overwhelmed. Antony's speech is not only about his dejection but about the power of imagination to transform the world.

The passage is followed by another exercise of the imagination, a panicky lie, which has a transforming effect on the world of the play. Mardian, lying on Cleopatra's behalf, acts the part of Cleopatra dying, and this double bit of pretense finally prompts Antony to suicide. After the final defeat, then, the action is shaped by a series of deliberate manipulations of reality—deceptions (as of Antony here and Caesar later), self-dramatizations (as in the cloud speech and the conversion of Dolabella), and finally Cleopatra's carefully staged spectacle of suicide. The long concluding movement of the play, more than one-fifth its length, is dominated by this sequence of imaginative transformations, which accompany and bring about a corresponding emotional movement of enhancement—from meanness and agitation of spirit to generosity and peace, leading from Antony's rage through Cleopatra's panic, through the false report and the attempted suicide, through Antony's death in Cleopatra's arms, to Cleopatra's final sovereign moments.

V

The process I have been describing—of imaginative transformation and enhancement, of making the insubstantial substantial, the questionable valuable—is very active in those final moments, and I want to approach them by way of an important and closely related pattern of imagery. A great deal has been made, critically, of what might be called horizontal oscillation in the play, its use of a back-and-forth movement in the alternation of scenes between Egypt and Rome, in the swings of Antony's emotions, and in many images—the vagabond flag upon the stream, for instance. And this has generally been interpreted as contributing either to a sense of ambivalence or of dissolution, or both. But there is another pattern of movement in language and action which is far more vividly impressed upon us, and which both controls and gives meaning to the horizontal. It might be called vertical, for contrast. The movement is both down and up, and the effect is one not of mere oscillation or breaking apart but of enrichment, renewal, and freedom. Put simply, it is a movement sometimes of descending into, but always of rising from, the generative slime, and it makes itself felt in the stage movement, the imagery, and the psychic action of the characters. But to put it simply is to run the risk of missing the fullness of its work upon us. For it is presented with great variety and suavity.

I want to stress the larger dramatic imagery here, but I would like to begin with one of the more frequently discussed verbal images as a way of making clearer the relation I perceive between the movements I am calling vertical and horizontal. When Caesar in a famous passage refers to the movement of the tide, he is not only indulging a typical bit of Roman political analysis, he is using imagery familiar to us from *Julius Caesar*, where it also stands for those currents politicians must study and follow:

> It hath been taught us from the primal state
> That he which is was wished until he were;
> And the ebbed man, ne'er loved till ne'er worth love,
> Comes deared by being lacked. This common body,

Like to a vagabond flag upon the stream,
Goes to and back, lackeying the varying tide,
To rot itself with motion.
(I, iv, 41–47)

The tide in the affairs of men goes this way and that in both plays, and he who does not seize it at the flood is drowned in it. And when Antony sees Octavia standing, as at that moment the whole Mediterranean world stands, between the two great competitors, he calls on a similar image, though gentler and more humanely felt:

the swan's-down feather
That stands upon the swell at the full of tide,
And neither way inclines.
(III, ii, 49–51)

But like many Roman judgments in the play this version of the tide image is not final. For tides do not move horizontally but, rather, vertically upon the varying shore of the world, and it is the vertical movement of the Nile from full to ebb—not aimless but fertilizing—that dominates the play.

The process by which the rise and fall of the tides is measured and used to sow the land is described at length by Antony for Caesar's benefit during their Bacchic feast, and runs through the play's imagery. *Antony and Cleopatra* begins with an accusation that Antony o'erflows the measure, but it is suffused with the suggestion that to o'erflow the measure is to moisten the earth and renew the world. Or, put another way, the tide of the affairs of men may be an endless oscillation, but the tides of nature endlessly create.

I hope this has given a useful notion of what I am calling vertical movement. In the play's stage imagery, it is most prominent when Antony is hoisted up to Cleopatra in the monument. I doubt whether one can overemphasize the force of this daring piece of stage mechanics. First of all we must pay full attention to Antony's condition. He has bungled his suicide, and we are meant to know that it hurts. For all his fortitude, he cries out in pain at least once. As early as *Romeo and Juliet*, Shakespeare had played the neat death off against the messy one, and here the messiness of the death, in which the hero must be seen as bungling, helpless, bleeding, in cruel pain, works against and with the wit, high language, and emblematic significance of his elevation. Up comes the dying Antony from the blood and mess to a final kiss, a final drink, a final cry of pain, and a final display of nobility. At the moment he reaches the balcony, Cleopatra explicitly strikes the note of renewal:

> Welcome, welcome! Die where thou hast lived,
> Quicken with kissing.[5]
> (IV, xv, 38–39)

Antony's movement here through and with what is low or messy to what is high and great is repeated more subtly but with equal theatrical force in the sequence of events leading up to and beyond Cleopatra's suicide. So much of importance is going on simultaneously in this last scene that it is difficult to talk about in any wholly perspicuous sequence. Perhaps it would be useful to begin by noting that there is more specific anticipation of the final death in this play than in any other Shakespearean tragedy. That is, there is more verbal reference to the particular circumstances in which Cleopatra will die. All the tragedies contain lines which may at least be construed as foreshadowing their end, and, not surprisingly, it is the love tragedies, *Romeo and Juliet* and *Othello*, that come closest to our play in this regard, with Romeo's dream, Othello's foreshadowing kiss, and his anticipation of chaos. But we have many more and more specific references to the nature and effect of Cleopatra's suicide—the serpent of old Nile, the breathless breathing forth of power, the am'rous pinches which are later echoed in the stroke of death like a lover's pinch, etc. I think Shakespeare may have been encouraged in this by the circumstance that this would be of all his plays the one in which the audience would be most familiar with the manner of the climactic death and most fascinated by it, and in which Cleopatra's way of dying would be one of the most famous things about this famous couple. For her death with the serpent at her breast was one way in which these lovers commanded imagination in posterity as they did in their lifetime. By anticipating it, Shakespeare is not only making capital out of his audience's state of mind, but he is using the fact of our state of mind as part of the stuff and meaning of his play. Among the other sensations of the death scene, we are aware of ourselves savoring the fame of famous events.

In the deaths of both Antony and Cleopatra, we feel once more the force of the play's focus on greatness as imaginative command. Their deaths are insisted upon—by Shakespeare, by themselves, by the people around them—as imaginative acts that sustain and enhance their nobility, as ways of imposing their greatness permanently on the play's multiple audiences. It is not the fact that they die, or even that they die by their own hand. What matters is their style of doing it, how they conceive and describe it, how their audiences react.

Cleopatra's death is a superb piece of poetic transformation which quite insists on its poetry. Its best-known lines draw attention to their own verbal magic—their echoes, condensations, comparisons, ambiguities. The scene as a whole insists, too, on its power to change vilest things into lasting pleasures and great achievements, outreaching the Roman standard of suicide it seems based upon. Hers is no terse, stoic acceptance of a sword in the belly but a conversion of death into something gentle, regenerative, sovereign. Death is like sleep, sexual pursuit becomes a strong (and sleep-like) toil of grace; the snake is the worm that quickens Nilus' slime, a baby sleeping and feeding at the nurse's breast.

Like most of the ambiguities in the play, the treatment of the language here and the treatment of death itself works to take a relatively plain statement and promote it vertically, to invest it with greater attractiveness and value. Similarly, the events surrounding Cleopatra's suicide are arranged in a way that makes us aware of vertical promotion. Their sequence suggests a pattern of enhancement, a rising free from limit. We build up from Cleopatra as a helpless prisoner, whom we have seen struggling in the arms of her captors and kneeling to Caesar; through her scene with the Clown, with its puns and homely language, its basket and snake and talk of mud; through the play's final scene of tending and adorning, the putting on of the robe and the crown—a moment of stage spectacle that we see in the process of being created as well as in its final visual splendor. Then, of course, she dies, having become fire and air, with a great evocation of peace and gentleness.

The quality of sensation projected by the actress at the moment of Cleopatra's death is one of the play's most concentrated expressions of the entire complex of feeling we have been charting. As Lear dies in a moment of heightened perception,

> Look on her. Look, her lips,
> Look there, look there.
> (V, iii, 312–13)

so Cleopatra dies in a moment of heightened sensation:

> As sweet as balm, as soft as air, as gentle . . .
> (V, ii, 311)

Lear focuses on Cordelia's lips, as his play has repeatedly focused on minute bodily particulars. Cleopatra dies in a large, enveloping sensual experience, which has the enriching ambiguity typical of the play. Is she describing, in these words, the gentleness of the asp like a baby at her breast, or the stroke of death like that of a lover, or is it her lover himself? For her words finally gather into that name of names, so often used simply as a superlative in the play, that infinite virtue uncaught by the snares of the world, though tangled in them, indeed adorned by them:

As sweet as balm, as soft as air, as gentle—
O, Antony!

VI

Like Cleopatra's death, the play as a whole can be taken as insisting on what poetry can do—and on the problematic status of that power. To make vilest things becoming, to take a gypsy's lust and, by fanning it, to convert it into a mesmerizing radiance of fire and air—well, such procedures are a kind of trick, but they also echo some of our deepest experiences outside the theater, notably the experience of sexual passion and the related phenomena of human charisma. And if it is a trick, it is not a deception; Shakespeare, like Antony and Cleopatra, hides nothing. We see the moral questionableness of the material at every step, yet the enhancement mounts. The world of the entire play is bound to weet that its heroes stand up peerless—though no one can miss the point that they are of the earth, dungy. In them, as in poetry, every passion, however mean or ugly, can be made fair and admired—and we are left astonished that this can be so.

Are we left enlightened? One way of describing the elusiveness of *Antony and Cleopatra* is to say that of all Shakespeare's plays it is perhaps the hardest to accommodate to a notion of authorial intention. As a result, it is nearly impossible to discuss the play without making some statement about how we are to receive its peculiar mixture of glamor and demystification. I would like to approach this question by way of a flight of biographical fancy, which I hope will be taken less as an assertion of possible fact than as a metaphor, a step toward describing the kind of understanding the play communicates. I find it helpful to think of *Antony and Cleopatra* as written at a moment when Shakespeare, for whatever reason, had become particularly self-conscious about his own career. At forty-three or forty-four, he would have had a reasonably clear sense of his own greatness. Even if he shared his culture's relatively low estimate of the importance of playwriting, he must have been conscious of the unusual power of his mind. The intellectual effort required to produce *Hamlet*, *Troilus and Cressida*, *Measure for Measure*, *Othello*, *King Lear*, and *Macbeth* in half-a-dozen years would have struck even the most modest of men as extraordinary. Like any great artist he might have wondered what his powers could have achieved in a more practical sphere:

I turn away and shut the door and on the stair
Wonder how many times I could have proved my worth
In something that all others understand or share.

Antony, too, was admirably fitted for success in practical life—and instead both he and Cleopatra had chosen to follow an aesthetic path, the path of imagination and pleasure, had chosen to live out their mutual attraction—and attractiveness—to the full. What value, what substance, could be found in such a career?

And there was the other side of the coin to consider. What was Shakespeare's responsibility for the moral impact of his art? If, like Antony, he had followed his imagination where it might lead, placing its promptings finally before the claims of practical success, he had at the same time led a most public life. Again like Antony (and like Cleopatra, too), he had continually addressed the world in the most calculated terms, attempting very deliberately to command its feelings. Like Antony, he knew how to make his followers weep. Had he done less harm than his heroes—or had he too corrupted honest men?

> Did that play of mine send out
> Certain men the English shot?

Essex's friends had of course been idiotic to arrange for a performance of *Richard II* on the eve of their rebellion, but one could see their point. Whatever Shakespeare may have intended, however orthodox the political "philosophy" of his history plays, the power of his art made the possibility of rebellion vivid, interesting, moving. In this, it loosened the fibers of authority and moral restraint. And which of the tragedies, with their immense indulgence of passion and fantasy, did not? Oh, they were perfectly correct on questions of right and wrong. *Macbeth* deprecated regicide; *Othello* made it clear one wasn't supposed to kill one's wife. But each was a risky adventure in feeling and knowledge. Certainly it could not be denied that imagination at its most importunate swept dangerously beyond moral lines. The power of language could make everything it touched precious, could, while the play lasted, make its own preciousness the center of value. In the figures of Antony and Cleopatra, Shakespeare may have recognized an appeal like that of supreme poetic fluency itself—the amoral splendor of the absolutely attractive.

In any literal sense, of course, such speculation is idle. We can never know Shakespeare's intentions, if he had any, and no intention can account for a work as great as *Antony and Cleopatra*. But the relation between poetry and the practical or moral life does give us a metaphor for our involvement with its heroes. As such it helps place the *showiness* of the play—its unparalleled emphasis on the quality of its own technique—and the similar showiness of Antony and Cleopatra. It also helps us in the difficult task of getting the play's ironies straight.

I do not think we are meant to "balance" the claims of Antony and Cleopatra with those of their critics; nor does one position dissolve or transcend the other. Rather, the main experience of the play is what I called vertical promotion. We are caught up in the process of enhancement. In the end, all the play's most questionable materials are transformed into elements of Cleopatra's final spectacle. They do not cease to be questionable, but the transformation sweeps us along. We accept it and enjoy it. At the same time, we are left with no confident way of locating or judging the process. Indeed—a further complication—we are left without a feeling of disturbance, with none of the moral vertigo, for example, that attends *Troilus and Cressida*. We are not allowed the comfort of knowing what we can "do" with the pleasure we feel; we are not even allowed the moral comfort of discomfort.

Shakespeare's position in all this may perhaps be glimpsed in the role of the messenger who brings Cleopatra the news of Antony's marriage to Octavia. What is his relation to these questionable lives he reports with such accuracy?

> O, that his fault should make a knave of thee,
> That art not what th'art sure of!
> (II, v, 102–103)

Though the poet is not, morally, to be confused with what he describes, still the good poet must be "sure" of the news he brings—and is thus in some sense implicated in it. Neither Aristotle's nor Sidney's excuses quite get him off the hook. Poetry makes nothing happen, says Auden, but he would have been more correct had he added—except for the things that happen when we read poetry. Poetry makes life seem very interesting, and, once aroused, there is no way to confine this interest to what is healthful, prudent, or community oriented. In *Antony and Cleopatra*, Shakespeare found a subject that richly indulged the ambiguity of the poet's position, a story that both challenged the claims of raw imaginative power and seductively breathed them forth. The play mounts no case against morality and public order; for certain instants, it simply leaves them behind.

The special theatrical quality of this experience can be felt in a question: what are we to make of a tragedy that finds its climax in an *easy way to die*? Like the acting it requires from its title characters, the action of *Antony and Cleopatra* puts a premium on sensual indulgence, on the unabashed exploitation of what is immediately attractive. Not for this play the suggestion that violent delights have violent ends, the idea which makes the action of *Romeo and Juliet* feel always like fire kissing powder. Instead we are drawn into the rhythm of indulgence itself, following out its becomings, seeking its own fulfillment, the sensual moment indefinitely prolonged, remembered, desired:

> There's not a minute of our lives should stretch
> Without some pleasure now.
> (I, i, 46–47)

> As sweet as balm, as soft as air, as gentle—
> O, Antony!
> (V, ii, 311–12)

We have seen how Cleopatra's last words focus on physical sensation. As an acting problem, that easy death must be made good by the actress' sensual conviction. Here, as throughout the play, we must be won over by the actors' ability to make the experience of sensation itself admirable and fulfilling—to demonstrate their commitment to pleasure in a way that makes an audience willing to entertain it as "the nobleness of life."

This special focus on the creation of pleasure as an end in itself—on sensuality in performance and as performance—places us in an unusual relation to the heroes of the play. Antony and Cleopatra are each other's best audience. They love each other, above all else, for the excellence of their performances ("Good now, play one scene / Of excellent dissembling") (I, iii, 78–79). If we may be said at all to identify with Antony and Cleopatra, it is their performances we identify with—with the ways in which they are most like the actors who play them, with their abnormal capacity to feel pleasure and desire and to transmit those feelings splendidly to the world. Our identification is the more breathless because we see them risking so much vulgarity and showing their bodies to be used and aging and greedy as well as attractive. We identify with their performances—rather than with the inner movement or constitution of their minds. There is nothing in Antony and Cleopatra that passes show. Indeed, the aim of their action is to find a show which passes everything—all obstacles and competitors—which shackles accidents and bolts up change.

Even more, perhaps, this is a play in which we identify with audiences, with Antony and Cleopatra as each other's audience, with ourselves as audience, and with the audience characters on stage. The play throws us into the position of Octavius in his tent, weeping at the death of a man we could not afford to tolerate among us, wondering (as we always wonder about Octavius) whether or not our tears are real. Our response to the play also resembles our response to and through Enobarbus, whose defection we regret, though in reason we cannot condemn it. As moral observers, we too would defect from

Antony—yet to give up on Antony is to desert the life of the play. If we want to go on living after Enobarbus dies, we must remain loyal to this great corrupter of honest men, we must, as Cleopatra says, die where we have lived.

Notes

1. The process of transformation is further extended by the play's final procession, which represents a transformation by Cleopatra of the triumph that her Roman conqueror has planned. Regally attired, solemnly and respectfully attended, she is now to be carried, not to humiliation in Rome, but to a famous Egyptian grave, and Caesar himself is glad to claim reflected glory from the spectacle. As an Egyptian procession has brought Cleopatra on-stage at the beginning of the play, a Roman one carries her off, but it, too, celebrates her greatness.

2. Redgrave comments, "You have to create, convincingly, the image of a man who held part of the world in thrall, and you have very little to do it with; all you have is his voluptuousness." (Margaret Lamb, *Antony and Cleopatra on the English Stage* [Associated Universities Press, 1981], p. 147.)

3. An influential and particularly explicit example is John Danby, *Poets on Fortune's Hill* (London, 1952), pp. 128–51.

4. In the role of Cleopatra, Shakespeare makes good use of the boy actor to reinforce this double impression. At the beginning, Cleopatra draws heavily on the boy actor's strong suits of playful bitchery, bright raillery, mockery of the "adult" Roman style, but concludes the play on a sustained level of mature emotion which severely taxes the boy's skills—even while calling attention to his limitations (including, specifically, his whory gestures). Watching the boy Cleopatra, an Elizabethan audience could feel both the theatrical shallowness of "boying" a woman's greatness and the power of *this* boy to go beyond the normal limits of his art. See *The Actor's Freedom: Toward a Theory of Drama*, pp. 141–45.

5. Following Pope's emendation at l. 38.

NORTHROP FRYE

Antony and Cleopatra

I've talked about *Hamlet* as the central Shakespeare play for the nineteenth and early twentieth centuries, when so many cultural factors revolved around the difficulties of uniting action and the consciousness of action. In the existentialist period of this century this theme was still in the foreground, but, with a growing sense of the absurdity of trying to rationalize a world set up for the benefit of predatory rulers, *King Lear* began to move into the centre in its place. I don't know what play will look most central in the twenty-first century, assuming we get there, but *Antony and Cleopatra* is, I think, the play that looks most like the kind of world we seem to be moving into now.

History goes in cycles to a large extent, and in our day we're back to the Roman phase of the cycle again. It's amazing how vividly Shakespeare has imagined a world so much more like ours than like his. There's no Tudor anxiety about who the Lord's anointed is or who his successor should be. We can see what the power relations are like in the conference on Pompey's galley. The Roman Empire has reached the stage of the second "triumvirate," or control by three leaders, Antony, Caesar and Lepidus. Lepidus, who holds a third of the world but not his liquor, is only a cipher, and as soon as the time is right he is swept into prison on a trumped-up charge by Caesar. Caesar and Antony are making an alliance, to be cemented by Antony's marriage to

---

Caesar's sister, Octavia, but we realize that they are only postponing a showdown. Enobarbus says so, speaking on Antony's side; Antony tells him to be quiet, but Caesar expresses his agreement, and remarks again after Antony's death that two such leaders "could not stall together" in the same world. After the conference ends, the triumvirate goes off the ship, because Pompey lacks the nerve to murder the lot of them and become master of the world himself. Having missed his chance, the officer who suggested it to him deserts him in disgust.

The defeat of Antony by Caesar does not centralize authority in the way that, for example, the defeat of Richard III centralizes authority in the House of Tudor. We're not in a closely knit kingdom anymore: there's only one world, so there's no patriotism, only more or less loyalty to the competing leaders. Late in the play the demoralized Antony challenges Caesar to a duel, and we see how clearly the creator of Tybalt understands that in *this* world personal duelling is an impossibly corny notion. There are any number of messengers in the play, and the air is thick with information and news, but nothing much seems to be getting communicated, although when something does happen it affects the whole world at once. But while there is one world, there are two aspects of it: the aspect of "law and order" represented by Rome, and the aspect of sensual extravagance and licence represented by Egypt. The lives and fortunes of millions depend, quite simply, on the whims and motivations of three people. The fact that two of them are lovers means that what is normally a private matter, the sexual relation, becomes an illuminated focus of contemporary history.

The historical Cleopatra was a highly cultivated woman who spoke seven languages and had had the best education her time afforded. It's true that she used her sex as a political weapon, but Queen Elizabeth used her virginity as a political weapon. All the efforts of Roman propaganda failed to disguise the fact that she was the one person the Romans were really afraid of. When the news of her death reached Rome, even the normally stodgy Horace was prompted into something like enthusiasm:

> Nunc est bibendum, nunc pede libero
> pulsanda tellus . . .

Now's the time to drink and dance, because Cleopatra's dead and everything's going to be wonderful. Virgil was more restrained, but even he puts the word *nefas*, shameful, into his allusion to her in the *Aeneid*. The spectre of an enemy equipped, not merely with an open female sexuality, which was frightening enough, but with terrible secret weapons like intelligence and imagination, was gone forever. (I'm not idealizing her—she was a tough and dirty fighter—but her qualities had survival value in her world.) Shakespeare's treatment of her is not historical: for one thing, the historical Cleopatra was Greek, not Egyptian, and we have to forget that in this play, where she's the very essence of Egypt. But we can see from the play why she still haunts history as well as literature.

Of the two aspects of the Roman-Egyptian world, Caesar belongs consistently to the Roman side, Cleopatra consistently to the Egyptian one, and Antony vacillates between the two. Near the beginning of the play, with Antony in Egypt, Cleopatra remarks sardonically: "A Roman thought hath struck him." But Antony, at least then, knows what a Roman thought is, and Cleopatra, quite genuinely, does not. The Roman way of life makes no sense of any kind to her, despite her previous experience of it, when she was attached to Julius Caesar. The most elementary way of misreading this play is to turn it into either a moral or a romantic melodrama, against or for Cleopatra. The moral view identifies Rome with the virtues of Rome, and Egypt with the vices of Egypt, and says what a pity it was that so great a man, instead of living up to his historical destiny, allowed himself to be debased by a sexy woman. The romantic view is expressed in the title of the second most famous play on the subject in English literature: John Dryden's *All for Love, or The World Well Lost.* (The play itself is better balanced.) Both views are cop-outs: what we have to make sense of is a tragedy, not a morality play or a sentimental love story.

We've seen Shakespeare working, in *Hamlet* and *King Lear*, on well-known stories that had been treated in earlier plays. In *Antony and Cleopatra* he was dealing with one of the best-known stories in the world, one that everybody had heard of and that was endlessly alluded to in every kind of literary genre. There was an earlier play (one of many) on this subject too: Samuel Daniel's *Cleopatra* (1594), which deals with events occurring after the death of Antony. According to Ben Jonson, "Samuel Daniel was a good honest man, had no children; but no poet." You may gather from this, correctly, that Jonson's judgments were not always notable for fairness. Shakespeare found a good deal of poetry in Daniel's play, and probably found in him too the emphasis on the horror of being part of Caesar's triumph in Rome as the main motive for Cleopatra's suicide. For the rest, Shakespeare's main source was Plutarch's *Lives*, which was available to him, in those easygoing days, in an English translation made from a French translation of the Greek. The incidents of the play almost all come straight from Plutarch, except that the impression of Antony we get from Plutarch is one of a rather brutal gangster: I hope the reasons why Shakespeare gives so different an impression of him will become clearer as we go on. For this, and for all the rest of the plays in this course, we have the Folio text only. Modern printed texts, where you get involved with Act IV, Scene xv, may give the impression of a cumbersome play, but any good production will show that the speed and economy of Shakespeare's storytelling are still at top level. Caesar and Antony also appear in Shakespeare's earlier play *Julius Caesar*, but I think it's a mistake to read our present play as a sequel, though we could look at a few details here that refer back to the earlier time.

Julius Caesar had set up the triumvirate pattern earlier in his career, when he got control of the western part of the Roman world, leaving Pompey in control of the east. Crassus, a slum-landlord profiteer, supplied the money and was the third member. Looking for a more heroic role, he led an expedition against the Parthians, on the eastern frontier of the empire: the Parthians captured and murdered him, and poured molten gold down his throat—the only evidence we have of what the Parthian sense of humour was like. I mention it only because Cleopatra uses the image as one of the things she would like to do to the messenger who brings the news of Antony's marriage. Pompey was murdered in Egypt, but his son, who had become a pirate, is still an influential figure in the world of *Antony and Cleopatra*. The rebels against Julius Caesar, Brutus and Cassius, were defeated and killed at the battle of Philippi by an army led by Mark Antony and Octavius Caesar, as he was then called. In this play Antony has a good deal to say about how much the Philippi victory depended on him and how little on his colleague, but in *Julius Caesar* he and Octavius both seem rather mean-minded and cynical, co-opting Lepidus but determined to treat him as a "property," always ready (especially Antony) to manipulate a crowd with tear-jerking speeches, but using the impetus of revenge for Julius Caesar's death to get power for themselves.

Both of them are relatives of Julius Caesar: Octavius was born his nephew, but was adopted as his son. The fact that Cleopatra had been Julius Caesar's mistress, and had borne him a son, Caesarion, makes an additional complication to the later play. Caesar tells his lieutenants how Cleopatra and Antony were publicly enthroned in Alexandria, along with "Caesarion, whom they call my father's son." We notice how often tragedy includes as a central theme a rupture within a family, as in *Hamlet* and *King Lear*, and in this play Caesar, and Antony by virtue of his marriage to Octavia, are both involved in inter-family feuds. There is, of course, a considerable difference between Roman and Egyptian views on what constitutes a permanent sexual relationship. In Rome there is no obstacle to Antony's marriage to Octavia because Cleopatra has no legal status as a wife; but in the closing moments of the play, when Cleopatra plans her entrance into the next world, it never occurs to her that anybody in that world would be stupid enough to regard Antony as still married to Octavia. Her only problem, as she sees it, is to get into the next world before her attendant Charmian, so that she won't have to get Antony pried loose from somebody else. The point here is not how primitive her views of the next world are, but the fact that she can't conceive of any world at all where she wouldn't continue to be Cleopatra.

I've often spoken of the theatre as the central character in all of Shakespeare's plays, and this play revolves around Cleopatra because she's the essence of theatre. Besides having the fattest female role in the entire range of drama, she's a woman whose identity is an actress's identity. One wonders how the lad who first attempted the part got along, and how much he liked expressing Cleopatra's contempt of having "Some squeaking Cleopatra boy my greatness"—a line that in any case took the most colossal nerve on Shakespeare's part to write, even if the context is logical enough. One occasionally hears some such question about the play as: "Did Cleopatra really love Antony or was she just play-acting?" The word "really" shows how wrong the assumption underlying the question is. Cleopatra is not an actress who can be Vivien Leigh or Elizabeth Taylor offstage: the offstage does not exist in her life. Her love, like everything else about her, is theatrical, and in the theatre illusion and reality are the same thing. Incidentally, she never soliloquizes; she talks to herself occasionally, but someone else is always listening and she always knows it.

The most famous description of her is in the speech of Enobarbus describing her appearance in the royal barge on the Cydnus. Enobarbus is a character who in this age of Brecht might be called an alienation character: it's part of his function in the play to comment on how the principals are doing as theatrical figures. He has several other aspects, one of them being a plain blunt Roman soldier, and one wonders if a plain blunt soldier would really talk about Cleopatra in the terms he does if he were not half in love with her himself. At the same time, he calls her Antony's "Egyptian dish," and has earlier commented to Antony himself about her carefully manufactured tantrums. He comes close to the centre of his own feelings, however, when he says that "vilest things / Become themselves in her," echoing Antony's earlier remark that she is someone "whom everything becomes." To translate this simply as "she can get away with anything" would be inadequate: it means far more than that. Pascal remarked in one of his aphorisms that if Cleopatra's nose had been an inch shorter the history of the world would have been different. But Shakespeare's Cleopatra could have coped very easily with a snub nose (actually the historical Cleopatra may have had one, as some of her coins suggest). She doesn't depend on any conventional attributes of beauty. The whole of Cleopatra is in everything she expresses, whether splendid, silly, mean, grandiloquent, malicious or naive, and so her essential fascination comes through in every mood. She has the female equivalent of the kind of magnetism that makes Antony a born leader, whose soldiers will follow him in the face of obvious disaster.

Of course there is a price to be paid for being in contact with such a creature, the price of being upstaged by someone who is always centre stage. At the beginning of the play we have this little whispered exchange among her attendants:

> Hush! here comes Antony.
> Not he: the queen. (I.ii. 75)

The words could not be more commonplace, yet they tell us very clearly who is number one in that court. Her suicide is motivated by her total refusal to be a part of someone else's scene, and she needs the whole fifth act to herself for her suicide show. Apart from Julius Caesar, who is a special case, Mark Antony is the only major hero of Shakespeare who dies in the fourth act. An obsolete proverb says that behind every great man there is a devoted woman, but Cleopatra is not a devoted woman and she's not standing behind anybody. Octavia, now, is the kind of woman who does exactly what she should do in a man's world, and she bores the hell out of Antony.

There is no character in Shakespeare whom Cleopatra resembles less than Falstaff, and yet there is an odd link between them in dramatic function. Both are counter-historical characters: they put on their own show oblivious to the history that volleys and thunders around them. But the history of Falstaff's time would have been the same without him, and Cleopatra, though very conscious of her "greatness" in her own orbit, hardly seems to realize that she is a key figure in *Roman* history as well. Her great betrayal of Antony comes in the middle of the battle of Actium, when she simply pulls her part of the fleet out of the battle. What is going on in her mind is probably something like: "What silly games these men do play: nobody's paying any attention to me at all." She may not even be aware that her action would lose Antony the battle, or that it would make any difference if it did. She says to Enobarbus, "Is Antony or we in fault for this?" and it seems clear that it is a real question for her, even though she's obviously dissatisfied with Enobarbus's patriarchal Roman answer that the fault was entirely Antony's for paying attention to a woman in a battle. We may still wonder why she insisted on entering the battle in the first place: the reason seems to be that Caesar was shrewd enough to declare the war personally on her, putting her in the spotlight of attention. So, although Antony could have won handily on land, she insists on a seafight, because there would be nowhere to see her in a land operation.

Let's look at Antony's death scene, in which, after a bungled attempt at suicide and mortally wounded, he makes his way to Cleopatra's monument and asks her to come down and give him her last kiss. But Cleopatra has already started on her private war to outwit Caesar's plan to make her part of his triumph in Rome. It sounds like a restricted operation, but it's as important to Cleopatra as the mastery of the world is to Caesar. So she apologizes to Antony, but she's afraid she can't come down "Lest I be taken." She must stay in the protection of a monument that would hold up a cohort of Roman legionaries for about a minute and a half. There's no help for it: "we must draw thee up." What follows is a difficult scene to stage, but nobody can miss the humiliation for Antony of this grotesque manoeuvre, to say nothing of the physical agony of the ordeal for a dying man. "Here's sport indeed! How heavy weighs my lord!" says Cleopatra. Our minds go back to an earlier scene, when, with Antony absent and Cleopatra stupefied with boredom, she proposes to go fishing, as she used to do with Antony:

> my bended hook shall pierce
> Their slimy jaws; and as I draw them up,
> I'll think them every one an Antony,
> And say "Ah ha! y'are caught." (II.v. 12–15)

To Antony's exhausted murmur, "Give me some wine, and let me speak a little," her answer is, "No, let me speak, and let me rail." When Antony is finally going, she says first, "Hast thou no care of me?" and then breaks into the tremendous rhetoric of her lament for her dead lover. I'm taking phrases out of their contexts a bit, and of course Shakespeare's really intense scenes are so delicately balanced that emphasizing and overemphasizing any single aspect are almost the same thing.

The reason why Antony is in this situation, and mortally wounded, is that when his fleet surrendered to Caesar he assumed that Cleopatra had betrayed him, and Cleopatra had to counter this threat with the most dramatic action possible: of sending to Antony, by her eunuch Mardian, a report of her death, which Mardian was urged to "word piteously." All of which still does not show that Cleopatra is a monster of selfishness. Selfishness is a product of calculation, and Cleopatra, at least at the moment of Antony's death, is not calculating. Her reactions are too instinctive to be called selfish: she's just being Cleopatra. And she's still being Cleopatra when, a few scenes later, she thinks of the humiliation of being in Caesar's triumph, and says with the utmost horror (echoing a phrase Antony had used earlier): "Shall they hoist *me* up?" (emphasis mine, but doubtless hers as well).

From now on, her whole strategy is directed to baffling Caesar's intention to include her in his triumph in Rome. She first has to make sure that this is his intention. The dying Antony has said to her: "None about Caesar trust but Proculeius." It would not occur to Cleopatra to trust anybody: what she does with all the people she meets is to ascertain, within a few seconds, whether she can get what she wants from them or not. Proculeius, precisely because he is trustworthy, walks into her monument and takes her prisoner; then Dolabella comes in. It is to him that she utters a prodigiously exaggerated eulogy of Antony: he doesn't fall for that, of course, being a Roman, but he's dazzled by her all the same, and in no time she's extracted the information she wants.

Caesar certainly does want Cleopatra to be part of his victory procession in Rome: her presence there "would be eternal in our triumph," he says. He has her under close guard, and keeps two of her children as hostages, dropping a veiled threat about their fate if she should fool him. That falls flat: Cleopatra is one of the least motherly heroines in literature, and hardly even knows that she has children. There is a scene (which I'm reading the way it usually is read and produced) in which, with Caesar present, she pretends to be outraged with her treasurer, Seleucus, for exposing some minor cheating of hers, reserving for herself some "trifles" that were part of the Roman loot. Caesar is amused by this, but assumes that if Cleopatra still wants such things she can hardly be meditating suicide, which is precisely what she hoped he would think. Then she arranges for a clown to bring a basket of figs to her past the Roman guard, poisonous serpents being under the figs.

This clown, brief as his scene is, is extraordinarily haunting: as with the more elaborate gravediggers' scene in *Hamlet*, he represents almost our only contact with the population of survivors on whose backs all these masters of the world are sitting. As a clown, he mixes up his words, as clowns conventionally do, but the way he mixes them makes him an eerie and ghoulish messenger from another world, and not at all the kind of world Cleopatra thinks of herself as entering. He hands on a recommendation to Cleopatra from a woman who has sought the same remedy for life: "how she died of the biting of it, what pain she felt; truly, she makes a very good report o' the worm." At the same time he strains Cleopatra's nerves nearly to the breaking point: he's garrulous; he doesn't want to shuffle off the stage; he knows very well what he's carrying and what it's for, and at any moment he could wreck her whole scheme. However, the stage is finally clear: her scheme has succeeded; the "worm" is ready to do its job. She wishes that the serpent, like its ancestor in Eden, could speak, and call "great Caesar ass." It's hardly necessary to add that she's greatly underrating Caesar: there isn't a syllable of disappointment or baffled rage from him when he discovers he's been circumvented. That's how things go sometimes, is his only reaction. Let's give them both a big funeral and attend it "in solemn show." They've earned that, at least.

All of which seems merely to be accumulating evidence that Cleopatra was Antony's evil genius. It's true that she herself doesn't seem to be really evil, in the way that Goneril and Regan are evil. No doubt she'd be capable of it, in some contexts. But what we see is a woman possessed by vanity, and vanity, whatever the moralists say, is a rather disarming vice, in a way almost innocent, exposing the spoiled child under the most infuriating behaviour of the adult. And sometimes we even wonder if she's such a simple thing as an evil genius at all. In the second scene of the play a "soothsayer" is introduced, making a not very glamorous living telling the fortunes of a group of giggly attendants on Cleopatra. We know that Shakespeare would never introduce such a character unless he were going to use him later, and later he duly appears, to tell Antony that his real evil genius is Caesar. (He's Egyptian, of course, but that seems to have nothing to do with it.) The mysterious quality called "luck," so important and so frequently mentioned in tales of legendary heroes, only works for Antony, the soothsayer says, when he's out of Caesar's range. Within Caesar's orbit, Caesar will have all the luck. So the really fatal misstep that Antony makes is not returning to Cleopatra but marrying Octavia. In his last days there's a temporary rally in his favour, and Cleopatra says to him:

> O infinite virtue, com'st thou smiling from
> The world's great snare uncaught? (IV.viii. 17–18)

The world's great snare is war generally, and war with Caesar in particular. The point is that most moralists would say that the world's great snare for Antony was Cleopatra herself, and Cleopatra's use of such a phrase means that she has a different point of view on the subject, perhaps one to be respected.

There's also a curious scene at the beginning of the third act, when one of Antony's generals, named Ventidius, has done what Antony should have been doing all along: fought with and defeated the Parthian army. One of his subordinates suggests that he follow up the victory in a way that will knock the Parthians out for much longer, but Ventidius says he's done enough. If he makes a more impressive victory than he has made, he'll be threatening Antony's "image," as we call it now, and Antony will find some way of getting rid of him. We're back to the smaller, calculating Antony of *Julius Caesar*, and the episode seems to be telling us that if Antony really did his Roman duty we'd find him a rather commonplace character, not the unforgettable tragic hero of this play.

There are different levels on which characters can be presented to us in literature. In pure myths characters may be gods or divine beings, though since Classical times this has been rather uncommon. Or they may be heroes of romance like the knights of Arthur's court, or like what Don Quixote dreamed of being, capable of incredible feats of strength, endurance and love. Or they may be leaders like Othello or King Lear or Bolingbroke, with nothing strictly supernatural about them, but with authority and a power of speech denied to ordinary mortals. Or they may be people roughly on our own level, or they may be unfortunate or foolish or obsessed people whom we feel to be less free than ourselves, and whom we look down on (I mean in perspective, not morally). At the beginning of the play Caesar and Antony are on the third level, social and military leaders. Caesar's greatest strength is his limitation to that role: he is single-mindedly devoted to leadership, and lets nothing else get in his way. He has gods, of course, but he seems to be indifferent to them, and one would never guess from this play that he himself was deified after his death. Thus:

1. Divine being, hero descended from gods, hero who is a protégé of the gods, etc.
2. Romantic hero and lover, human but not subject to ordinary human limitations.
3. Kings and other commanding figures in social or military authority.
4. Ordinary people.
5. Foolish, obsessed, unfortunate people; people assumed to be in a state of less freedom than we are.

Antony is a leader, we said, but he has a heroic dimension that makes him a romantic legend, on the second rather than the third level, even in Caesar's eye, as when Caesar recalls his tremendous powers of endurance in his earlier campaigns, drinking "the stale of horses" and the like. A bystander remarks that his soldiership is "twice the other twain," meaning Caesar and Lepidus, whatever Lepidus may count for. His immense physical vitality (Plutarch calls him the "new Bacchus" or Dionysus) and his great personal magnetism mean that any army following him feels drawn together into a fighting community. In front of the most certain defeat, his men, or some of them, are still fighting with high morale and joking about their wounds. In his last wretched days, when he is only, as his soldiers call him, the ruin of Cleopatra's magic, he still seems like a kind of force of nature. Even his blunders are colossal, and, as Enobarbus says, there is a glamour in being part of so majestic a lost cause.

The story of Enobarbus is the clearest illustration of Antony's power as a leader. Enobarbus, we said, is a commentator on the action; his detachment makes him use rational categories, and causes him to be especially sensitive to the decline of rationality in Antony. He contrasts the courage of Caesar, guided by a cool head, with the courage of Antony, which is increasingly guided by panic, "frighted out of fear," as he says, so that in a sense Antony's reason has been taken prisoner by Caesar. He then draws the inference that the rational thing for him to do would be to desert to Caesar. But his reason has betrayed him. He finds himself at once in the deep cold hell of the deserter, no longer trusted by those he has left, never to be trusted by those he is trying to join. Then comes the news that Antony, aware of his desertion, has sent on all his possessions and his "treasure." What he discovers in that moment is that his identity consisted of being a part of Antony's cause, and that he is now nothing, just as a hand severed from the body is no longer a hand. It's significant, I think, that he does not commit suicide: he simply lies down in a ditch and stays there, because he's already dead.

The great romantic heroes are normally great lovers too, and Antony's love for Cleopatra gives him again a dimension that puts him beyond the usual human categories. We may look at the extraordinarily concise opening scene. Two fairly anonymous Romans speak of Antony's "dotage" and his spending his energies in cooling a "gipsy's lust" (the Gypsies were believed at that time to have come from Egypt, and the term is Roman racism). Then they eavesdrop on the first encounter we have between Antony and Cleopatra. The important part of it for us is Cleopatra's "I'll set a bourne how far to be beloved," and Antony's response, "Then thou must needs find out new heaven, new earth." However the scene is staged, it's framed by the two visiting Romans, so that it's in a deliberately confined area, yet out of this confined area comes the declaration of a love that bursts the boundaries of human experience altogether. The two Romans, like most tourists, have seen and heard what they expect to see and hear, and have no notion of what they really have seen and heard, which is a statement of what another very great, love poet, John Donne, calls "Lovers' Infiniteness."

As for Cleopatra, the queen of Egypt was a goddess, an incarnation of Isis, the goddess of the sea, in whose "habiliments," according to Caesar, she publicly appeared. She is also described by Enobarbus as enthroned on her "barge" on the water, as though she were a kind of Venus surrounded by love spirits. The effect she produces is so close to being that of an incarnate love goddess that Enobarbus speaks of how even the holy priests "Bless her when she is riggish [sexually excited]." It is after Antony dies that in her laments for him she speaks of him as a divinity whose legs bestrid the ocean and whose eyes were the sun and moon. We may, with Dolabella, consider this just the rhetorical grief of a very rhetorical person, but then there is that curious episode of soldiers hearing a mysterious music which means that Hercules, Antony's patron, has deserted him.

This scene, Act IV, Scene iii, is the only moment in the play that looks in the least supernatural, and we may think it at first a bit out of key: something that Shakespeare found in Plutarch and thought maybe he ought to include, but that doesn't really belong. I don't think that critical judgment will quite do. If one is explicitly writing romance or myth, characters can go into extra-human categories without trouble, according to the conventions of what's being written; but *Antony and Cleopatra* is on the historical level of credibility. On that level, anything above the human may be suggested, but it must almost always be associated with failure. The desertion of Antony by Hercules means that Antony has failed to become a pagan incarnation, a Hercules or Dionysus walking the earth. Such heroic incarnations always fail: that's one of the things Greek tragedy is about. Agrippa, on Caesar's side, remarks that the gods always give great spirits flaws to keep them on the human level. There's a truth in this I want to come back to, but not all tragedy is about heroes who had flaws preventing them from living up to their heroism. Some tragedies are about heroes whose "flaws" were their virtues, whose heroism was simply too destructive a force to the world around them to survive in it. Antony was perhaps not one of those, but he comes so near to being one that what emerges from the deepest centre of this immensely profound play is Cleopatra's bitter complaint:

> It were for me
> To throw my sceptre at the injurious gods,
> To tell them that this world did equal theirs,
> Till they had stolen our jewel. (IV.xv. 75–78)

What is true of heroism is true of love as well. There are no superhuman lovers, and all attempts at such love have been tragic. Antony's page, who kills himself to avoid having to kill Antony, is named Eros, and it seems clear that Shakespeare uses the name for the sake of its resonances, and for the aspect of the play in which it is a tragedy of Eros:

> Unarm, Eros, the long day's task is done,
> And we must sleep. (IV.xiv. 35–36)

In one of his more manic phases in the same scene, Antony speaks of himself and Cleopatra as becoming the model for lovers in the next world, gazed at by all as the two who, so to speak, made it:

> Dido, and Aeneas, shall want troops,
> And all the haunt be ours. (IV.xiv. 53–54)

The reference to Dido and Aeneas is deeply ironic, as it's both right and wrong. Aeneas rejected Dido's love; she burned herself on a funeral pyre; Aeneas went on to Italy but had first to visit the lower world to gain a prophecy of the future greatness of Rome; he met Dido in the lower world; she cut him dead and went off to find her first husband. Nevertheless, Dido is one of the most famous lovers in literature, and Aeneas is famous by virtue of his association with her. The Aeneas who went on to Italy and made a dynastic marriage with someone called Lavinia is, despite Virgil's best efforts, almost an antihero. Antony's tragedy is in many respects like the tragedy of Adam as seen later by Milton. Adam falls out of Eden because he would rather die with Eve than live without her: theologically he may have been wrong, but dramatically everyone applauds his decision. Success in heroic love being impossible, better to fail heroically than to succeed in mediocrity.

Here we have to return to Agrippa's observation. There is a character in one of Blake's Prophecies who says, at the end of a long poem, "Attempting to become more than man we become less." It is because Antony is so much bigger a man than Caesar that he is also, at other times, so much smaller. Along with Cleopatra, he is often not simply ordinary but silly and childish. Caesar never descends to that level, because he never rises above his own: he has no dreams of divinity, and so no awakenings into the "all too human," as Nietzsche calls it. Cleopatra is often spoken of as though she had charms or love potions or magic spells or other apparatus of a witch. She hasn't any of these things: what gives the illusion of them is the intensity of her humanity, and the same thing is true of Antony. But intense humanity is a two-way street.

One yardstick to contrast Rome and Egypt, and which this time does illustrate the superiority of Rome, is the treatment of messengers. Caesar is invariably courteous to his messengers, and so is Antony at the beginning of the play, when the messenger who brings the bad news from the eastern front is even encouraged to include a comment on Antony's lackadaisical response. But Cleopatra's treatment of the messenger of the marriage to Octavia shows her at her impossible worst, and Antony soon shows that he has caught the infection, when he orders Caesar's messenger Thidias to be flogged. There is, it is true, another element here: it almost looks as though Cleopatra, feeling that Antony's number is up, would be ready to do a deal with Caesar, and of course her repertoire of deals is very limited. Enobarbus, one feels, also suspects that Cleopatra is ready to come to some kind of terms with Caesar, and this is the moment when he decides to leave Antony. The childish petulance in Antony's action comes, first, from the fact that it's obviously Cleopatra that he wants to take the whip to, and, second, that he's reacting in a small-minded way to disaster, by retreating from the present into fantasy and reminiscence of the past. Antony never recovers his original control, and later tells the eunuch Mardian how close he has come to death for bringing the (false) news of Cleopatra's death. But still his lowest moment in the play is the pitiful complaint in his speech to Thidias:

> He [Caesar] makes me angry with him. For he seems
> Proud and disdainful, harping on what I am
> Not what he knew I was. (III.xiii. 141–43)

One pattern of imagery that runs all through the play is the contrast of land and sea, of a solid and a liquid world, an imagery that reinforces the contrast between Rome and Egypt. I spoke of the first scene, where a Roman begins the play with:

> Nay, but this dotage of our general's
> O'erflows the measure . . . (I.i. 1–2)

This is a Roman view of someone taken over by Egypt, the land that owes its fertility, in fact its very existence, to the annual overflowing of the Nile. The metaphors associated with Rome are often geometrical, as in Antony's apology to Octavia, "I have not kept my square," implying something solid. On Pompey's galley there is a discussion between Enobarbus and Pompey's lieutenant, Menas, in which the words "land" and "sea" echo like a cuckoo clock; and Cleopatra, the "serpent of old Nile," as Antony calls her, is constantly associated with seas and with two rivers, the Nile and the Cydnus. It is she, as is said earlier, who insists that the battle of Actium should be a sea fight, and it is the fleet that finally betrays Antony.

I said a moment ago that in tragedy we sometimes get forms of heroism that are too big for the world as we know it, and so become destructive. If the wills of Antony and Cleopatra had been equal to the passions they express in their language, there wouldn't have been much left of the cosmos. "Let Rome in Tiber melt," says Antony at the beginning of the play; "Melt Egypt into Nile," says Cleopatra later. From the scene of Antony's attempted suicide on, the play is full of images of the world dissolving into chaos, of the sun burning its sphere, of cloud shapes becoming as indistinct "As water is in water." The chaos is social as well as cosmic, because with the loss of such a leader the hierarchy on which all existence depends collapses, as Lear's world after his abdication collapses into the world symbolized by the storm. Cleopatra says of Antony:

> The soldier's pole is fall'n: young boys and girls
> Are level now with men. (IV.xv. 65–66)

The entire history of the word "standard," which is not even used, lies behind these images. The images of dissolution point to the fact that Caesar becomes master of the world because he knows the substance, location and limits of the world that can be mastered: for a short time, one may master anything that will stay in place. Antony has fallen into the world of process and metamorphosis, a far bigger world than Caesar's, but a world that no one can control unless he can also control death itself. Cleopatra comes to feel that to choose death with Antony is a greater destiny than Caesar, who is "but Fortune's knave," can ever reach; and she speaks of transcending the world of the moon and of the corruptible elements below it

> I am fire and air; my other elements
> I give to baser life. (V.ii. 288–89)

difficult as it is to envisage a discarnate Cleopatra.

One cannot read or listen far into this play without being reminded that the action is taking place about thirty years before what Shakespeare's audience would have considered the turning point of history, the birth of Christ. There are references to Herod of Jewry, which are in Plutarch but have overtones for the audience that they would not have for Plutarch, and Caesar, with his victory practically in sight, remarks, "The time of universal peace is near," where again the audience knows more of his meaning than he does. It would have been strange if Christ had been born into a world whose temporal master was a protégé of Hercules, ruling the world probably from Egypt. It is partly in this context that the upper limits of Antony and Cleopatra become so significant: of Antony as a failed pagan or heroic incarnation, of Cleopatra as a goddess of love, of the sea, and of the overflowing Nile. The Egypt of this play is partly the biblical Egypt, whose Pharaoh was called in the Bible "the great dragon that lieth in the midst of his rivers," and whose ruler here is the serpent of old Nile whom we last see nursing a baby serpent at her breast.

There are some books on mythology that tell you things about the actual grammar of mythology that you won't find in more conventional handbooks. I referred earlier to Robert Graves's *The White Goddess*, a book that appeared about forty years ago, which tells us of a goddess personifying the fertility of the earth, who takes a lover early in the year, then turns him into a sacrificial victim, then erases the memory of him and starts the next year with a new lover. We remember that Cleopatra hates to be reminded that she once was the mistress of Julius Caesar, and she apparently does not react to the name Herod, though she had been involved with him too. And when she is finally dead—at least so far as our knowledge of such things goes—Caesar looks down on her and comments that:

> she looks like sleep,
> As she would catch another Antony
> In her strong toil of grace. (V.ii. 344–46)

The old dispensation, as the theologians call it, has rolled by, carrying its symbols of the skin-shedding serpent, the sea, the dying and renewing life of the earth. And, whatever happens to human fortunes in the next thirty years, it is still there, ready to roll again.

JONATHAN GIL HARRIS

"Narcissus in thy face": Roman Desire and the Difference It Fakes in Antony and Cleopatra

> But what if the Devil, on the contrary, the Other, were the Same? And what if the Temptation was not one of the episodes of the great antagonism, but the mere insinuation of the Double? What if this duel developed in the space of the mirror?
>
> Michel Foucault[1]

This essay examines the relation between Elizabethan versions of Ovid's Narcissus myth and Shakespeare's *Antony and Cleopatra*. In doing so, it may seem to tiptoe through that tired terrain which Stephen Greenblatt has termed "the elephants' graveyard of literary history"[2]—source study. I do not intend to suggest that Shakespeare had read contemporary versions of the myth, although there are a number of telltale fingerprints in the play—borrowed phrases, motifs—suggesting this may have been the case. Rather I wish to use the tale of Narcissus to reread *Antony and Cleopatra* in a way that challenges orthodox understandings of gender difference in the play, in particular the status of Cleopatra as the quintessentially female object and origin of heterosexual desire—both the desire of her Roman suitors and, perhaps just as important, the desire of her heterosexual male spectators and readers, past and present. Hence this essay engages in "source" study of another kind: a critical reappraisal of the source of heterosexual eros in Elizabethan versions of the Narcissus myth as well as in Shakespeare's play.

From *Shakespeare Quarterly* 45, no. 4 (Winter 1994): 408–25.

I

Criticism of *Antony and Cleopatra* has repeatedly returned to Shakespeare's representations of Rome and Egypt, a topographical and cultural opposition that is undeniably central to the play. Much attention has been devoted to showing how, in contrast to Rome's "measure" and Lenten restraint, Egypt is represented as a land of excess in the thrall of an endless Bacchanal.[3] What is perhaps most notable about many past accounts of the Rome/Egypt opposition, however, is the extent to which these accounts have also elaborated an absolute gender polarity or, more accurately, a gender hierarchy. Rome has been characterized as a male world, presided over by the austere Caesar, and Egypt as a female domain, embodied by a Cleopatra who is seen to be as abundant, leaky, and changeable as the Nile. Significantly, it is this changeability, manifest in her legendary "infinite variety" (2.2.236), that has prompted critics such as George Brandes to style Cleopatra somewhat negatively as "the woman of women, quintessentiated Eve."[4] Within this disparaging assessment of Cleopatra as the archetype of a fallen femininity, there lurks a fascination with her as the irrepressible origin of male desire. For example, G. Wilson Knight's notorious observation that "Cleopatra and her girls at Alexandria are as the Eternal Femininity waiting for Man" is accompanied by the claim that she is "all romantic vision, the origin of love, the origin of life."[5] Whether viewed as the wily perpetrator of original sin or the redemptive source of romantic love, Cleopatra has been cast within literary criticism as the Ur-Woman, the archetypally female origin of male heterosexual eros.

Not surprisingly, more recent criticism has taken issue with such sexist interpretations of Cleopatra and her "quintessentiated" femininity.[6] In the wake of feminist, poststructuralist, and cultural-materialist critiques of gender essentialism, most modern Shakespeare scholars are inclined to be far more skeptical about claims that Shakespeare possessed a unique insight into a timeless "femininity." Nevertheless, despite the historicizing impulse that has rescued Cleopatra from the negative pole of an oppressively essentialist gender opposition, much criticism continues to abide by the gendered topographical binaries that dominate romantic and formalist interpretations of the play.[7] In a powerful reading that undermines many of the conventional assumptions about Cleopatra's "femininity," Janet Adelman claims, for example, that "the contest between Caesar and Cleopatra, Rome and Egypt, is in part a contest between male scarcity and female bounty."[8] Leonard Tennenhouse asserts that "Cleopatra is Egypt," and that by virtue of her difference from patriarchal Roman "measure," "she embodies everything that is not English according to the nationalism which developed under Elizabeth as well as to the British nationalism later fostered by James. . . . She contrasts

Egyptian fecundity, luxury and hedonism to Rome's penury, harshness and self denial."[9] I would argue that the play is far less secure in asserting the differences that Adelman's and Tennenhouse's assessments seem to uphold. While Cleopatra may appear to incarnate everything exotic and bountifully "feminine," the play suggests at crucial moments that the relationships between Egypt and Rome, Cleopatra and Antony, are less ones of opposition than of specularity—a specularity that, as we shall see, parallels and even critically interrogates the historically specific relation between the Cleopatra of the play's first performances and her Jacobean audience.[10]

Instances of specularity recur throughout the play. Gnaeus Pompey "would stand and make his eyes grow in . . . [Cleopatra's] brow" (1.5.2); Caesar fills the front line of his army with deserters from Antony's army, so that the latter would "seem to spend his fury / Upon himself" (4.6.10–11); the defeated Antony sees himself reflected in the changing clouds of the Egyptian sky (4.14.1–14); the triumphant Caesar glimpses himself in the "spacious mirror" of Antony's demise (5.1.33). The self-scrutinizing gaze of Rome's triumvirs is thus obliquely but suggestively aligned with that of Narcissus, rapt in contemplation of his reflection on the surface of Ovid's spring.[11] Yet critics have more customarily, albeit indirectly, associated Narcissus with Cleopatra and her quintessential "femininity." If essentialist interpretations have regarded Cleopatra's lack of coherent selfhood, her inconstancy, as characteristic of her "sex," there has also been a paradoxical tendency to emphasize her excessive love of self as a uniquely "feminine" quality. For example, Anna Jameson in 1832 noted "her consistent inconsistency" yet lambasted her "love of self."[12] Likewise, Schlegel noted Cleopatra's narcissistic "royal pride [and] female vanity."[13] A. C. Bradley drew attention to Cleopatra's "comic vanity" in the tirade against the messenger,[14] which contains the play's one explicit reference to Narcissus: "Hadst thou Narcissus in thy face, to me / Thou wouldst appear most ugly" (2.5.96–97). Cleopatra invokes Narcissus here primarily to contrast his surpassing beauty with the ugliness of the messenger's shocking news about Antony's marriage to Octavia; but the allusion serves also as a sly reminder of Cleopatra's own narcissism, displayed in her insistence earlier in the scene that the messenger tell her only what she wants to hear, even if it deviates from the truth. She berates the messenger precisely because he does not have Narcissus in his face: he has failed to reflect her desire.[15]

Curiously, however, other moments in the play suggest that Cleopatra has less in common with Narcissus than with his reflection. When Enobarbus says of her "she makes hungry / Where most she satisfies" (2.2.237–38), he reprises an important motif in early modern English versions of the Narcissus myth. In Ovid's text Narcissus stares hungrily at his reflection in the spring and, trying in vain to kiss it, utters "inopem me copia fecit"—"My very plenty makes me poor" (*Metamorphoses* III, 1. 466).[16] Tudor and Stuart writers reworked this line to emphasize the thirst or hunger-inducing insubstantiality of the narcissistic reflection. Edmund Spenser compared his own gaze to that of "Narcissus vaine / whose eyes him staru'd: so plenty makes me poore."[17] In Henry Reynolds's 1630 *Mythomystes*, Narcissus is described as growing "thirsty as his thirst he slakes."[18] And in Thomas Edwards's 1595 poem "Narcissus," to which I shall soon return in greater detail, Narcissus complains of his reflection that "Neuer the greedie Tantalus pursued, / To touch those seeming apples more than I."[19] Cleopatra is thus accorded by Enobarbus the paradoxical power of the narcissistic reflection—like the reflection, she is depicted as possessing both an ineluctable power to "make hungry" and a frustrating insubstantiality. To this extent Cleopatra may appear to conform to the conventional misogynist archetype of the "hard-to-get" temptress, an assessment endorsed by critics like Knight with his reading of Cleopatra as the "Eternal Femininity waiting for Man." But I shall argue that the identification of Cleopatra with the hunger-inducing satisfaction of the narcissistic reflection generates resonances that seriously disrupt the essentialist perception of her as the "Eternal Femininity."

II

The motif of the hunger-inducing reflection was just one feature of the many appropriations of the Narcissus myth in early modern England.[20] In addition to Arthur Golding's English translation of Ovid's entire *Metamorphoses* in 1567, there were a number of versions of the tale in wide circulation before 1630. Most united in condemning Narcissus for his pride; he was, according to both the 1560 anonymous translator and Richard Brathwayte in his poem "Narcissus Change" (1611), guilty of a hubris comparable to Lucifer's.[21] Significantly, such conventional attacks on pride were often made to serve a Neoplatonic critique of appearances: Henry Reynolds inveighed against Narcissus's reflection as a "deceiptfull shadow";[22] "the transitory thinges of this world are not to be trusted," argued the author of the 1560 translation.[23] For these writers, therefore, Narcissus's crime was less self-love than the fatal overvaluation of a mere reflection; he misrecognized surface for depth, an image for the real thing, an effect for the source. As Reynolds remarked in his version of the tale, Narcissus mistook the "deceiptfull shadow" of his reflection for a "sun-beame,"[24] an oxymoronic juxtaposition that highlights his debilitating confusion of origin and effect.

For writers like Reynolds, Echo—the disembodied nymph spurned by Narcissus—assumed allegorical importance not only as the authentic and legitimate object of a heterosexual desire opposed to Narcissus's self-rapture but also as the representative of a cosmic origin opposed to "deceiptfull shadow": "*adore Ecco*," Reynolds commanded his readers, "This Winde is the Symbole of the Breath of God."[25] As Barry Taylor remarks in his excellent study of Neoplatonism and the Narcissus myth in early modern England, "Echo represents the 'reflex' of the image produced in the mind by the breath of God, which conduces to intellectual unity and the direction of the soul's parts towards God. Narcissus, on the contrary, is the soul which denies this process and attends instead to the reflection supplied by the sense and 'corporeal shadows.'" In symbolizing the Neoplatonic origin, Echo offers the "possibility of a re-engagement with truth through the restoration of a heterosexual mutuality which stands for all forms of 'natural' relationship."[26] Within the Neoplatonic interpretation of Ovid's tale, therefore, Echo functions powerfully as a twin figure of legitimacy: she is the cosmically sanctioned origin of both "true" understanding and "natural" male heterosexual eros.

The Neoplatonic understanding of Narcissus's crime is partially evident also in Thomas Edwards's 1595 "Narcissus," which is a somewhat elliptic rewriting of the story as it appears in *Metamorphoses*. Edwards's Narcissus is not the antisocial Sylvan solipsist of Ovid's poem; instead he is an urban sex-tease who plays it fast and loose and is proud of his substantial wardrobe. Narcissus, who narrates most of the poem, is accosted by a never-ending stream of suitors, both male and female. He accepts jewels and garments as gifts from them and, in the process, undergoes a curious transformation: "like a lover glad of each new toy," he exclaims, "So I a woman turned from a boy."[27] When Edwards's Narcissus stares into the spring, therefore, he falls prey to a double misrecognition. He follows Ovid's protagonist in believing his reflection to be substantial, but he parts company with the classical Narcissus in also believing it to be a woman: "my lips hers to have touched, / I forc'd them forward, and my head down crouched."[28] Narcissus perceives his reflection to be not only female but also spellbindingly exotic. He compares his discovery to that of "the English globe-incompasser" Francis Drake, who "by same purueying found another land." In a fascinating variation on the paradoxical Ovidian motif of riches coupled with poverty, satiety with hunger, the intensity of Narcissus's gaze serves to deprive him of sight: in a further development of the trope of the European witness in the New World, he declares himself to have been struck blind by "gazing on this Orient sunne."[29] The confusion of reflection and celestial source hinted at here is made explicit with Edwards's oxymoronic description of Narcissus's image (reminiscent of Reynolds's yoking of "deceiptfull shadow" and "sun-beame") as a "Sun-shine-shadow."[30] This disjunction serves to underline Edwards's Neoplatonic interpretation of Narcissus's crime as a failure to recognize the "true" source of his desire: Narcissus himself is the "sun" that produces the image on the spring's surface.

In directing attention to Narcissus as the source, Edwards deviates from other Neoplatonic versions of the myth in that he notably fails to include Echo in his tale. Thus the customary Neoplatonic redress to Echo as the origin of legitimate heterosexual desire and allegorical incarnation of "the breath of God" is also omitted. In the process Edwards invites a subtly different understanding of the source of male heterosexual eros: in the world of his poem, the "real thing" is neither Echo nor any female object of desire but Narcissus himself, "a woman turned from a boy." His "heterosexual" desire, therefore, is in a crucial sense homoeroticized, its origin and object disclosed as male. Edwards's Narcissus eventually understands his predicament. But unlike Ovid's Narcissus, for whom the realization that he has fallen in love with his own reflection proves fatal, Edwards's protagonist remains very much alive, musing wistfully and not particularly repentantly on the nature of his self-love.

Edwards's poem contains three important motifs: the projection of Narcissus's own sunlike qualities onto the surface of the spring; the misrecognition of the reflection as female and exotic; and the abrupt realization that this seductive image is, in fact, a reflection of a male source. As I shall show, all these motifs may be discerned in *Antony and Cleopatra.* Like Edwards's poem, that play stages an orientalist discourse of the Other which blatantly problematizes itself in the process of elaboration, revealing its "exotic" object of "heterosexual" desire to be a chimera conjured up and misrecognized by the narcissistic male gaze. Just as Edwards's Narcissus discovers that "this Orient Sunne" has an occidental origin, so do the Romans who kiss "this orient pearl" (1.5.41)—one of the play's many metonymies for Cleopatra's erotic power—find themselves desiring something far closer to home.

III

Roman desire is characterized by contradiction in a number of ways. In terms of the opposition between Egypt and Rome, desire is more obviously an attribute of the former: it is to be expected of Egypt and its voluptuous citizens, who "trade in love" (2.5.2), but not of Lenten Rome and its "cold and still conversation" (2.6.120), exemplified by Octavia. Yet when it comes to Cleopatra, Roman desire is seemingly uncontainable. She is the object of a lingering fascination that has ensnared Julius Caesar, Gnaeus Pompey, and Mark Antony alike. What are we to make of this history of desire? Is it enough to assert, as numerous critics have done over the centuries, that Cleopatra's desirability is simply so transcendentally enormous that Rome's normally sober rulers cannot help but be bowled over by her "infinite variety"?[31] Or does the play suggest that there is something in the very structure of Roman desire itself which produces Cleopatra as desirable?

Near the beginning of the play, Octavius Caesar accounts for the rebellious Sextus Pompey's immense popular support with the following speech:

> It hath been taught us from the primal state,
> That he which is was wish'd until he were;
> And the ebb'd man, ne'er loved till ne'er worth love,
> Comes dear'd by being lack'd.
> (1.4.41–44)

The sense of this rather difficult passage becomes clear in the last line. It is part of received Roman wisdom that desire is linked to the object's absence: Romans want only what they do not or cannot have.[32] Sextus Pompey, precisely because he lacks power, has become desirable as an alternative to the present Roman leadership. The speech Antony makes after hearing of his hated wife Fulvia's death expresses precisely this law of Roman desire:

> There's a great spirit gone! Thus did I desire it:
> What our contempts doth often hurl from us,
> We wish it ours again; the present pleasure,
> By revolution lowering, does become
> The opposite of itself: she's good, being gone:
> The hand could pluck her back that shov'd her on.
> (1.2.119–24)

As with the Roman plebeians' desire for Pompey, Antony's attraction to Fulvia is triggered by her absence—by the fact that he does not, cannot, have her: "she's good, being gone." He suffers the same mood swing upon receiving the (inaccurate) news that Cleopatra has died: a mere twenty lines after denouncing her as a "vile lady" who has "robb'd" him of his sword (4.14.22–23), he contemplates suicide in order to "o'ertake . . . Cleopatra, and / Weep for . . . pardon" (ll. 44–45); he even fantasizes "couch[ing]" with her in the Elysian fields (l. 51). If Roman desire emerges in response to an absence it attempts to fill or repudiate, it can be seen to parallel the Renaissance axiom "Nature abhors a Vacuum,"[33] alluded to in Enobarbus's account of Antony's first meeting with Cleopatra, when Cleopatra was so desirable that even the air "but for vacancy, / Had gone to gaze on Cleopatra too, / And made a gap in nature" (2.2.216–18). This fantastic "gap in nature" provides an enabling figure for the intolerable vacuum into which Roman desire imperially projects itself. But what do Romans see when they project their desire into such gaps?

The answer to which the play repeatedly gestures is that the desiring Roman gaze fixes on a reflection, or projection, of itself. Like Narcissus, the spectator misrecognizes himself (or his image) as Other. Maecenas, noting the grief that Antony's death paradoxically prompts in Caesar, exclaims, "When such a *spacious* mirror's set before him, / He must needs see himself" (5.1.34–35; emphasis added); within the space created by Antony's absence, in other words, Caesar supplies his own image and, seemingly mourning Antony, grieves for himself. Caesar here conforms to the law of Roman desire, wanting what he cannot have, in at least two ways. Like Antony grieving for the much-despised Fulvia upon her death, Caesar's hand would pluck him back that shoved him on. But Maecenas's observation about the "spacious mirror" into which Caesar gazes suggests that, like Narcissus, Caesar also wants the paradigmatic instance of what he cannot have—his reflection, misrecognized as an ontologically discrete entity.

A comparable if comic misrecognition of the projected self as Other within the "spacious mirror" of absence is Lepidus's drunken perception of the Egyptian crocodile:

> LEPIDUS. What manner o' thing is your crocodile?
> ANTONY. It is shap'd, sir, like itself; and it is as broad as it hath breadth: it is just so high as it is, and moves with its own organs: it lives by that which nourisheth it; and the elements once out of it, it transmigrates.
> LEPIDUS. What colour is it of?
> ANTONY. Of its own colour too.
> LEPIDUS 'Tis a strange serpent.
> ANTONY. 'Tis so. And the tears of it are wet.
> (2.7.40–48)

What does Lepidus see? Antony's litany of tautologies creates a "gap in nature" where the crocodile should be and Lepidus's "'Tis a strange serpent" suggests that he fills the space with his mind's eye. Lepidus's apprehension of the crocodile may serve as a comic diversion, but it is also far more than that: the manner in which he sees the "strange serpent" is how Rome "sees" Cleopatra. This is no mere analogy. Cleopatra is very much implicated in the exchange between Antony and Lepidus. Indeed, for all his tautologous nonsense, Antony could well be describing Cleopatra: not simply because Lepidus's remark recalls Antony's familiar name for "my serpent of the old Nile" (1.5.25); nor because the reference to the crocodile's tears may suggest Cleopatra's willingness to pretend a sadness she does not feel (see 1.3.3–5); but primarily because it is the crocodile's very vacancy that associates it with Cleopatra or, at least, with the way in which Roman desire takes her as its object.

This assertion may seem paradoxical given that Cleopatra is traditionally praised for being the most vivid, alive, and present of Shakespeare's female creations.[34] The play indisputably invites us to regard Cleopatra as an authentic character, tragically misunderstood by her Roman suitors: "Not know me yet?" she asks Antony after he has subjected her to a torrent of perhaps undeserved recrimination (3.13.158). Her question provides a salutary reminder of the gulf that separates Roman (mis)characterizations of her and the "real" Cleopatra presented to us in, for example, her exchanges with Mardian, Charmian, and Iras. Moreover, this "real" Cleopatra possesses a vitality that is in large part the effect of the constant reminders the play text gives us of that irreducible residue of presence, her body. Whether it is the carnal tang of her remarks ("Now I feed myself / With most delicious poison" [1.5.26–27]; "Ram thou thy fruitful tidings in mine ears" [2.5.24]) or the abundance of stage directions the text gives her ("embracing" Antony [1.1.37]; "striking" or "haling up and down" the messenger [2.5.61, 62, 64]), her insistent, melodramatic physicality lends her a seemingly undeniable presence. More than any other of the play's characters, Cleopatra is "in thy face," possessed of a corporeality that seems to cry out for recognition.

But such reminders of her physicality are supplemented by a counternarrative in which her very vividness is shown to be the effect of a Roman desire for her presence, prompted by the gaps and absences that repeatedly afflict the play's attempts to represent her. A. C. Bradley once expressed a wish to "hear her [Cleopatra's] own remarks" about his analysis.[35] His wistful desire to obtain an "authentic" Cleopatra replicates a desire that the play itself repeatedly expresses and frustrates. For all of Cleopatra's undeniable corporeality, her body has an odd habit of disappearing altogether at precisely those moments when it seems most overwhelmingly present.

Think, for example, of Enobarbus's account of Cleopatra on the river Cydnus, which is often cited as proof of Cleopatra's intoxicating desirability.[36] Enobarbus paints a portrait of a world in which subjection to imperial power is subjection to erotic desire: Cleopatra's pages are Cupids, and even the winds that follow her are lovesick. In a manner that recalls Elizabethan notions of the power exerted by the sovereign's displayed body, Cleopatra's power appears to be predicated on the visibility of her eroticized body to her subjects, who abandon all activity to gaze on her.[37] But what do her subjects see? Because Enobarbus is known for the plainness of his speech (Pompey commends it at 2.6.78), it is easy to neglect the way in which his rhetoric actively and ingeniously produces Cleopatra as desirable only according to the Roman logic of desire: that is, she exerts a seductive power by virtue of her paradoxical absence within Enobarbus's depiction of her.

Enobarbus presents a wealth of detail in the opening lines of his account. He describes the deck, the sails, even the river water that, "amorous" of the oarsmen's strokes (2.2.197), caresses Cleopatra's barge. The detail is profoundly synaesthetic; the purple sails are "perfumed" (l. 193), and the procession is accompanied by the "tune of flutes" (l. 195). But when Enobarbus comes to describe Cleopatra herself, he is remarkably vague:

> For her own person,
> It beggar'd all description: she did lie
> In her pavilion—cloth of gold, of tissue—
> O'er-picturing that Venus where we see
> The fancy outwork nature.
> (ll. 197–201)

Here is little or no detail of "her own person." Unlike the objects around her, Cleopatra "beggar[s] all description." Enobarbus's reference to the portrait of Venus only underlines Cleopatra's "O'er-picturing" unrepresentability: her "cloth of gold" thus encloses what is effectively a "gap in nature." The speech serves as a rhetorical counterpart of a rococo mirror, its extraordinarily ornate and copious frame enclosing a subtly camouflaged glass in which Enobarbus's Roman listeners glimpse whatever they want to see. Just as Antony's nondescription of the crocodile provides Lepidus with the "spacious mirror" in which he glimpses a "strange serpent," so does Enobarbus's nondescription of Cleopatra allow Agrippa to imagine a "rare Egyptian!" (l. 218). Agrippa thus conforms to the law of Roman desire, filling a "gap in nature" with a phantom that compensates for and repudiates Cleopatra's absence. Little wonder that "she makes hungry, / Where most she satisfies." If she is an "Egyptian dish," as Enobarbus calls her (2.7.122–29), she is a food that curiously vanishes at the moment she appears to be most vividly apprehended by her Roman gazers;[38] in effect, she is the "vacancy" that Antony fills with "his voluptuousness" (1.4.26).

IV

The Romans play Narcissus not only when looking on Cleopatra.[39] The narcissistic component of their desire is also hinted at in Octavius's description of his namesake and sister as one "whom no brother / Did ever love so dearly" (2.2.150–51) and as "a great part of myself" (3.2.24). He uses much the same language in eulogizing Antony: gazing into the "spacious mirror" of Antony's absence, Caesar grieves for "my brother, my competitor, / In top of all design; my mate in empire, / Friend and companion in the front of war, / The arm of mine own body" (5.1.42–45). Antony's revealing transformation by Caesar from "brother" to "mate" and, finally, "arm of mine own body" shows that the desire initiated in *Antony and Cleopatra* by the narcissistic reflection need not only be heterosexual.

Caesar's eulogy for Antony provides a point of departure for a consideration of both the play's depiction of male homosocial and homoerotic desire and also the extent to which the two may overlap. As Bruce Smith has remarked, Shakespeare portrays in *Antony and Cleopatra* "a dramatic universe in which the male protagonists find their identities, not in romantic love or in philosophical ideals, but in their relationships with each other."[40] Such relationships in the play often conform straightforwardly to the triangular structure of homosociality described by Eve Kosofsky Sedgwick: women mediate between (Roman) men as exchangeable commodities, and in a fashion that intensifies the bonds of friendship or rivalry between the men. As female commodities of exchange, Cleopatra and Octavia—for all their differences—find an unlikely common ground. Octavia's position in the homosocial triangle is transparent: for Octavius Caesar and Antony, she is a token of exchange whose primary purpose is to "knit [their] hearts / With an unslipping knot" (2.2.126–28). Cleopatra serves a comparable function as she is exchanged among Rome's rulers as a "morsel for a monarch" (1.5.31); despite the strength she appears to wield within such transactions, that strength is called into question by the play's final emphasis on Octavius Caesar, for whom she is primarily a spoil of war whose acquisition and public display would attest to his victory over Antony.

Sedgwick claims that in modern Western culture the continuum between male homosocial and homosexual desire is "criss-crossed with deep discontinuities."[41] But it seems to me that relations between Roman men in *Antony and Cleopatra* repeatedly open up the possibility of slippage from the homosocial to the homosexual. This is especially true in the play's depiction of the Roman triumvirate, a version of the homosocial triangle in which Lepidus plays the part normally reserved for the mediating woman: "[H]earts, tongues, figures, scribes, bards, poets cannot / Think, speak, cast, write, sing, number, hoo! / His [Lepidus's] love to Antony. But as for Caesar, / Kneel down, kneel down, and wonder." To Enobarbus's mocking words, Agrippa replies, "Both he loves." Enobarbus goes on to describe Lepidus's function in the triumvirate with a richly suggestive image: he claims that Antony and Caesar are Lepidus's "shards, and he their beetle" (3.2.16–20)—that is, they are the wings that carry the beetle aloft. Like Octavia, Lepidus holds together the feuding rivals. In the process, he is feminized: Enobarbus describes him as suffering from "green-sickness," or love-anemia (3.2.6)—the conventional ailment of virginal maidens—pining, as does Octavia, for both of the men. Act 3, scene 2, provides an illuminating instance of *Antony and Cleopatra*'s treatment of homosocial rivalry and its homoerotic underbelly. While it may be countered that Enobarbus's mocking of Lepidus marks an attempt to assert a discontinuity between legitimately "masculine" homosocial bonding/rivalry and comically "feminine" homosexual love-anemia, it is important to note that the homoerotic impulses attributed derisively to Lepidus are not confined to him, as Caesar's remarkable eulogy for Antony, with its transition from "brother" to "mate," indicates. In erotic triangles where men mediate between men, homosocial and homosexual desires become endlessly substitutable; the difference asserted by Enobarbus between the "beetle" and the "shards," the lowly insect and the soaring wings that elevate it, surely points to a difference of power rather than desire. Both Caesar and Lepidus love Antony; in doing so, both are characterized as desiring a part of their own bodies (be it "shard" or "arm"); both thus participate within the same economy of narcissistic desire glimpsed in Caesar's loving tribute to his sister as "a great part of myself."

The homoerotic dynamic that informs the bonds between the members of the Roman triumvirate provides, I would argue, a template for all Roman desire in *Antony and Cleopatra*—even desire that is putatively "heterosexual." It is here that Thomas Edwards's "Narcissus" comes in handy as a device for decoding the origins of Roman desire. As I have suggested above, Edwards's poem offers three motifs through which the homoerotic origins of Narcissus's "heterosexual" desire are articulated: the projection and/or displacement of his attributes onto the reflective surface of the spring; the misrecognition of this reflection as female; and, finally, the recognition that his object of adoration is the reflection of a male source, is a "woman turned from a boy." All three motifs find suggestive counterparts in Shakespeare's representations of the ways in which Roman desire takes Cleopatra as its object.

The first motif—the projection and/or displacement of the desiring subject's attributes onto the object of desire—is evident in Cleopatra's accounts of her love-making with Antony and Gnaeus Pompey. If Cleopatra is associated by Enobarbus with the hunger-inducing insubstantiality of the narcissistic reflection, she herself confirms the suggestion that Romans play Narcissus when gazing at her. She recalls how, after a night of Bacchanalian revelry with Antony, she "drunk him to his bed; / Then put my tires and mantles on him, whilst / I wore his sword Phillipan" (2.5.21–23). This cheerfully kinky episode involves far more than an instance of the carnivalesque gender inversion customarily identified with Shakespeare's Egypt. The effeminated Antony, Cleopatra implies, is aroused by his own Phillipan-packing reflection—an autoerotic adventure that in its exquisite narcissism surely demands to be seen as less typically Egyptian than Roman.

An equally revealing insight into the origin and object of Roman desire is afforded by Cleopatra's description of Gnaeus Pompey. As I have already noted, she styles him as a Narcissus staring at and erotically aroused by his own misrecognized reflection:

> . . . great Pompey
> Would stand and make his eyes grow in my brow,
> There would he anchor his aspect, and die
> With looking on his life.
> (1.4.31–34)

What is remarkable about Cleopatra's description of Gnaeus Pompey is its deployment and transformation of standard Ovidian motifs. We find here not only an arresting image of narcissistic self-contemplation but also an eroticized version of the paradoxical "*inopem me copia fecit*" tag: Pompey's apprehension of his "life" is the occasion for his erotic "death." Most evident in her description, however, is the projection of Pompey's own attributes onto Cleopatra. The more he looks at her, the more he manifests himself in her face, as is implied by the perverse suggestion that his eyes grow in her forehead. As a result of this specular encounter, Cleopatra indeed has "Narcissus in [her] face."[42]

The transformation of Cleopatra wrought by Antony's and Pompey's narcissistic desire brings to mind Slavoj Žižek's gloss on Lacan's infamous claim that woman is a symptom of man: "so, if woman does not exist, man is perhaps simply a woman who thinks she does exist."[43] Žižek's proposal is perfectly illustrated by Edwards's Narcissus, who becomes "a woman turned from a boy," believing his object of desire to be female. The same is true, of course, for Antony, who simultaneously displaces his own attributes onto Cleopatra and is effeminated. It is here that the second motif from Edwards's "Narcissus"—the desiring subject's conviction that his (misrecognized) reflection is female—may be discerned. The Romans' narcissistic perceptions of Cleopatra prompt a critical reevaluation of those very qualities that audiences and readers have not only attributed to her but also believed to be representative of an "Eternal Femininity." Her allegedly "female" attributes demand in many instances to be understood as displaced or misrecognized Roman characteristics. A particularly good example is Cleopatra's much-noted "infinite variety." The impression of her "variety" is in part created by the panoply of subject-positions she is accorded by the alternately desiring and disgusted Antony: "enchanting queen" (1.2.125); "my chuck" (4.4.2); "my nightingale" (4.8.18); "Triple-turn'd whore," "grave charm," "right gipsy" (4.12.13, 25, 28). Cleopatra's "variety" provides the specular image—is, in many respects, the very effect—of Antony's own. His displacement onto her of his own vacillations exemplifies Catherine Belsey's observation that Tudor and Stuart patriarchal ideology denied women "any single place from which to speak for themselves"; in the process, women acquired "a discontinuity of being, an 'inconstancy' which [was] seen as characteristically feminine."[44]

The process of narcissistic displacement which informs the Roman construction of Cleopatra's contradictory "feminine" identity may be discerned in a number of other plays from the Jacobean stage. Perhaps the best example is provided by John Webster's *The Duchess of Malfi*, a play whose deployment of motifs from the Narcissus myth is hinted at in the Cardinal's weary lament at the play's conclusion: "When I look in the fishponds, / Methinks I see a thing arm'd with a rake / That seems to strike at me" (5.3.3–5).[45] This speech provides the paradigmatic instance of the way in which the play's powerful characters apprehend and/or misrecognize their own reflections as evil forces distinct from them. In particular, Ferdinand, the tyrannical duke of Calabria, attacks his own shadow at the climax of his lycanthropic madness (5.2.38), and he repeatedly displaces his own attributes onto the Duchess, his twin sister, misconstruing them as her distinctively "feminine" vices. She acquires for him the deceptive and salacious qualities that he is incapable of recognizing in himself: he warns her that "they whose faces do belie their hearts / Are witches . . . and give the devil suck," an inadvertent self-description that the Duchess acknowledges with her wry response, "This is terrible good counsel" (1.2.230–32). Ferdinand's projection of his vices onto his sister is most manifest, perhaps, when he accuses her of possessing a heart "Fill'd with unquenchable wild fire" (3.2.117) a mere two scenes after he has insanely fantasized raping her to "quench [his] wild-fire" (2.5.48). When read alongside the narcissistic projections of *Antony and Cleopatra*, these instances offer a remarkable disclosure of the unacknowledged masculine sources of "female" identity in Jacobean patriarchal ideology.

But where *The Duchess of Malfi* appears to offer its audiences and readers a genuine "flesh, and blood" protagonist (1.2.369) who counters her brother's narcissistic projections, *Antony and Cleopatra* in at least one way defers indefinitely any apprehension of an authentic Cleopatra. We are, to some extent, invited to distinguish between the Cleopatra that is a Roman projection and the "real" Cleopatra who stands in seeming contrast to male images of her. By encouraging this distinction, Shakespeare would appear to be reworking a theme found in his earlier comedies: the conflict between female characters as they are perceived by their male counterparts and as they present themselves to their audiences. Consider, for example, the much-scorned Helena in *A Midsummer Night's Dream*, transfigured by Demetrius's love-potioned gaze into "goddess, nymph, perfect, divine!" (3.2.137); or the homely Luciana in *The Comedy of Errors*, mistaken by her "brother-in-law" Antipholus of Syracuse as a "sweet mermaid" and "siren" (3.2.45, 47).[46] What distinguishes *Antony and Cleopatra* from these earlier plays is the way in which it places a question mark next to the "reality" of the Cleopatra whom we are encouraged to dissociate from the projections of her Roman suitors.

Crucially, it is not only Mark Antony or Gnaeus Pompey who mistakenly believe themselves to see the "real" Cleopatra when "looking on" their own lives. In the last act the relationship between Cleopatra and her spectators is reworked in a way that, like the dénouement of Thomas Edwards's "Narcissus," serves to complicate the status of the seemingly exotic, apparently female object of desire on display to the audience. Cleopatra expresses revulsion at the prospect of being transformed in one of Caesar's Roman triumphs into a degraded object of spectacle. But she goes even further—she claims to abhor above all the notion of being represented on the stage: "The quick comedians / Extemporally will stage us ... and I shall see / Some squeaking Cleopatra boy my greatness / I'the posture of a whore" (5.2.215–20). On the Jacobean stage the boy-actor playing Cleopatra was here called upon to express disgust at the prospect of seeing a boy-actor playing Cleopatra. Such self-reflexivity cannot help but achieve an effect similar to that created by Enobarbus in his description of Cleopatra on the river Cydnus: in each instance "she" becomes curiously disembodied, an effect generated by her absence. Unlike Enobarbus's accomplished rhetorical sleight of hand, Cleopatra's reference to the "squeaking Cleopatra boy" blatantly discloses the artifice of the "authentic" queen.

Indeed, the above speech may at first glance strike the reader as one instance of an "alienation effect" all too common on the Shakespearean stage.[47] Attempting to guess a Jacobean audience's response (if there ever is such a thing as a unified response) to the speech is, of course, a treacherous task. But I think it fair to assume that this moment of theatrical self-reflexivity—at least in its early performances—differs from others largely because of its capacity to interrogate an audience and its desires. If alienation effects frequently empower spectators by comforting them with the reminder that what they are watching is simply a play, *Antony and Cleopatra*'s moment of self-reflection could have had an altogether more challenging effect on its Jacobean audience. With this episode the third motif from Thomas Edwards's poem—Narcissus's realization that the origin and object of his desire is a "woman turned from a boy"—finds a powerful parallel. Like Edwards's Narcissus, who abruptly realizes that the woman he sees in the spring is his own reflection, the play's earliest audiences were confronted with an unavoidable reminder of how the surpassingly seductive Egyptian Queen on whom they had been gazing was, like many of them, English and male.

Cleopatra, the "serpent of the Nile," is coded in terms that make her legible as a threatening Other to both Roman and Jacobean body politics. But the play also unleashes a series of potentially subversive images of Cleopatra as the same. "Hush, here comes Antony," Enobarbus announces early in the play—only to have his vocalized stage direction flatly contradicted by the apparition of Cleopatra: "Not he, the queen," Charmian retorts (1.2.76). Enobarbus's misrecognition is symptomatic. Here and at other crucial moments, Cleopatra not only lacks the absolute gender and racial alterity that her audiences and readers, as well as her Roman suitors, have ascribed to her; like the radiant reflection that Edwards's Narcissus beholds, she is shown to be no "Orient sunne" herself but literally an image of another male sun: "Think on me," Cleopatra declaims, "That am with Phoebus' amorous pinches black / And wrinkled deep in time" (1.5.27–29). Cleopatra here provides a telling figure for how she is fashioned by (and out of) the animating "sunshine" of her European male lovers, fashioned ultimately—as her speech about the boy Cleopatra reveals—from the same matter as her theatrical spectators. Poor old Lepidus may, after all, have hit the nail on the head when he drunkenly tells Antony: "*your* serpent of Egypt is bred now of *your* mud by the operation of *your* sun. So is *your* crocodile" (2.7.26–27; emphasis added). In his unwitting but suggestive adaptation of the Neoplatonic figure of the sun as origin, together with his use of the colloquial indefinite *your*, Lepidus inadvertently provides yet another reminder of the way in which *Antony and Cleopatra* offers a compelling and sustained critique of the origin of male heterosexual eros. Like Edwards's "Narcissus," Lepidus's speech deviates from conventional Neoplatonic accounts of desire in hinting that the play's primary "feminine" object and origin of desire, the "serpent of the Nile," is no Ur-Woman but the specular image of a sun that is *yours*—a term that, in its second-person inclusivity, may be taken as addressing not only the male "suns" of Gnaeus Pompey, Julius Caesar, and Antony but also the "infinite variety" of those Narcissuses—spectators, readers, and critics—who have found themselves in thrall to their own seductive images of "Cleopatra."

Notes

A version of this essay was prepared for the 1994 Northeast MLA conference panel "Shakespeare's Erotic Economies." I am grateful to the panel chair, Heather Findlay, and Alan Sinfield, Michael Neill, and Charles Mahoney for their comments and critiques over the course of this essay's long gestation.

1. Michel Foucault, "La Prose d'Actéon," *Nouvelle Revue Française* 12 (1964): 444: "Mais si le Diable, au contraire, si l'Autre était la Même? Et si la Tentation n'était pas un des episodes du grand antagonisme, mais la mince insinuation du Double? Si le duel se déroulait dans un espace de miroir?" (translation mine).

2. Stephen Greenblatt, "Shakespeare and the Exorcists" in *Shakespeare and the Question of Theory*, Patricia Parker and Geoffrey Hartman, eds. (New York, 1985), 163. I do not propose to reopen the debate over the nature and extent of Ovid's influence on *Antony and Cleopatra*; a useful summary of the various critical positions and conjectures on this issue is offered in *A New Variorum Edition of Shakespeare*: Antony and Cleopatra, ed. Marvin Spevack (New York, 1990), 594–95.

3. Both old and new criticisms have abided by this basic opposition. For an instance of the former, see George Brandes, *William Shakespeare: A Critical Study*, trans. William Archer, Mary Morison, and Diana White (London, 1902): "Just as Antony's ruin results from his connection with Cleopatra, so does the fall of the Roman Republic result from the contact of the simple hardihood of the West with the luxury of the East. Antony is Rome. Cleopatra is the Orient" (475). Modern feminist readings of the play informed by psychoanalytic perspectives have critically reevaluated the topographical opposition—and the gender opposition with which it has often been complicit—without necessarily disturbing it. Janet Adelman, for example, construes the opposition between Rome and Egypt as a struggle between "male scarcity and female bounty" in *Suffocating Mothers: Fantasies of Maternal Origin in Shakespeare's Plays, Hamlet to The Tempest* (New York, 1992), 177; see also her earlier study, *The Common Liar: An Essay on* Antony and Cleopatra (New Haven, CT, 1973). Edward Said's critique of European orientalism has enabled powerful analyses of the opposition's complicity with early modern colonialist discourse; see, for example, Ania Loomba, *Gender, Race, Renaissance Drama* (Manchester, UK, 1989): "in colonialist discourse, the conquered land is often explicitly endowed with feminine characteristics in contrast to the masculine attributes of the coloniser. . . . All Egyptians, represented and symbolised by their queen, are associated with feminine and primitive attributes—they are irrational, sensuous, lazy and superstitious" (78–79).

4. Brandes, 462. The tendency of critics in the first half of the twentieth century to view Cleopatra and Antony's relationship as an agon that has mythic analogues in the tales of Venus and Mars or Omphale and Hercules has doubtless contributed to the critical willingness to view both characters as archetypes of their sexes. For a summary of such archetypal readings of Antony and Cleopatra, see Spevack, ed., 655–60. Feminist criticism of the play has questioned Cleopatra's archetypal "femininity": Janet Adelman, for instance, argues that Cleopatra is not simply Omphale subduing the Herculean Antony but also the androgynous figure of *Venus armata* (*The Common Liar*, 92). For other discussions of the way in which Cleopatra problematizes rather than embodies "femininity," see Clare Kinney, "The Queen's Two Bodies and the Divided Emperor: Some Problems of Identity in *Antony and Cleopatra*" in *The Renaissance Englishwoman in Print: Counterbalancing the Canon*, Anne M. Haselkorn and Betty S. Travitsky, eds. (Amherst, MA, 1990), 177–86; and Jyotsna Singh, "Renaissance Antitheatricality, Anti-feminism, and Shakespeare's *Antony and Cleopatra*," *Renaissance Drama* N.S. 20 (1990): 99–121. All quotations of *Antony and Cleopatra* follow the Arden Shakespeare, ed. M. R. Ridley (London, 1954). Quotations of all other Shakespeare plays follow the *Riverside Shakespeare*, ed. G. Blakemore Evans (Boston, 1974).

5. G. Wilson Knight, *The Imperial Theme: Further Interpretations of Shakespeare's Tragedies* (London, 1950), 297 and 304.

6. For a useful summary of the assumptions that have dominated discussions of Cleopatra, see L. T. Fitz, "Egyptian Queens and Male Reviewers:

Sexist Attitudes in *Antony and Cleopatra* Criticism," *Shakespeare Quarterly* 28 (1977): 297–316. See also Malcolm Evans, *Signifying Nothing: Truth's True Contents in Shakespeare's Text* (Brighton, UK, 1986), in which he attempts to retrieve Cleopatra's "infinite variety" from those who would morally reconstrue it as a representative "feminine" inconstancy. Assessing the conventional interpretations of Cleopatra's variety, Evans concludes that "the hint here of another discourse, one which may disturb the 'truth' of the patriarchal order, is, however, recuperated for that order by the firm attributions that trail behind this figure—the 'woman's wiles,' 'female enchantment,' etc." (165).

7. There have been a number of notable exceptions. Critics who have challenged the gender binaries of the play, albeit from very different standpoints, include Constance Brown Kuriyama, "The Mother of the World: A Psychoanalytic Interpretation of Shakespeare's *Antony and Cleopatra*," *English Literary Renaissance* 7 (1977): 324–51; Murray M. Schwartz, "Shakespeare through Contemporary Psychoanalysis" in *Representing Shakespeare: New Psychoanalytic Essays*, Murray M. Schwartz and Coppélia Kahn, eds. (Baltimore, MD, 1980), 21–32; Madelon Gohlke, "'I wooed thee with my sword': Shakespeare's Tragic Paradigms" in Schwartz and Kahn, eds., 170–87; Peter Erickson, *Patriarchal Structures in Shakespeare's Drama* (Berkeley, CA, 1985), esp. 131–33; Jonathan Dollimore, "Shakespeare, Cultural Materialism, Feminism and Marxist Humanism," *New Literary History* 21 (1990): 471–93; Singh, esp. 99–100, 114–16; Theodora A. Jankowski, *Women in Power in the Early Modern Drama* (Urbana, IL, 1992), esp. 156–60; and Valerie Traub, *Desire and Anxiety: Circulations of Sexuality in Shakespearean Drama* (London, 1992), esp. 134, 142.

8. Adelman, *Suffocating Mothers*, 177.

9. Leonard Tennenhouse, *Power on Display: The Politics of Shakespeare's Genres* (London, 1986), 144.

10. In foregrounding the specularity of the play's female Egyptian and male Roman characters, my argument owes a substantial debt to Luce Irigaray's analysis of male constructions of the feminine Other as the self-same; see her *Speculum of the Other Woman*, trans. Gillian C. Gill (Ithaca, NY, 1985), especially "Any Theory of the 'Subject' Has Always Been Appropriated by the 'Masculine,'" 133–46.

11. Shakespeare hints at Roman rulers' capacity for self-knowledge through specular encounter also in *Julius Caesar*, when Cassius tells Brutus that "since you know you cannot see yourself / So well as by reflection, I, your glass, / Will modestly discover to yourself / That of yourself which you yet know not of" (1.2.66–69).

12. Anna Jameson, *Shakespeare's Heroines: Characteristics of Women, Moral, Poetical, and Historical*, 2d ed. (London, 1833), 256 and 271.

13. August W. von Schlegel, *A Course on Dramatic Art and Literature*, trans. John Black, rev. A.J.W. Morrison (London, 1846), 416.

14. A. C. Bradley, *Oxford Lectures on Poetry* (London, 1909), 299.

15. Arguably, such a reading of Cleopatra's narcissistic pride acquires weight from the play's insistent identification of her with "crocodiles" and "serpents" of the Nile, creatures associated not only with deception and temptation but also with pride. One may recall the third verse of Spenser's "Visions of the Worlds Vanitie": "Beside the fruitfull shore of muddie Nile, / Vpon a sunnie banke outstretched lay / In monstrous length, a mightie Crocodile, / That . . . Thought all thinges lesse than his disdainful pride" (*The Works of Edmund Spenser: A Variorum Edition*, ed. E. Greenlaw et al., 9 vols. [Baltimore, MD, 1932–49], 8:175).

16. *The Metamorphoses of Ovid*, trans. Mary M. Innes (Harmondsworth, UK, 1955), 86. Interestingly, Frances Quarles appended Ovid's tag to a portrait depicting an infected breast, his emblem of postlapsarian corruption; see *Emblems, Divine and Moral*, ed. Augustus Toplady and John Ryland (London, 1839), 44. This demonstrates how the motif of plenty making poor, or of satiety prompting hunger, lent itself to numerous interpretations. Quarles's identification of Narcissus's complaint with a contaminating femininity responsible for the Fall potentially reinforces readings of Cleopatra as an Egyptian Eve; I would argue, instead, that *Antony and Cleopatra*'s preoccupation with mirrors and reflections makes it difficult to avoid pursuing a reading of Enobarbus's remark based on the more literal narcissistic resonances of Ovid's tag. Janet Adelman discusses Quarles's emblem in *Suffocating Mothers*, 5–6.

17. Spenser, 8:209.

18. Henry Reynolds, *Mythomystes: Wherein a Short Survay is Taken of the Nature and Value of True Poesy and Depth of the Ancients above our Moderne Poets* (London, 1630[?]), sig. N4v.

19. Thomas Edwards, *Cephalus and Procris. Narcissus.* (London, 1882), 52.

20. For a thorough discussion of Neoplatonic readings of the Narcissus myth, see Louise Vinge, *The Narcissus Theme in Western European Literature up to the Early Nineteenth Century*, trans. Robert Dewsnap et al. (Lund, Sweden, 1967), esp. 123–27, 148–51, and 185–86; see also Barry Taylor, *Vagrant Writing: Social and Semiotic Disorder in the English Renaissance* (Toronto, Canada, 1992), esp. 86–89 and 185–88.

21. Anonymous, *The Fable of Ouid Treting of Narcissus in Edwards*, 146; Richard Brathwayte, *The Golden Fleece, Whereto Bee Annexed Two Elegies, Entitled Narcissus Change and Aesons Dotage* (London, 1611), sig. D7.

22. Reynolds, sig. O1.

23. Edwards, 148.

24. Reynolds, sig. N4v.

25. Reynolds, sig. P3v.

26. Taylor, 88 and 186.

27. Edwards, 48.

28. Edwards, 52.

29. Edwards, 51.

30. Edwards, 49.

31. Past generations of critics agree with the Romans about Cleopatra's "transcendental" desirability. See, for example, Arthur Symons: "*Antony and Cleopatra* is the most wonderful, I think, of all Shakespeare's plays, and it is so mainly because the figure of Cleopatra is the most wonderful of Shakespeare's women. And not of Shakespeare's women only, but perhaps the most wonderful of women" (*Studies in the Elizabethan Drama* [New York, 1919], 1).

32. This notion was, of course, proverbial; see M. P. Tilley, *A Dictionary of the Proverbs in England in the Sixteenth and Seventeenth Centuries* (Ann Arbor, MI, 1950), W924. The idea is expressed elsewhere in Shakespeare's plays; see, for example, *All's Well That Ends Well*, 5.3.61–63, or *Much Ado About Nothing*, 4.1.217–22. But the insistence with which the notion is articulated in *Antony and Cleopatra* to explain specifically Roman behavior serves to deprive it (at least in this play) of its conventionally universal application.

33. See R. W. Dent, *Shakespeare's Proverbial Language: An Index* (Berkeley, CA, 1981), N42.

34. Critics from Margaret Cavendish in the Restoration to Derek Traversi in the twentieth century have paid homage to Cleopatra's vividness and vitality. Traversi's assessment is in some ways typical: "Cleopatra, though the creature of the world which surrounds her, can at times emerge from it, impose upon her surroundings a vitality which is not the less astonishing for retaining to the last its connection with the environment it transcends" (*An Approach to Shakespeare*, 3rd ed., 2 vols. [Garden City, NY, 1969], 2:223–24).

35. Bradley, 298.

36. For example, Harley Granville-Barker asks: "What is the best evidence we have (so to speak) of Cleopatra's physical charms? A description of them by Enobarbus" (*Prefaces to Shakespeare* [Princeton, NJ, 1947], 435).

37. Discussions of the power exerted by the displayed monarch's body in early modern Europe include Michel Foucault, *Discipline and Punish: The Birth of the Prison*, trans. Alan Sheridan (New York, 1979); and Ernst Kantorowicz, *The King's Two Bodies: A Study in Mediaeval Theology* (Princeton, NJ, 1955). Studies that specifically examine the iconography of Queen Elizabeth's displayed body include Marie Axton, *The Queen's Two Bodies: Drama and the Elizabethan Succession* (London, 1977); and Leonard Tennenhouse, *Power on Display*. Tennenhouse makes the intriguing observation that *Antony and Cleopatra* is "Shakespeare's elegy for the signs and symbols which legitimized Elizabethan power. Of these, the single most important figure was that of the desiring and desired woman, her body valued for its ornamental surface, her feet rooted deep in a kingdom" (146). In its depiction of an erotically ornamental, pageantlike display of royal female power, Enobarbus's account of Cleopatra's procession at Cydnus would in many ways appear to confirm Tennenhouse's assertion; however, as I go on to argue, the curious lack of physical detail offered by Enobarbus about Cleopatra's displayed body suggests that her power subsists in her very invisibility, her publicly paraded absence—the "*inopem me copia fecit*" of the narcissistic reflection.

38. Phyllis Rackin's response to Enobarbus's speech is notable for its conjunction of traditional homage to Shakespeare's imaginative poetic power with suggestive insight into the "defect" that paradoxically underwrites the panegyric's effect of "perfection": Enobarbus "suddenly abandons his characteristic ironic prose for the soaring poetry that creates for his listeners a Cleopatra who transcends anything they could see with the sensual eye or measure with the calculating and rational principle of the soul. . . . It is a commonplace of the older criticism that Shakespeare had to rely upon his poetry and his audience's imagination to evoke Cleopatra's greatness because he knew the boy actor could not depict it convincingly. But he transformed this limitation into an asset, used the technique his stage demanded to demonstrate the unique powers of the very medium that seemed to limit him. Like Cleopatra's own art, the economy of the poet's art works paradoxically, to make defect perfection" ("Shakespeare's Boy Cleopatra, the Decorum of Nature, and the Golden World of Poetry," *PMLA* 87 [1972]: 201–12, esp. 204).

39. Other early Stuart playwrights attribute narcissistic traits to Roman desire. In a tantalizingly suggestive passage, Elizabeth Cary invokes Narcissus's "*inopem me copia fecit*" to describe how Antony would have reacted to Maryam, Queen of the Jews, if he had only succeeded in disentangling himself from Cleopatra: "Too much delight did bare him from delight, / For either's love the other's did confound" (*The Tragedy of Maryam, The Fair Queen of Jewry*, ed. Barry Weller and Margaret W. Ferguson [Berkeley, CA, 1994], 1.2.185–86).

40. Bruce R. Smith, *Homosexual Desire in Shakespeare's England: A Cultural Poetics* (Chicago, 1991), 59. I would like to thank Charles Mahoney for his thoughtful comments on this issue.

41. Eve Kosofsky Sedgwick, *Between Men: English Literature and Male Homosocial Desire* (New York, 1985), 2.

42. Cleopatra's speech offers an intriguing counterpart to Ovid's account of Narcissus: like Echo, Cleopatra is excluded from a circuit of desire whose origin and terminus is male. Perhaps this exclusion can help explain a puzzling reference that seems to lurk in Cleopatra's description. Pompey's eyes, she claims, "grow" in her "brow": the phrasing here invokes the inescapable image of the cuckold's budding horns. Is Cleopatra half-comically suggesting that she has been cuckolded by a Pompey who "betrays" her by making love, albeit unwittingly, to himself?

43. Slavoj Žižek, *The Sublime Object of Ideology* (London, 1989), 75. I am grateful to Heather Findlay for drawing this passage to my attention.

44. Catherine Belsey, *The Subject of Tragedy: Identity and Difference in Renaissance Drama* (London, 1985), 149. For a reading similar to my own of the patriarchal construction of a contradictory "feminine" identity, see Loomba, 75–79 and 125–30.

45. All quotations from *The Duchess of Malfi* follow the New Mermaids text, 3rd ed., ed. Elizabeth M. Brennan (London, 1993).

46. To this short list there could be profitably added a number of Shakespeare's other plays. The examples most pertinent to an analysis of *Antony and Cleopatra*, perhaps, are *Much Ado About Nothing*, *Othello*, and *The Winter's Tale*. All three plays subject to critical scrutiny the derogatory assumptions men make about women—Benedick's hyperbolic conviction that Beatrice is a "harpy" who "speaks poniards" (2.1.271, 247), Claudio's denigration of Hero as a "rotten orange" (4.1.32), Iago's unsubstantiated belief that Emilia has cuckolded him, Othello's mischaracterization of Desdemona as a "strumpet" and "cunning whore of Venice" (4.2.82, 89), or Leontes's jealous invectives against the irreproachable Hermione as an "adult'ress," "traitor," and "bed-swerver" (2.1.88, 89, and 93).

47. The term, of course, is Bertolt Brecht's. For critical analyses of this speech and the issue of the boy Cleopatra, see Michael Jamieson, "Shakespeare's Celibate Stage: The Problem of Accommodation to the Boy-Actress in *As You Like It*, *Antony and Cleopatra* and *The Winter's Tale*" in *Papers Mainly Shakespearean*, G. I. Duthie, ed. (Edinburgh, 1964), 21–39; Rackin, 201; Michael Shapiro, "Boying her Greatness: Shakespeare's Use of Coterie Drama in *Antony and Cleopatra*," *Modern Language Review* 77 (1982): 1–15; Kathleen McLuskie, "The Act, the Role, and the Actor: Boy Actresses on the Elizabethan Stage," *New Theatre Quarterly* 10 (1987): 120–30; Terence Hawkes, *That Shakespearian Rag: Essays on a Critical Process* (London, 1986), 83; Dollimore, 490; Graham Holderness, "'Some Squeaking Cleopatra': Theatricality in *Antony and Cleopatra*" in *Critical Essays on* Antony and Cleopatra, Linda Cookson and Bryan Loughrey, eds. (Harlow, Essex, UK, 1990), 42–52; and Lorraine Helms, "'The High Roman Fashion': Sacrifice, Suicide, and the Shakespearean Stage," *PMLA* 107 (1992): 554–65.

SUSAN SNYDER

Meaning in Motion: Macbeth *and Especially* Antony and Cleopatra

Decades ago, R. A. Foakes spoke out persuasively for a new approach to Shakespeare's imagery that would go beyond the categories of Caroline Spurgeon. Specifically, he appealed for more attention to dramatic imagery, including props and stage effects; and for analysis and classification of images on bases other than subject matter.[1] More recent times have witnessed a new concentration on the direct imagery of stage production, with a corollary withdrawal from verbal imagery—for fear of committing the new cardinal sin, reading the play as a poem. A few critics remained faithful to "the poetry," assuming that *Hamlet* can be apprehended in the same way as, say, *Paradise Lost.* Yet drama is a temporal art, much more so than poetry, and its essence is action. Perhaps one reason that image-critics of the traditional sort and theater-oriented critics have had little to say to each other is that the former are, for the most part, still attending only to image-patterns created by static subject matter, recurring objects like jewels or qualities like darkness. But verbs have their effect in Shakespeare's language as well as nouns and adjectives. Images create other patterns through repeated *motion*, and it is this dynamic aspect of imagery that connects most naturally with stage movements and groupings.

Not that the dynamics of images have been completely ignored. Few critics will discuss poison or disease references in *Hamlet* without pointing

---

From *Shakespeare: A Wayward Journey*, pp. 62–77.

out their characteristic common movement—spreading unseen, mining all within, and at last breaking forth to betray the inner corruption that can no longer be contained. Yet it is not sufficiently recognized that a recurrent motion connects these images with others in the play whose "subject" is not poison or sickness: for example, with Hamlet's early prediction that "foul deeds will rise, / Though all the earth o'erwhelm them, to men's eyes" (1.2.262–63),[2] and with his later one that the hidden, decaying body of Polonius will eventually give away its whereabouts by smell (4.3.37–38).

In one play, *Richard II*, a very pronounced pattern of iterated motion has attracted critical comment. First Paul A. Jorgenson and later Arthur Suzman pointed out the persistent up-and-down action that informs not only verbal images as diverse as buckets, scales, plants, and the sun, but gesture and stage movement as well—gages thrown down and taken up, kneeling and rising, and most tellingly of all, in the Flint Castle scene that marks the real end of his temporal power, Richard's descent from the upper stage to the level where his challenger awaits him:

> Base court, where kings grow base
> To come at traitors' calls. . . .
> Down, court! Down, king!
> For night-owls shriek where mounting larks should
> sing. [*Exeunt from above.*][3]
> (3.3.180–83)

It is possible to go further than Jorgenson or Suzman have in relating this imagery to dramatic structure. *Richard II* has a built-in structural ambivalence: politically, Richard's course is downward and Bolingbroke's is upward, but in audience sympathies Bolingbroke is the one who falls while Richard rises. Many of the up–down images convey versions of this ambivalence, either in themselves or as qualified one by another. The equation of Richard with the setting sun, for instance, suggests a natural, right transition "from Richard's night to Bolingbroke's fair day" (3.2.218). But this image is associated with a less natural, more awesome phenomenon when Salisbury imagines Richard not only as the sun setting but as a shooting star, plummeting suddenly to the base earth and presaging "storms to come, woe, and unrest" (2.4.19–22). Richard's own choice of Phaeton rather than Apollo in the Flint Castle speech reminds us that his night is an abrupt, violent thing, a violation of natural process rather than the timely closing of day. Night owls forcibly displace the larks of day that *should* be singing. When in Act 3, scene 4 the Gardener speaks in his own idiom of Richard's flourishing and fall—"He that hath suffered this disordered spring / Hath now himself met with the fall of leaf" (48–49)—the abrupt passage from spring to fall of leaf carries the same implication that Richard's decline, while inevitable, is unnatural. So, too, the later image of the scales (84–89) is more ambivalent than it seems. Bolingbroke prevails because his side is heavy with allies, while Richard's contains only himself and his "light" vanities. Straightforward enough, except that in changing his metaphor the Gardener has also changed, in fact reversed, the values that he and other speakers have established for up and down. Up has been the desirable position, yet this vision of Bolingbroke solid in power and popularity and Richard dangling vainly in the air suggests that up can be bad as well as good. The suggestion carries over into the deposition scene that follows, when Richard applies the opposition of up and down to himself and his rival, and reverses the values back again—or does he? In his simile of the two buckets (4.1.184–90), the King is once again on the down side, freighted with tears, while Bolingbroke dances in the air. But this lightness of Bolingbroke's recalls the implications of "light" in the Gardener's scale conceit, especially when Richard calls his successor "empty." The ambiguity may well be conscious on the speaker's part as well as the playwright's. Bolingbroke is empty in being free of Richard's griefs, the weight of tears, but also in lacking proper sanction as a king; without the weight of tradition and inheritance his position is shaky.

Another motion-system of oppositions shapes *Macbeth*. The Macbeths conceive and execute their crime in terms of perversions of natural flow, especially stopping up and leaping over. Legitimate monarchy, passing from one king to his rightful successor, finds its movement in slow, ordered growth. "I have begun to plant thee," says Duncan to Banquo, "and will labor / To make thee full of growing" (1.4.28–29). His son Malcolm, finally king of Scotland after the dreadful interlude of the Macbeths, plans his restoration of order in the same terms: "What's more to do / Which would be planted newly with the time . . ." (5.8.65–66). But in the earlier scene, while Duncan foresees slow but flourishing development for loyal followers and names Malcolm his eventual successor, Macbeth responds with something quite opposite—varieties of convulsive motion. Malcolm's nomination as Prince of Cumberland is "a step / On which I must fall down or else o'erleap" (1.4.48–49).

Stopping and leaping over, disrupters of ordinary flow, return to haunt the imaginations of both Macbeths as they work themselves up to their crime. Lady Macbeth shows why they must violate natural motion in order to do what they do. She calls on the murderous spirits to thicken her blood so as to block the rush of pity that would naturally respond to thoughts of such a murder:

> Stop up th'access and passage to remorse,
> That no compunctious visitings of nature
> Shake my fell purpose. . . .
> (1.5.44–46)

Night must interfere with the ordinary line of vision to cut off both murderer and judging heaven from the sight of the deed. At the same time, she feels propelled past difficulties, leaping past "this ignorant present" to "feel . . . The future in the instant" (1.5.56–58). Her husband in his own soliloquy (1.7.1–28) is obsessed in a parallel way with cutting off the normal progression from cause to result, and wishes rather to trammel up consequence, to stop with his single murderous blow the whole process of reaction and new initiative. The prospect of consequence after death he addresses with overleaping, another form of blotting-out—"We'd jump the life to come." Later on he is more aware of the dangers of "vaulting ambition," which overleaps itself only to fall on the other side. But his lady retains her faith in stopping-up, even imagines violently cutting off the literal flow of nursing and life itself in her helpless infant.

In that savage truncation of the next generation, as many have noticed, what begins as an image later turns into dramatic fact. There are apparently no Macbeth children to rule after him in orderly succession. It is Banquo's issue who will move forward, generation after generation, an endless line stretching out to the crack of doom. Macbeth's fury at this vision (4.1.150–54) is displaced onto Macduff, possibly a traitor but guilty mainly of having a "line." Behind this insistence on Macbeth's truncated line and his obsession with cutting off others in retaliation lies the original crime, presented to Duncan's sons as a violent stopping up of the natural flow of life from father to children: "The spring, the head, the fountain of your blood / Is stopped, the very source of it is stopped" (2.3.100–101).

Like the cutting off of progeny, other violations of natural motion eventually turn against the Macbeths. The natural laws they depend on (in spite of trying to thwart them), become unreliable. Dead men, like Banquo, refuse to lie still. "This is more strange / Than such a murder is," says the shaken Macbeth in the banquet scene (3.4.83–84), his turn of phrase inadvertently revealing how one action answers the other: unnatural stoppage calls forth unnatural movement. The witches' prophecies give Macbeth confidence exactly because he trusts in natural process and law: men are born of women, trees don't move.

> Who can impress the forest, bid the tree
> Unfix his earthbound root? Sweet bodements, good!

Rebellious dead, rise never till the wood
Of Birnam rise, and our high-placed Macbeth
Shall live the lease of nature. . . .
(4.1.95–99)

But the rebellious dead have already risen, and their refusal of natural stasis will be reprised in the sleepwalking of Lady Macbeth. The fixity of the forest and the universality of the birth process prove no more reliable. Only when the Macbeths are trapped and extinguished by their own perversions of natural motion can the old orderly rhythm be reinstituted, as in Malcolm's final speech:

this, and what needful else
That calls upon us, by the grace of Grace
We will perform in measure, time, and place.
(5.8.72–74)

Antony and Cleopatra is similarly bound together by kinetically linked images that reinforce apparent movements and gather in less obvious ones. Here the clash of Rome against Egypt and Antony's tragic dilemma are enacted through the imagistic opposition of solid fixity or speedy directness against beautiful, unpurposive motion.

The play's first scene presents without delay the opposed forces that are working and will continue to work on Antony—Egypt in Cleopatra's changeable, demanding charm and Rome in the harsh judgments of Philo and Demetrius. Philo's opening lines set up the contrast between what he stands for and what he sees in the Alexandrian court:

Nay, but this dotage of our general's
O'erflows the measure. Those his goodly eyes,
That o'er the files and musters of the war
Have glowed like plated Mars, now bend, now turn,
The office and devotion of their view
Upon a tawny front. His captain's heart,
Which in the scuffles of great fights hath burst
The buckles of his breast, reneges all temper,
And is become the bellows and the fan
To cool a gypsy's lust.
Flourish. Enter Antony, Cleopatra, her Ladies, the train, with eunuchs fanning her.
Look where they come!

Take but good note, and you shall see in him
The triple pillar of the world transformed
Into a strumpet's fool.
(1.1.1–13)

Uniting the images of speech and action are two opposed ideas: one of steadfast, rigid immobility—a fixed *measure* and *temper*, the orderly *files* of ranked soldiers, the hard solidity of *plated Mars*, the unmoving *pillar of the world*—and the other of fluid, shifting movement, of overflowing, bending, turning, fanning. This last is reinforced by stage action when Cleopatra enters with eunuchs fanning her.

Philo's disapproving stand is simple enough, but the scene goes on to explore and complicate the values of fixity and flux. *Measure*, a positive notion in Philo's speech, is undercut in Antony's "There's beggary in the love that can be reckoned" (1.1.15). Roman measure has no room for a new heaven or a new earth.[4] Similarly, Antony makes Rome's solidity yield to his larger vision of human fulfillment:

Let Rome in Tiber melt, and the wide arch
Of the rang'd empire fall! Here is my space.
Kingdoms are clay; our dungy earth alike
Feeds beast as man. The nobleness of life
Is to do thus; when such a mutual pair
And such a twain can do't, in which I bind,
On pain of punishment, the world to weet
We stand up peerless.
(35–42)

The stable pillars and arches of Rome dissolve into fluidity, a fluidity however that is seen as expanding and completing rather than destroying. In what sense can Antony find positive value in dissolution? Against the Roman message, with its implications of purposive action and thinking for the future, he sets up the ideal of the immediate moment perfectly fulfilled: "There's not a minute of our lives should stretch / Without some pleasure *now*" (48–49, my italics). This is Cleopatra's gift, the full realization of all moments and moods.

Fie, wrangling queen!
Whom everything becomes—to chide, to laugh,
To weep; whose every passion fully strives
To make itself in thee fair and admired.
(50–53)

Antony celebrates a mode of life like the fanning motion which is the visual background to his words, directed to no end except motion itself and the beautifying of the moment. His word *becomes* is an important one. Cleopatra's moods serve no consistent purpose except to realize themselves, and her, perfectly. Later uses of the word will bring out the link between gracing the moment and expanding into fuller being. For now, Philo and Demetrius sway the balance back again, posing against this hint of identity expanding infinitely a contrary notion of identity as defined by Roman duties. Philo uses *become* negatively, for *degenerated into*: Antony's martial heart "is become the bellows and the fan. . . ." In his eyes, Antony by seeking escape from Roman measure has simply fallen below it, diminished and negated the self that is based on his Roman achievements. "He comes too short of that great property / Which still should go with Antony" (60–61).

On this note the scene ends. Its very structure carries out the opposition of fixity and flux, framing Antony's hyperboles and Cleopatra's quicksilver shifts with the unyielding judgment of the two Roman onlookers who open and close the scene.[5] An equally intractable, though silent, presence is the Roman message itself. The lovers can describe arabesques of constant motion around it, but they cannot blow it away. Antony's tragedy will be played out between these two imagistic poles, of solid stillness (or direct, purposive motion) and continual shifting activity, with their ambiguous implications for the self.

The images that follow continue and fill out the pattern set in the first scene. Cleopatra's Nile journey, as later described by Enobarbus (2.2.200–215), is all beautiful, self-fulfilling, self-justifying motion. The barge will eventually land somewhere, but there is no sense of direction toward an end in the action of sails and oars. On the contrary, the sails are there to dally with the "love-sick" winds and the oars to keep time with flutes while playing similar games with the water, which is "amorous of their strokes." The point is in the process—as it is also with the fans plied by pretty boys "whose wind did seem / To glow the delicate cheeks which they did cool, / And what they undid did." So, too, Cleopatra's waiting women make "their bends adornings," achieving nothing beyond the graceful movements themselves.

Antony calls Cleopatra his serpent of old Nile, and water with its unending shift and flow is clearly her element as solid earth is natural to the Roman soldier Antony. While Shakespeare is not so eager as Plutarch to blame Antony's decision to fight Caesar by sea rather than by land on his passion for Cleopatra,[6] she certainly gives instant support to the choice—"By sea! What else?" (3.7.28)—and her only forces mentioned in the play are naval ones. The Cleopatra who first caught Antony's heart on the river of Cydnus dreams in terms of their favorite river-sport of catching him again and again with her angle and bended hook (2.5.10–15). Enobarbus, who first identified her with winds and waters (1.2.155), at Actium defines the slippery changeability of her element in relation to stable land when he warns Antony not to "give up yourself merely to chance and hazard, / From firm security" (3.7.48–49).[7] Cleopatra's actions have the ebb and flow of water: laughing Antony out of patience and then laughing him back in (2.5.19–20), meeting his sadness with dancing and his mirth with sudden sickness (1.3.3–5). Her verbs, so to speak, are intransitive, objectless like the movements of winds and waves and fans. Hopping forty paces in the street, as Enobarbus recalls her doing (2.2.239), has no object beyond spirited activity. It is surely no way to *arrive* anywhere. Even when Cleopatra is being apparently purposeful, sending messages to the absent Antony (1.5.66–81), what counts is not the message but the act of sending. It hardly needed the "twenty several messengers" (65) already dispatched to make Antony understand her love and longing for him, yet she goes on from there to vow extravagantly, "He shall have every day a several greeting, / Or I'll unpeople Egypt" (80–81).

Roman movement, when there is any at all, is direct, efficient, transitive. The best example is Caesar's incredibly rapid passage with his troops from Italy to Epirus, which so impresses Antony and Candidius (3.7.20–25; 54–57; 74–75). Antony's first bemused image is of Caesar, supposed so far away, *cutting* the sea like a sword to conquer Toryne near Antony's own camp (3.7.22–23). For the most part, though, Rome evokes images of stationary firmness. Opposed to Cleopatra's constant movement is Octavia, who is "holy, cold, and still" in her behavior (2.6.124), "still" too in her judgment (4.15.29), who seems "a body rather than a life, / A statue than a breather" (3.3.21–22). Antony's marriage to her is a *binding* (2.5.59), Maecenas hopes she will *settle* his heart (2.2.251–53), and he himself vows his reform to her in terms of fixed, straight lines: "I have not kept my *square*, but that to come / Shall all be done by th'rule" (2.3.6–7, my italics).

From this Roman perspective, Egyptian movement looks stupid and degrading in its lack of purpose. Caesar's verbs to describe Antony's "pleasure now"—tumbling on the bed of Ptolemy, keeping the turn of tippling, reeling, standing the buffet—have no beauty in them (1.4.16–21). Jostling with knaves "that smell of sweat," no longer commander of himself or his situation, Antony in Caesar's eyes is at the mercy of the moment, like the vulgar populace whose loyalties shift with every tide. Caesar might say of him, as he does of the despised public,

> This common body,
> Like to a vagabond flag upon the stream,
> Goes to, and back, lackeying the varying tide,

To rot itself with motion.
(1.4.44–47)

In the Roman's contemptuous image, watery instability is simply servitude—"lackeying the tide"—and unpurposive motion leads only to helpless decay. Pompey even finds a kind of stasis in Antony's pleasures of the moment: for him Antony is a tame animal tethered in a field of feasts (2.1.23). Indeed, Antony in his Roman mood can also see the restless motions of pleasure as imprisoning. In the expansive sentiment of "Let Rome in Tiber melt," it was the world he would "bind" to admire in the activities of Cleopatra and himself the full nobleness of life. When struck by Roman thoughts, however, he sees *himself* as immobilized, "bound . . . up / From mine own knowledge" (2.2.96–97), pinned down by strong Egyptian fetters (1.2.122). He can even share Caesar's disdain for the undirected flux of public opinion, now flowing for no good reason toward Pompey—"our slippery people" (1.2.192). Later, after he has failed to stand firm at Actium, Antony harks back to that Roman norm of fixed, straight lines to image his disgrace: "I have offended reputation—/ A most unnoble *swerving*" (3.11.48–49, my italics). And, as if in response to his own lack of fixity, others now fall away from him—kings, captains, Enobarbus, Fortune, the god Hercules—in a pattern of repeated desertions that shapes most of Act 4.

Nowhere after the first scene does the opposition between Roman fixity and Egyptian fluidity come into sharper focus than in 2.7, the feast aboard Pompey's galley. The setting itself is suggestive. But only a film version could give us as direct dramatic image the solid ship on ever-shifting water, secured in a place by a single cable. In this play written for the bare Shakespearian stage, it is words and gestures that must keep us aware of the chancy, changeable element that surrounds this gathering of Romans. Drink is the main reminder, of course. The characters reel and stagger in varying degrees, Lepidus most and Caesar and Menas least, and finally join in the dance whose dizzying motion is indicated in its refrain—"Cup us till the world go round." Verbal imagery reinforces the effect of Roman *terra firma* threatened and undermined by other, alien elements or perversions of its own. The Romans are ill-rooted plants at the mercy of the wind, Lepidus is sinking in quicksands, cares drown in Bacchus's vats, Menas wishes the whole world could "go on wheels" (2.7.1–3; 60; 117; 93–94). In answering Lepidus's drunken catechism Antony invokes Egyptian undulation directly, the swell and ebb of the Nile and the serpentine crocodile it breeds, which like Cleopatra lives by no other law than itself. Caesar is inevitably ill at ease amid all this living for the moment. He cannot, as Antony counsels, "be a child o' the time" (101). That is Antony's way, the way he learned in Egypt, but not Caesar's.

If Caesar has misgivings about flux undermining firmness, they are justified. While Antony is being a child of the time, Menas urgently reminds Pompey that he need only cut one cable to set the whole Roman government adrift and manipulate it at his own pleasure. Order and stability are worth something, after all, and in a play not notably sympathetic to Rome Shakespeare makes us feel here, at least, how vulnerable and how necessary Roman order is. Where Caesar offers in his bearing a dramatic image of fixity at the reeling feast, Menas is the other image of Rome—direct, purposive action. He dogs Pompey's steps relentlessly about the stage to prod him to the decisive act. "Wilt thou be lord of all the world? . . . Wilt thou be lord of the whole world? . . . Let me cut the cable" (62–72). Menas's urgent movements and speech-rhythms are another kind of Roman counterpoint to these self-fulfilling Egyptian Bacchanals. The plot to cut the cable comes to nothing, because of Pompey's ambiguous but nevertheless inhibiting honor. Caesar, the real man of the future, who will later cut the sea, has no such inhibitions.

The galley scene is typical of *Antony and Cleopatra* as a whole in its ambivalence about the values of fixity/direct-drive and flux. Menas's plan of action, which involves cutting throats as well as cables, makes the boasting talk of Egyptian tourist attractions seem trivial; but Antony, the child of the time, is more alive than cautious, calculating Caesar. When the Nile's flow quickens Egypt, Antony tells Lepidus, it brings forth grain and also crocodiles. So it is with Antony's Egyptian excess, as Janet Adelman observes: "it too will breed serpents as well as crops. But the man of measure—the man who never overflows—will not breed at all."[8]

Both aspects of breeding, positive and negative, come through in the play's persistent references to melting, merging, and "becoming." As in Antony's speech in the first scene Rome's hard outlines melt to allow a new heaven and a new earth, so later we learn that Egyptian life breaks down normal divisions between day and night (2.2.187–88), between land and water again (2.5.79), even between male and female. Cleopatra recalls how she and Antony expanded, into each other's roles, he wearing her tires and mantles and she his sword Philippan (2.5.22–23). What was play then becomes a more profound merging later, in Antony's startling invitation to her:

> Leap thou, attire and all,
> Through proof of harness to my heart, and there
> Ride on the pants triumphing.
> (4.8.14–16)

Hard-and-fast limits ("proof of harness") give way, in his imagination at least, before the leaping, pulsing motion that fuses separate selves. Antony has also said that every passion becomes Cleopatra, gracing her by its full realization; later she will likewise expect him to "become / The carriage of his chafe" (1.3.84–85), make his anger an ennobling thing. "Be'st thou sad or merry," she says of him in his absence, "The violence of either thee becomes, / So does it no man else" (1.5.62–64). The Roman notion of "becoming" is conversely narrow: soldierly dress becomes Romans, reveling does not (Caesar's "say this becomes him" after that unattractive list of Antony's activities in Egypt is obviously ironic). *Becoming* means "fitting for Roman," and any other kind of becoming is degeneration—as in Philo's image Antony has degenerated into a mere appliance catering to Cleopatra's lust. Egypt finds even negative passions "becomings," ways to fuller being. When Enobarbus claims that "vilest things become themselves" in Cleopatra, it is impossible to disentangle in the knotted sense "vilest things are graces" from "vilest things are fully realized." In this paradoxical merging of earnings divisions between good and bad also give way to the expansiveness of endless process.[9]

Rome, in contrast, finds true being only in sharp outlines and distinctions. Caesar is aware in his own way of the melting of sex distinctions between Antony and Cleopatra—as adulterating Antony's soldier-self, not enlarging it: " [Antony] is not more manlike / Than Cleopatra, nor the queen of Ptolemy / More womanly than he" (1.4.5–7). For Caesar that self of Antony's is defined by hardship and his unyielding sameness in the face of it, the retreat from Modena when, in spite of eating strange flesh and drinking horses' urine, his cheek "so much as lank'd not" (1.4.56–72). Later events bear out to a certain extent Caesar's view of identity as persisting in one's own ways, observing one's own boundaries. After Antony has yielded at Actium to Cleopatra and her fluid element instead of standing fast on his own, images of wayward movement express disintegration rather than fuller being. Antony is "unqualitied"; he has left himself, lost his way forever, lost command (3.11.19–20; 3–4; 23). Melting is not completion but loss, as authority melts *from* him (3.13.91). Like Caesar, he seeks "Antony" in past exploits of war:

> He [Caesar] at Philippi kept
> His sword e'en like a dancer, while I struck
> The lean and wrinkled Cassius; and 'twas I
> That the mad Brutus ended. He alone
> Dealt on lieutenantry, and no practice had
> In the brave squares of war. Yet now—
> (3.11.35–40)

Antony is very Roman here. He defines his past self by opposition, between himself and Cassius, himself and Brutus, himself and Caesar. And his typically Roman images combine direct, efficient action ("struck," "ended") with the right-angled solidity of "squares."

But the Egyptian notion of identity has not been dropped. I have been looking at the two scenes that follow the defeat at Actium, 3.11 and 13. While both of them give full expression to Antony's Roman mood, both also swing up eventually from despair to an affirmation of self that includes Cleopatra. Indeed, the first seems to discard Roman values entirely for Egyptian ones: "Fall not a tear, I say; one of them rates / All that is won and lost. Give me a kiss; / Even this repays me" (3.11.68–70). The second affirmation is more comprehensive. When Antony exclaims, "Where hast thou been, my heart?" (3.13.175), he is recovering both his own essence and the Cleopatra he had earlier thought lost to him ("what's her name / Since she was Cleopatra?" (99–100). Thus restored, Antony can in the same speech proclaim himself tripled in strength and valor, and call for one other gaudy night of feasting (3.13.181–88). In the final movement of Act 4, Antony again feels his outline dissolving like the dragonish cloud (4.14.2–14), melting into indistinctness like water in water. It is important here that this newly endangered identity is not simply the Roman soldier but the fused self of warrior and lover. His earlier promise, on leaving Cleopatra for Rome, to make peace or war according to her wishes (1.3.69–71) was only words: the peace he concluded with Caesar was pure Roman policy and its seal, his marriage to Octavia, could not have been less to Cleopatra's liking. In the last battle it is finally true that he has "made these wars for Egypt and the queen" (4.14.15). Again the pendulum swings to affirmation. Antony dies affirming both sides of that greater self—a Roman by a Roman valiantly vanquished, still relishing wine and Cleopatra's kiss.

Still, Antony can bring together incompatible modes of life only when he has no more life to live. Images of fixity and flux have acted out kinetically the terms of his dilemma, the fixity necessary to define the self and the fluidity necessary to transcend the self's limitations. However much Antony wants to encompass both, he cannot be fixed and constantly moving at the same time, calculate and seize just the right moment for action while living every moment for its own sake. *Antony and Cleopatra* is distinctive among Shakespeare's tragedies not only in its relative lack of high-drama scenes, which Bradley noted,[10] but in a corollary lack of dramatic build-up. Actium is a turning point, to be sure, but there is no long sequence building toward it as the early scenes of *Macbeth* build toward the murder of Duncan or the early scenes of *King Lear* toward Lear's self-exile and madness on the heath. In *Antony and Cleopatra*, although we are reminded in various ways that the triumph of Caesarism is inevitably coming,[11] scenes tend to be complete in themselves. Each fulfills the potential of the immediate situation, and if it links with what follows it is by ironic juxtaposition rather than as part of a sustained dramatic crescendo. Pleasure is a term in Antony's tragedy, and its quality of immediacy ("pleasure now") is bound to create a different kind of structure than such motives as power and revenge. Bradley also observed, with some regret, Shakespeare had passed up the opportunity to make intense drama of inner conflict out of the contrary pulls of Rome and Cleopatra on Antony.[12] Such a conflict, though, would necessarily undercut Antony's capacity—which is both his weakness and his greatness—to fulfill each moment wholeheartedly. He cannot, as Ernest Schanzer remarks, be shown like Brutus or Macbeth, "with himself at war"; rather, "he is like a chronic deserter, forever changing sides."[13]

In the end both Antony and Cleopatra are for stillness over constant flux. Once Cleopatra challenged the hard pillars and arches of Eternal City with something softer, more alive, more mobile: "Eternity was in our lips eyes, / Bliss in our brows' bent" (1.3.35–36). But that claim was undercut by its situation (Antony is leaving her) and even by its form. "Eternity was" is a contradiction. Ultimately she must be something less malleable, "marble constant" (5.2.240), and commit her volatile self to the act "which shackles accidents, and bolts up change" (6). Yet her death is not, any more than Antony's, a simple submission to Roman fixity. It is not just that her mode of dying combines Egyptian means with Roman end. Beyond that, image and reference project the sense that in dying both lovers rise to the moment one last time and do it so perfectly as to arrest time. Each strains toward death as to lover's embrace (4.14.99–101; 5.2.293–96). Cleopatra prepares again for Cydnus (5.2.277–28), catching up that perfect moment out of the flux of time. Even Caesar sees in the dead queen not so much cessation as eternal attraction, "as she would catch another Antony . . ." (347). At Antony's suicide what the onlookers sense is time itself frozen:

> The star is fall'n.
> And time is at his period.
> (4.14.108–9)

This effect of rising *through* constant motion to timelessness is what distinguishes the resting point of Antony and Cleopatra from the hard immobility of Rome. The paradox comes across most compactly in the climax of Cleopatra's rhapsody on the dead Antony, the last of the fish images.

> His delights
> Were dolphin-like; they showed his back above
> The element they lived in.
> (5.2.87–89)

What meanings attach to flux and superior solidity in this vision of the dolphin's firm back gleaming above the dancing, shifting sea? For Kittredge, who was later followed by Dover Wilson, Cleopatra means that "as the dolphin shows his back above the water, so Antony always rose superior to the pleasures in which he lived." This separates Antony's superiority from his pleasures, opposes them in fact. But "delights" are the agents of his rising: it is they who show his back above the sea. Another gloss, this one from the *Riverside Shakespeare*, says that Antony "in his pleasures . . . rose above the common as a dolphin rises out of its element, the sea."[14] Now the pleasures have been dissociated from the sea, which is simply "the common." But the sea with its unceasing flux is the element in which those uncommon pleasures lived. Antony's delights are both flux, the succession of moments, and that which ultimately lifts him above flux—because the moment is fully realized. Finally, then, the motion patterns convey not only the essential, tragic incompatibility between stillness and flux but also a hint of transcendence.

Image-patterns created by actions may shape other plays as well. Indeed, the whole question of motion in Shakespeare's verse invites further study. Years ago, F. C. Prescott pronounced that Portia's "the quality of mercy is not strain'd" was not poetry, because it presented an abstraction rather than the concretes that characterize true poetry.[15] Prescott would doubtless grant more pictorial respectability to Portia's following words, "It droppeth as the gentle rain from heaven / Upon the place beneath" (*Merchant of Venice*, 4.1.183–84). But in fact the whole passage has a poetic force, which is more kinetic than visual: the tightness of "strained" easing into the free release of "droppeth," heaven's benign gesture refusing even the constraint of a single line to spill over into the next. Even critics who would reject Prescott's dogmatism have not paid enough attention to the peculiarly kinaesthetic qualities of Shakespeare's word-painting. His descriptive passages typically depend more on verbs than on adjectives. Consider Perdita's "Daffodils, / That come before the swallow dares, and take / The winds of March with beauty" (*The Winter's Tale*, 4.4.118–20); or Romeo's warning, "Night's candles are burnt out, and jocund day / Stands tiptoe on the misty mountain tops" (*Romeo and Juliet*, 3.5.9–10); or even the Shakespeare of the sonnets.

> Full many a glorious morning have I seen
> Flatter the mountaintops with sovereign eye,
> Kissing with golden face the meadows green,
> Gilding pale streams with heavenly alchemy.
> (Sonnet 33)

It is *kissing* and *gilding*, not *golden*, that makes us feel the sun lighting up a landscape, just as outdaring the swallow and taking the March winds express the daffodils' brave yellow better than any color-adjective could. To return to our beginning: drama's essence is action, and Shakespeare—in his lyric verse as well as his plays—is preeminently a dramatic artist.

Notes

1. Foakes, "Suggestions for a New Approach to Shakespeare's Imagery," *Shakespeare Survey* 5 (1952): 81–92.

2. All Shakespeare references in this essay are to the *Complete Works of Shakespeare*, ed. David Bevington, 4th ed. (New York: HarperCollins, 1992).

3. See Jorgenson, "Vertical Patterns in *Richard II*," *Shakespeare Association Bulletin* 23 (1948): 119–34, and Suzman, "Imagery and Symbolism in *Richard II*," *Shakespeare Quarterly* 7 (1956): 255–70.

4. In *The Common Liar: An Essay on* Antony and Cleopatra (New Haven and London: Yale University Press, 1973), Janet Adelman discusses the play's images, including many that I cite below, in terms of measure and overflow (122–31).

5. The contrast between hard Roman efficiency and the lush prodigality of Egypt comes out in Antony's own speech patterns. Compare the leisured, expansive quality of his "Let Rome in Tiber melt" speech with the brusque economy of this interchange with the Roman messenger:

Messenger. News, my good lord, from Rome.
Antony. Grates me, the sum.

(1.1.18; I follow the Folio punctuation, a comma between Antony's terse phrases. Alexander omits the comma, but the phrases make better sense separated.)

6. "Now Antonius was made so subject to a womans will, that though he was a great deale the stronger by land, yet for Cleopatraes sake, he would needes have this battell tryed by sea," North's Plutarch (1579), cited in the New Arden edition, ed. M. R. Ridley (Cambridge, Mass., 1954), 274.

7. Compare in this same scene the Roman soldier: "Let th'Egyptians / And the Phoenicians go a-ducking; we / Have used to conquer standing on the earth / And fighting foot to foot" (64–67).

8. *The Common Liar*, 130.

9. On the double meaning of "becoming," cf. Adelman, *The Common Liar*, 144; "process—infinite variety—is her decorum."

10. "Shakespeare's *Antony and Cleopatra*," *Oxford Lectures on Poetry* (London: Macmillan, 1909), 283–84.

11. Direct reminders are the soothsayer's warning Antony that Caesar's daemon will defeat his in any contest (2.3.18–31) and Caesar's own prophecy the *pax romana*, "The time of universal peace is near" (4.6.5). Awareness comes more indirectly from the stress on Antony's age and Caesar's youth, and from the overplot movement in which Caesar eliminates a "world-sharer," first Pompey and then Lepidus, creating the expectation that Antony will be eliminated in his turn. The conflict between Antony and Caesar, "half to half the world opposed"

(3.13.9), is imaged by Enobarbus as two jaws inevitably grinding against each other (3.5.13–15), a picture which combines Roman stillness and directness in its slow but inexorable motion.

12. *Oxford Lectures*, 285–87.

13. *The Problem Plays of Shakespeare* (London: Routledge, 1963), 135.

14. *Antony and Cleopatra*, ed. G. L. Kittredge (Boston: Ginn, 1941); New Cambridge, ed. (Cambridge: Cambridge University Press, 1950); *Riverside Shakespeare* (Boston: Houghton Mifflin, 1974).

15. *The Poetic Mind* (New York: Macmillan, 1922), 44.

THOMAS M. GREENE

Pressures of Context in Antony and Cleopatra

The folio volume of Plutarch's *Lives of the Noble Grecians and Romans Compared*, translated at thirdhand from Amyot's French by Sir Thomas North, may well have been the heaviest book Shakespeare ever held in his hands, as well, arguably, as the most useful to his theater. Shakespeare's debts to Plutarch as well as his departures have been carefully studied, and not least in the case of *Antony and Cleopatra*. But there remains an important and doubtless insoluble question about the playwright's adherence to his source in that play, a question that repays attention even though it may always remain open. It has to do with the rudimentary philosophy of history and, so to speak, morality of history to be gleaned from Plutarch's biographies.

The one overwhelming, infinitely complex historical development represented in the *Lives* is the transition from the Roman republic to the Roman empire. If the lives of those Romans chronicled can be said to cluster around a single story, it is precisely that gradual alteration of an oligarchy slowly and painfully turning into an autocracy. Plutarch's assessment of this immense event is not simple. On the one hand, he saw it as irresistible. "It was predestined," he wrote in the *Life of Antony*, "that the government of all the world should fall into Octavius Caesars handes."[1] In the *Life of Brutus*, this belief in destiny acquires a religious inflection. Plutarch states that his protagonist failed through divine intervention to hear at Philippi of a naval victory that would have determined his tactics: "The state of Rome (in my opinion) being now brought to that passe, that it could no more abide to be governed by many Lordes, but required one only absolute Governor: God, to prevent Brutus that it should not come to his government, kept this victorie from his knowledge."[2] The bloody time of Roman troubles had reached such a nadir that only an emperor could restore peace. This, despite Plutarch's greater admiration of Brutus than of his enemies, who did not in any case leap to empower a single governor. But that belief in a divine destiny coexists in the *Lives* with a nostalgia for the republic and a censure of Mark Antony for subjugating Rome.

> Antonius desire was altogether wicked and tyrannical: who sought to keepe the people of Rome in bondage and subjection, but lately before rid of Caesars raigne and government. For the greatest and most famous exployte Antonius ever did in warres (to wit, the warre in the which he overthrew Cassius and Brutus) was begon to no other ende, but to deprive his contriemen of their libertie and freedom.[3]

Plutarch's fatalism tinged with regret confers a certain tragic aura upon his composite narrative of republican decline and imperial emergence, spread across at least nine lives.

Did Shakespeare share that fatalism and that regret? *Antony and Cleopatra* contains some indications that he did, although some of them are refracted through the cant of the play's politicians and have to be assessed independently. Sextus Pompey, even in a speech of transparently hollow rhetoric, does accurately allude to the bloody history that led up to the present historical moment, including his father's fall from power and defeat at Pharsalus, the assassination of his father's enemy Julius Caesar, the libertarian ideals of Caesar's assassins, and their defeat at the battle of Philippi by his present interlocutors.

> To you all three,
> The senators alone of this great world,
> Chief factors for the gods: I do not know
> Wherefore my father should revengers want,
> Having a son and friends, since Julius Caesar,
> Who at Philippi the good Brutus ghosted,
> There saw you labouring for him. What was't
> That mov'd pale Cassius to conspire? And what
> Made the all-honour'd, honest, Roman Brutus,

> With the arm'd rest, courtiers of beauteous freedom,
> To drench the Capitol, but that they would
> Have one man but a man?
> (2.6.8–19)[4]

In Pompey's mouth this speech is nothing but fustian and the triumvirs he addresses disdain to make any response to it. Still, its presence in the play matters. It invokes a vision of relative republican liberty, "beauteous freedom," whose demise the actions represented in the play are helping to ensure.

So a republican nostalgia is not lacking from *Antony and Cleopatra*. Even if formulated by an opportunist, it is there for the spectator/reader to ponder. But the play also seems to hint that the coming of the Augustan empire is right and necessary. As his future victory becomes increasingly obvious, Octavius frames it in the most favorable terms.

> The time of universal peace is near.
> Prove this a prosp'rous day, the three-nook'd world
> Shall bear the olive freely. (4.6.5–7)

"Freely," not quite, but the prophecy of universal peace is in fact more or less accurate, even as a self-advertisement coming from a frigid and faceless prig. Does Cleopatra recognize the hand of fate when she calls him "Fortune's knave, / A minister of her will" (5.2.3–4)? It would seem so. She means to depreciate his actions but is obliged to see him as an embodiment of fate.

Thus specific remarks in the play can be shown to reflect something of Plutarch's dualistic and tragic attitude toward the massive turn of history he chronicles. What changes in Shakespeare's version—and this will really be my main preoccupation—is his brilliant use of moral paradox to construct a mirror hall of dramatic ironies. Plutarch himself was not an ironist, even though his biographies contained plenty of opportunities for one. Shakespeare not only reimagined in varying degrees Plutarch's cast of characters; he not only lyricized the narrative with a soaring obbligato of supreme poetry; he also exploited Plutarch's dualism by generating out of it relentless dramatic ironies, ironies so pervasive, so lucid, so penetrating, that they control the play's crafting throughout. They pit against each other the values of a supposedly heroic, spartan, individualistic Roman past, undermined by civil war, against the values of a peaceful, comfortable, subjugated empire, resting on centralized power. Both versions of Rome are then also pitted in turn against Egypt as an anti-Rome: self-indulgent, capricious, childlike, passionate, and feminized. Two sets of values becoming three sets are played off against each other with an ironic intelligence too Olympian to hint at a preference. The play really calls for a Bakhtinian study of its radical dialogism, which is essentially un-Plutarchan. One might indeed argue that it represents Shakespeare's profoundest departure from the *Parallel Lives*.

* * *

Antony and Cleopatra is the most gorgeous of Shakespeare's tragedies, bathed as it is in clear Mediterranean light illuminating grandiose, sharp-edged figures of universal history. It is also the tragedy that contains the most joy, and not least at its ostensibly tragic end. But it is also the play of Shakespeare most sensitive to the *perspectivism* of human understanding. It begins in fact with that play with perspective which governs the action throughout. In the first scene, the action is bracketed by the comments of two Roman observers, Philo and Demetrius, who are patently there only as voices to express dismay at the perceived deterioration of Antony's virile stature. Having played their roles as commentators, they disappear for good behind the scenes. But their roles are not negligible; essentially we see the first scene through their disapproving eyes. We are not invited to share as such their opinion of the action, but we are made aware of an alternative perspective upon it. The bracketing is twofold. Their dialogue literally brackets the rest; they are alone on stage at the opening and again at the close. But they also stand as one pictures them to one side of the stage watching what happens, in such a way that we watch with them. They impose an angle of simplistic ethical judgment upon the scene that influences without determining the audience's angle, thus creating a double perspective that heightens and complicates the dramatic atmosphere. It is this second kind of bracketing that matters most and is in fact an essential characteristic of the play.

This play with perspective performed by minor characters is an important and constant element. It is notable that Antony and Cleopatra are never alone on stage with one another. They speak and act without exception in front of observers who tend to precede them on stage and to linger after their exits with choral commentary. Janet Adelman first noticed this.

> The most characteristic dramatic technique in *Antony and Cleopatra* is the discussion of one group of characters by another. In its purest form, it is strikingly simple: a group of minor characters who are alone on stage discuss an action that is about to take place among the protagonists; the protagonists then appear on stage, act, and disappear; and a group of minor characters, frequently the same as the initial group, are left to discuss the action. The scene is thus

> framed so that the major characters become in effect actors and the minor characters their interpretive audience. This pattern appears with astonishing consistency throughout the play.[5]

Adelman rightly saw in the play the important function of conspicuous spectatorship. Any given speech or act is denied the centrality it might have received because the audience is aware of an alternative, generally judgmental, viewpoint embodied on stage. Cleopatra is rarely on stage without Iras and Charmian, who are capable of teasing her (as at 1.5.67ff.) and of criticizing her tactics (as at 1.3.6ff.). On the Roman side, Antony, Octavius, and Pompey all have their followers who become their observers, often entering first and exiting last, predicting and judging retrospectively what their betters have just said and done. This means that all the action in the relevant scenes is framed, both temporally and visually. Without the framing figures, *Antony and Cleopatra* would be a different play. What would the lovers say to one another if they were alone?

Among those choral witnesses who observe and frame the protagonists, one has a privileged role. Enobarbus is a genial creation—large-spirited, lucid, shrewd, and gifted with a flair for sarcasm.[6] One of his funniest scenes is his splendid duet with Agrippa (3.2) on the shortcomings of Lepidus—a rare moment in the play of unclouded irony. Enobarbus is entirely Roman, but as a Roman he has a breadth of appreciation denied the shallower Philo and Demetrius. He admires Cleopatra and he enjoys Egypt. He is a bridging figure who is not drugged by love. He is also one of the few important characters in the play who consistently tell the truth. In many scenes, he is alone the framing presence. It is only when he discovers that his master's judgment is warped by Cleopatra's (in 3.7) that his loyalty is shaken, and when he concludes that his master can no longer recover the "self" he once respected, he chooses to abandon him. But in the end his understanding of Antony's character proves to be insufficiently complex, and his failure kills him. During the last minutes of his life, he ceases to be an observer but is himself observed by sentries who are created for that purpose and whose talk frames his death. He is the incidental victim of those divisions acted out in the main narrative of the play.

The framing of the action by observers within a given scene is doubled by another kind of framing, only slightly less noticeable but carrying at least as much dramatic weight. This becomes clear if one considers how the close of scene 1 ("I am full sorry / That he approves the common liar, who / Thus speaks of him at Rome" [1.1.59–61]) spills over to color ironically the opening of scene 2 with the charming and childlike gush of Charmian as she plays with the fun of hearing her fortune told: "Lord Alexas, sweet Alexas, most any thing Alexas, almost most absolute Alexas, where's the soothsayer that you prais'd so to th' Queen?" (2.1.1–3). This comes pouring out with a kind of innocence that is engaging but which might be said to be threatened invisibly by the ethical code of Philo and Demetrius. Iras, Charmian, and company embody a racy, irresponsible, feminine subculture centered on sex and unaware of politics. Their irresistible scene with the soothsayer is not allowed, so to speak, its autonomy, but is caught up, for the audience, in a dialectic the characters cannot imagine. The "Roman" male perspective will linger faintly through the rest of the second scene. Antony's first dismissal of the Roman messenger in scene 1, under the nervous taunts of Cleopatra, helps to define the attention he gives the messenger in the following scene. The close of *that* scene in turn ("Our pleasure . . . require[s] / Our quick remove from hence" [1.2.194–96]) sets up the opening of the following (Cleopatra: "Where is he? . . . See where he is, who's with him, what he does" [1.3.1–2]). The audience, which already knows who is with him and what he is doing, hears these lines as evidence of Cleopatra's ironic ignorance. This ironic bracketing is the absolute rule in *Antony and Cleopatra*, and it continues to the end.

A few of the most obvious instances can be cited. Sextus Pompey's remark to his subordinates at the close of 2.1:

> how the fear of us
> May cement their divisions, and bind up
> The petty difference, we yet not know.
> (2.1.47–49)

leads immediately to the tense meeting of the triumvirs in 2.2 in which their divisions are thinly and precariously cemented. When Antony, in the opening lines of 2.3, says to Octavia, "The world and my great office will sometimes / Divide me from your bosom," (2.3.1–2) we have just heard this exchange referring to Cleopatra a moment earlier:

> *Maecenas*: Now Antony
> Must leave her utterly.
> *Enobarbus*: Never; he will not.
> (2.2.233–34)

A few scenes later, the quasitriumphal entry of Ventidius after his victory in Syria at 3.1 follows immediately upon the drunken banquet on Pompey's ship. Cleopatra's second scene with the hapless reporter of Antony's marriage in 3.3 ends with a little hope for its failure ("All may be well enough" [3.3.47]), hope that then colors the opening of 3.4 where Antony, ominously, is venting to Octavia his anger against her brother. Antony's painful moral deterioration in 3.13, where he has Thidias whipped, is performed against the closing lines of 3.12 in which Octavius gives his envoy his instructions:

> *Caesar*: Observe how Antony becomes his flaw,
> And what thou think'st his very action speaks
> In every power that moves.
> *Thidias*: Caesar, I shall.
> (3.12.34–36)

This command to Thidias to observe is also of course an invitation to the audience, which can only deplore, along with Enobarbus, what Antony's action speaks at this point. By the opening of the fourth act, where Antony's decline earns him a kind of sardonic pity from his enemy, Caesar's final devastating exclamation "Poor Antony!" (4.1.16) at the close of 4.1 imposes a terrible pathos on his victim's pitiful query as the next scene opens: "He will not fight with me, Domitius?" (4.2.1). This ironic montage, this commentary by a given scene upon its successor, is sustained through the play; each scene frames its successor.

The spectator's impression of zigzagging through ethnic and moral opposites is intensified of course by the imperial immensity of the geographical space covered. That sense of imperial space is already present in Plutarch's book, where the lives of Pompey and Caesar and Antony, among others, invite the reader to follow dramas of power politics enacted against a vast geographical horizon. Shakespeare in his corresponding tragedy was clearly sensitive to the theatrical usefulness of that magnitude. All three scenes in Alexandria during Antony's absence (1.5, 2.5, 3.3) are colored in complicated ways by the surrounding action to the west, which they in turn color. No other play of his moves through such magnificent itineraries: not only the repeated alternations between Alexandria and Rome, but the pauses at Misenum with Pompey, in Syria with Ventidius (disclosing Parthia in the far distance), at Athens with Octavia, and of course at Actium. We hear an account of Antony's conduct after the battle of Modena. Fulvia dies at Sicyon. A single speech of Caesar's contains a sonorous role call of exotic place names.

> He hath assembled
> Bacchus, the king of Libya, Archelaus
> Of Cappadocia, Philadelphos, king
> Of Paphlagonia.
> (3.6.69–71)

And so on. This impression of imperial space is heightened by the frequent motif of the messenger, already introduced in the first scene, the anonymous figure who has crossed the necessary distances to bring some message or bulletin. Shakespeare understood from Plutarch the greater ease and amplitude of movement that an empire permits the historical agent, as he swung his theatrical locations across the known world to underscore the swings of atmosphere and ethos.

The dialogue between scenes loses none of its ironic bite however as the contested geographical space narrows after Actium. By 3.13 Octavius is in Egypt, and as the intervening space narrows, the dialogue quickens with a flurry of shorter scenes commenting rapidly on each other. The closing of the distance separating the two camps seems to accelerate the pace of the intense scenic interaction, heightening the pathos of Antony's decline. The distance collapses altogether only in the very last scene when, for the first time, Octavius and Cleopatra are brought face to face. But even there, within that scene, the ironic framing is brilliant.

> *Cleopatra*: He'll lead me, then, in triumph?
> *Dolabella*: Madam, he will, I know't.
> *Flourish. Enter Proculeius, Caesar, Gallus, Maecenas, and others of his Train.*
> *Flourish and shout within*: Make way there! Caesar!
> *Caesar*: Which is the Queen of Egypt?
> *Dolabella*: It is the Emperor, madam. [Cleopatra kneels]
> *Caesar*: Arise! You shall not kneel:
> I pray you rise, rise, Egypt.
> *Cleopatra*: Sir, the gods
> Will have it thus, My master and my lord
> I must obey.
> (5.2.109–17)

The particular tension of this meeting is determined by the little exchange before Octavius's entrance.

It might plausibly be said that the framing devices that organize *Antony and Cleopatra* are common or even unavoidable in all drama. But few plays if any use it systematically with the self-consciousness, the consistency, and the dramatic skill that Shakespeare does here. Another way to describe this effect would be to say that context, always an important dramatic element, is made to exercise an even heavier and more pervasive pressure here than is the case in other plays. If irony can be defined very broadly as the pressure of context, then *Antony and Cleopatra* needs to be read as an unbroken tissue of ironies. No other play by Shakespeare matches the kind of Bakhtinian interplay that he sustains in this one. Not only is everything framed, but everything serves as ironic frame for something else. The comments of Philo and Demetrius provide a lens for our perception of the lovers, but their gift for imaginative play ("Tonight we'll wander through the streets" [1.1.53]) provides a lens by which to judge their observers. The framing functions just as firmly in the final scenes as in the earlier ones, since so many of the ironies are retrospective. Cleopatra's outwitting of Octavius in the last act casts a corrosive shadow backward upon his frigid and humorless self-assurance. Everything in the play seems bracketed—not only each scene but each character, event, symbol, and even word. The relevant question would then be whether the play ever provides an unbracketed element. The evidence would suggest a negative answer.

It is essential to the bracketing effect that its oppositions not privilege any specific ethical or cultural perspective over another. The irony does not stem from an ethical code supported by the play which a given character can be perceived to transgress. The oppositions are left unresolved, not only between a republican past and an imperial future, not only between Rome and Egypt, but between war against love, victor against loser, truth against policy, restraint against passion, Caesar against Antony, and Antony against Cleopatra. We are always watching an action, hearing a speech, judging a character, with a contextual alternative in mind. The framing structure, within scenes and between scenes, produces a flurry of shifting perspectives, angles, lenses, and sidelights that prevent any single character or scene or code from attaining what might be called the purity of absolute authority.

* * *

The mind of Antony, the main character in the play, is itself a theater of ironic contexts. All of his words and actions could be said to be bracketed. Antony at the opening is a man of large stature who commands and deserves respect for his distinguished if checkered past. His passion for Cleopatra, however compromising in the eyes of the world, does not at the opening shrink his stature for the audience. His taste for pleasure reflects a love of imaginative life, and his love of the queen testifies to his appreciation of the rare and exotic. Shakespeare suppresses what Plutarch saw as his role in enslaving Rome. It is notable that neither in this play nor in *Julius Caesar* does Shakespeare introduce the action that Plutarch found most revolting in Antony's life, his bargain to exchange the life of his uncle for the life of his enemy Cicero. But as the play progresses, it stages a moral deterioration that subverts Antony's selfhood. *Selfhood* is perhaps a vague term, but in this case it is the right one; the problem of Antony's "self" is foregrounded in the dialogue. It is the theme of Philo's first speech, the first speech in the play, and it seldom disappears. Antony is a bridging figure, not truly a Caesar, but no longer governed by the republican ethos. He is not only divided between the values of Egypt and Rome, but between the values of two eras.

For Plutarch, a believer in the effectiveness of human agency, Mark Antony was a guilty man. In Shakespeare he is an anachronism trying spasmodically and ineffectually to escape from anachronism. His actions receive less than his full volition because it is forever divided, as the opening two scenes already make clear. The staginess of his vows in scene 1 ("Let Rome in Tiber melt . . . !" [1.1.33]) anticipates his revulsion in scene 2 ("Would I had never seen her!" [1.2.152]). Who is Antony? Philo implicitly poses the question in the first scene.

> Sir, sometimes when he is not Antony,
> He comes too short of that great property
> Which still should go with Antony.
> (1.1.57–59)

Antony in his own self-analysis compares his variability to the turnings of the wheel of Fortune.

> What our contempts doth often hurl from us,
> We wish it ours again. The present pleasure,
> By revolution low'ring, does become
> The opposite of itself.
> (1.2.123–26)

The collapse at Actium is only the most scandalous example of a radical indecision that may even be traceable in the botched suicide. The judgmental voices within Antony's own mind allow us to discern within his own character that interplay of contexts and perspectives we find in the play as a whole. Any given action of his is ironized by an internal reservation. To Cleopatra he is both a Gorgon and a Mars. "Antony / Will be himself," she says to him teasingly (1.1.42–43). But she touches on a sensitive matter. "I shall entreat him / To answer like himself" (2.2.3–4), says Enobarbus of Antony later to the nervous Lepidus before the taut meeting of the triumvirs. But Antony's own excuses to Caesar for his negligence later in the scene suggest that he is not always himself. "I . . . did want / Of what I was i' the morning" (2.2.76–77) he confesses, and a moment later: "Poisoned hours had bound me up from mine own knowledge" (2.2.90–91). The knowledge is not easily attained. "If I lose mine honour, / I lose myself" (3.4.22–23) he will tell Octavia with the deliberate duplicity he uses toward her.

The theme surfaces most visibly after Actium. His lieutenant Canidius says: "Had our general been what he knew himself, it had gone well" (3.10.25–26). The despondent Antony advises his attendants to flee to Caesar and adds "I have fled myself," (3.11.7), this "myself" functioning not only as intensifier but as direct object of the verb. "Let that be left" he goes on, "Which leaves itself" (3.11.19–20). In the context of the whole play, these self-accusations gather resonance. Who is leaving whom? The man who fled at Actium is not apparently the true man; he is a wraith, an after-effect, an unreality. Iras's comment is relevant: "He is unqualitied with very shame" (3.11.44). At one of his worst moments, after the whipping of Thidias, he tells Caesar's envoy to report back to his master that he, Antony, is angry: "For he seems / Proud and disdainful, harping on what I am / Not what he knew I was" (3.13.141–43). Here the ontological theme verges toward an embarrassing pathos, not untinged with ridicule. A minute earlier he had said, with a feeble bravado that is almost touching: "I am Antony yet!" (3.13.91).

As the problematic of selfhood accumulates contexts and perspectives, the ironies grow denser and each usage carries more complicated weight. Each speech and action is more markedly framed. When the dispatch of Thidias leads Antony to assume a pathetic bluster, Cleopatra tells him: "Since my lord / Is Antony again, I will be Cleopatra" (3.13.185–86). But ironically he has never been so unlike his ideal self, and it is at this point that Enobarbus decides to leave him. After the loss of a second naval battle in act 4, attributed by Antony to the treachery of Cleopatra, he invokes in his rage the example of Herculean suicide and speaks of subduing his "worthiest [i.e., most worthy] self" (4.12.47). But to have to claim worthiness is to risk its loss. Antony is actually worthier two scenes later when, his rage abated, he compares his insubstantiality to a cloud's: "Here I am Antony, / Yet cannot hold this visible shape" (4.14.13–14). He speaks as though his selfhood were utterly dissipated. The whole play seems to be questioning its ontology.

It would be reductive to understand the divisions in Antony's makeup as due simply to his infatuation with a woman, although this reduction has often been made. The infatuation is there, but it is contracted during a century of political and cultural change profound enough to confuse strong men. The long and bloody time of troubles required for the Roman republic to be transformed for better and for worse into an empire involved moral adjustments that were difficult to negotiate.[7] Heroism now counted for less than organization. During the prolonged period of transition as power kept changing hands, the stability of a leader in the midst of the political whirligig was severely tested. Shakespeare's Octavius passes this test, but the play focuses on the more interesting man who fails it.

> My very hairs do mutiny; for the white
> Reprove the brown for rashness, and they them
> For fear and doting.
> (3.11.12–14)

It is the diachronic tension in Antony's mind as well as the ethnic tension between two cultures and the personal tension between a wife and a seductress that produces the interaction of contexts leading him to defeat and death. Within the irresolute theater of his mind, each of his acts might reasonably be described as bracketed by counter-impulses, by the counter selves that gain and lose the upper hand, thus ensuring the moral vulnerability of any single action.

* * *

Words and symbols in *Antony and Cleopatra* are divided and undermined by irony. Who can be depended on to tell the truth? Antony lies. Octavius lies. Cleopatra kills her lover with a lie. Pompey lies. Lepidus lies. Thidias and Proculeius lie. Mardian lies. Octavia, whose every instinct is truthful, makes mistakes through her innocent misunderstanding of her position. Enobarbus alone, an inveterate ironist, succeeds in speaking truth, his prose sometimes set off (as in 1.2) against the verse of his interlocutors. Most of the lies in the play doubtless can be scored up to the "necessary" deceptions of intrigue, political and erotic. But sometimes even a statement that is factually correct falls short of exact correspondence to reality. Is it possible to tell the whole truth in the play without recourse to sarcasm?

Decretas, a follower of Antony, takes the sword of his semi-suicide to Octavius, hoping to gain credit by bringing his intended master a token of good news.

> He is dead, Caesar,
> Not by a public minister of justice,
> Not by a hired knife, but that self hand
> Which writ his honour in the acts it did
> Hath, with the courage which the heart did lend it,
> Splitted the heart. This is his sword,
> I robb'd his wound of it: behold it stain'd
> With his most noble blood.
> (5.1.19–26)

Is that true? Well, yes and no. Antony is indeed dead, although he had not yet died when Decretas snatched the sword up. Antony had often showed "courage," though not at Actium and not when he asked Eros to use the sword upon him. What exactly does Decretas mean by "a public minister of justice"? That sounds like a euphemism for a soldier, who is not always known to be careful about justice. What then about Antony's honor? He has undeniably gained esteem in the eyes of the world. But then one has to remember that Antony has defiled the word in his systematic manipulations of his wife with a line worth quoting a second time: "If I lose my honor, / I lose myself" (3.4.22–23). That remark is intended to deceive but is choked in turn with ironies beyond his awareness. But quite aside from this single debasement, the word *honor* at this historical period is seriously tarnished. It is a relic from an earlier world when it may have had true meaning. Its roots in social practice now are poisoned. It has been too often misapplied to continue to have validity. If anything, it reflects back on the speaker who is condemned to misuse it. Within this single word a diachronic struggle makes itself heard.

Decretas finishes by saying that the sword in his hand is "stain'd" with Antony's "noble blood." But it's the word *noble* that's really stained. This is a word, like *honor*, that looks back to the ideals of an earlier age and sounds anachronistic in this one. Octavius had used the word to address his new brother-in-law while warning him not to break his vow: "Most noble Antony!" (3.2.27). For Lepidus, desperate to keep the triumvirate intact, it was an all-purpose epithet: "Noble friends" (2.2.17) at the stiff reunion of the three; "'Tis noble spoken" (2.2.96) a few minutes later after Antony's quarter-apology; "Noble Antony" as the meeting breaks up (2.2.169). But for Antony in the first scene of the play, "The nobleness of life / Is to do thus" (embracing Cleopatra) (1.1.36–37). In Mardian's fictive account of Cleopatra's death, her dying words are: "Antony, most noble Antony!" (4.14.30). There comes through in these usages and others in the play a hollowness of referentiality. The word itself is divided ironically; it carries with it memories and legends of a less sophisticated era when something like nobility might have been conceivable, but its vulnerability to abuse in the present cleaves it in two. One has to measure the *proportion* of validity in any given usage, while realizing that its earlier grounding in practice has largely leaked away. Through the pressure of context, there is ironic conflict within the boundaries of a single word. Perhaps it is impossible to speak the truth where language has been so damaged.

Contextual pressure is also there to problematize the symbolic object that Decretas holds in his hand. The sword of course has been a loaded metaphor from the beginning, as when Antony says that "our Italy / Shines o'er with civil swords" (1.3.44–45), or when Cleopatra says "Upon your sword / Sit laurel victory" (1.3.99–100), or when Antony says of Octavius: "He at Philippi kept / His sword e'en like a dancer, while I strook / The lean and wrinkled Cassius" (3.11.35–37). Agrippa makes explicit a sexual resonance of the symbol which it will retain:

> Royal wench!
> She made great Caesar lay his sword to bed;
> He ploughed her, and she cropped.
> (2.2.226–28)

Antony complains to Cleopatra after Actium that his sword was "made weak by my affection [for her]" (3.11.67), meaning presumably by "sword" his virile martial determination. Earlier, Cleopatra had gleefully recalled her theft of the sword while cross-dressing her drunken lover.

> Ere the ninth hour, I drunk him to his bed;
> Then put my tires and mantles on him, whilst
> I wore his sword Philippan.
> (2.5.21–23)

This is a good example of a detail lifted from Plutarch that lights up with epiphanic brilliance in the English text. The sword as symbol veers back toward concreteness when Antony pathetically proposes a private duel with Octavius to settle the war, "sword against sword / Ourselves alone" (3.13.27–28). That invitation earns him the scathing judgment of his observer Enobarbus:

> Yes, like enough! High-battled Caesar will
> Unstate his happiness, and be staged to the show
> Against a sworder!
> (3.13.29–31)

It is the privilege of Enobarbus's irony throughout the play to cut through the structural ironies. To be "high-battled," which is to say master of a powerful army, doesn't require one apparently to wear an actual sword. The kind of swordplay Antony is proposing is a thing of the past. It is preposterously histrionic, so that to be a sworder for Enobarbus is to be a comic fake. That remark deepens the irony a few minutes later when Antony in the same scene boasts: "I and my sword will earn our chronicle: / There's hope in't yet" (3.13.175–76).

Thus the symbol that had been at first a clear-cut token of martial and sexual capacity becomes undermined as the play progresses. It also is bracketed. It is losing its sharpness when, in the closing lines of this same painful scene 3.13, Enobarbus decides to abandon his master.

> When valor preys on reason,
> It eats the sword it fights with: I will seek
> Some way to leave him.
> (3.13.198–200)

Here the sword as military judgment is set against the hollow bravado of valor, a word, like *honor* and *noble*, that is leaking relevance. The sword as symbol is divided between the positive connotation of military judgment and the negative accusation of bluster. Basically the heroism of the sword is vestigial, and it too is bracketed ironically by its context. The spectator hears that irony acutely when Antony, after the loss of the second naval battle, says to Mardian: "O, thy vile lady! / She has robb'd me of my sword" (4.14.22–23). Just how inadequate a sworder he has become will be apparent soon when, as the symbol veers back again to concreteness, he calls upon Eros to stab him, and then, after Eros's exemplary suicide, he bungles his own. His hopeful speech as he falls upon his sword suggests not only a military but a sexual incapacity:

> But I will be
> A bridegroom in my death, and run into't
> As to a lover's bed.
> (4.14.99–101)

As the sword as symbol loses its potency in the course of the play, it becomes more and more obviously an outmoded and bracketed metaphor, reflecting the perceived decline of its possessor. Decretas, the thief of the sword, discovers, crestfallen, that Octavius cares nothing for the fetish by which he had expected to gain credit. His speech and his gesture are futile.

One intriguing puzzle in *Antony and Cleopatra* is the function of that haunting scene (4.3) in which a group of nocturnal sentries hears mysterious music underground. One of them offers an interpretation of it that the audience is invited to accept:

> 'Tis the god Hercules, whom Antony lov'd,
> Now leaves him.
> (4.3.16–17)

There is no later reference back to this scene, and its presence in the play remains somewhat enigmatic. In Plutarch, the god who is understood to leave is Bacchus. But Plutarch also wrote that the Antonys were supposed to be descended from Hercules, whose visual representations Mark Antony was said to resemble. It is to this tradition that Antony refers in his last anger against Cleopatra.

> The shirt of Nessus is upon me, teach me,
> Alcides, thou mine ancestor, thy rage.
> (4.12.43–44)

One way to interpret the sentries scene would be to see it as one more desertion of the condemned leader, a last signal of his doom. According to this reading, the incident would simply register his pathos and loneliness by extending the desertion of his followers to his divine patron.

But oddly enough, this scene is pivotal in the final evolution of the hero. In the action that follows, he acquires a kind of heroic poise humanized by his and our knowledge of certain defeat. This already emerges in the little scene that immediately follows the sentries (4.4), that scene, perhaps the most *charming* in the play, however deeply overshadowed, in which Cleopatra is helping to arm her lover for the day's fighting. When we last saw him (in 4.2), he was reducing his followers to tears with a calculated and repellent sentimentality. Now he is hopeful, affectionate, and spirited.

> *Cleo*: Sooth law, I'll help: thus it must be.
> *Ant*: Well, well,
> We shall thrive now. . . .
> *Cleo*: Is not this buckled well?
> *Ant*: Rarely, rarely:
> He that unbuckles this, till we do please
> To daff't for our repose, shall hear a storm.
> (4.4.8–9, 11–13)

Cleopatra on her side is adorable, all the more winning since she knows their cause is lost. Her closing speech deepens retrospectively the ironic shadow bracketing their gaiety.

> He goes forth gallantly. That he and Caesar might
> Determine this great war in single fight!
> Then, Antony—but now—Well, on.
> (4.4.36–38)

The day will prove prosperous for their armies, allowing a tiny flicker of hope to precede the final defeat. The tragic joy of this successful day provides a glimpse of the lovers at their most endearing.

> *Cleo*: Lord of lords,
> O infinite virtue, com'st thou smiling from
> The world's great snare uncaught?
> *Ant*: Mine nightingale,
> We have beat them to their beds.
> (4.8.16–19)

Antony is smiling, as we have seldom seen him. The audience's knowledge of his approaching defeat is there to frame the scene ironically, as always. But what it now brackets is a kind of tender and reckless happiness that is new. Somehow the tragic perspectivism now works to intensify the bravery of the gaiety.

If one asks what is the cause of Antony's alteration, the single intervening event is the apparent desertion by Hercules. One is obliged to see that little scene as pivotal. It is notable that Shakespeare chose to reverse the sequence of events in Plutarch, who had placed the divine desertion after the minor victory. Perhaps what had appeared to the sentries as a loss to Antony needs to be perceived as a symbolic gain, as a purging of that self-indulgent bluster and manic bravado that had sapped his leadership. The Herculean Antony is the enraged soldier who wants to lodge Lichas on the moon, the man Enobarbus came to despise.

> Now he'll outstare the lightning: to be furious
> Is to be frighted out of fear, and in that mood
> The dove will peck the estridge.
> (3.13.194–96)

In his final scenes, Antony is no longer "frighted out of fear."

This change is important, although it is not so absolute that the man we know disappears. He will still give way to the outburst in 4.13 that leads to Cleopatra's deception and his own death. His closing speeches do not lack a familiar staginess. His selfhood is still a work in progress when he dies. But in the post-Herculean scenes he becomes a presence whose loss we can mourn. He offers a cheerful and valiant resistance to the structural ironies that have heretofore qualified his greatness. It is true that his moment of profoundest tragedy, when he compares himself to an insubstantial cloud (4.14.2ff.), is bracketed ironically by his mistaken belief that Cleopatra has betrayed him.

His dying minutes with Cleopatra are flawed by the terrible advice he gives her to trust both Caesar and Proculeius, advice she is too clever to take. It is also true that his last lines are tarnished by a discredited rhetoric.

> The miserable change now at my end
> Lament nor sorrow at; but please your thoughts
> In feeding them with those my former fortunes
> Wherein I liv'd, the greatest prince o' the world,
> The noblest; and do now not basely die,
> Not cowardly put off my helmet to
> My countryman—a Roman, by a Roman
> Valiantly vanquished.
> (4.15.51–58)

This dying speech is sardonically and unavoidably framed by all that has preceded it. Antony is cheering Cleopatra up and himself as well, but as a summary of a life and death, his speech contains too much gilding to be accurate. The whole play is there to provide a skeptical bracket. What has changed is that an audience is prepared now to understand Antony's need to oversimplify at the end. The ironies that have accumulated over four acts have not been dissipated. But as they infiltrate the anachronistic language, they inform without dispelling our sympathy for the flawed greathearted hero.

Cleopatra for her part makes a splendid death by turning it into a performance, implicitly accepting the framing of all action by turning her monument into a stage. Dolabella seems to acknowledge this.

> Caesar . . .
> thyself art coming
> To see perform'd the dreaded act which thou
> So sought'st to hinder.
> (5.2.329–32)

Cleopatra as a consummate actress is so accomplished that she has sometimes lost the respect of credulous readers. They should remember her lover's description: "She is cunning past man's thought" (1.2.145). To those who judge harshly her conduct with Thidias and Seleucus, one can only quote her reply to the enraged Antony: "Not know me yet?" (3.13.157). It is as though Cleopatra has concluded that her only course through the dizzying crosscurrents of her spacious world is to regard it as a theater. Her conduct throughout the play has been just as ironized, of course, as everyone else's, and not least in her funniest scenes during Antony's absence from Egypt. She is not exempt from overacting: "Pity me, Charmian, / But do not speak to me" (2.5.118–19). Sometimes her improvisations are fatally bungled, as at Actium and at her lover's death. But in her supreme hour, her staginess presents itself as the only viable solution to the deadly interplay of moral pressures. In act 1, when she felt called upon to improvise an adequate speech at Antony's departure, she found herself stuck (1.3.86–91). But at the close, she finds her marvelous lines. Her grief is acted out with magnificent hyperbole, and her death is transfigured by the lyricism of her suicidal aria. Cleopatra undeniably wins the play.

At the last curtain Octavius stands in charge on the stage, frustrated in his conquest. The audience has no way of gauging the sincerity of his tributes, but there is no reason to doubt his recognition of the ironies attending his victory: "High events as these / Strike those that make them" (5.2.360–61). The pathos the lovers have earned, he says, equals his own glory. This is only the last of the remarks in the play implying the futility of action (1.2.123–24, 2.1.5–8, 4.14.47–49, 5.1.27–29). Caesar, like the supposed losers, stands framed by the pressure of context, overshadowed by uncontrollable history and reaching a bitter insight in his failing splendor.

Notes

1. Geoffrey Bullough, ed., *Narrative and Dramatic Sources of Shakespeare*, 8 vols. (London: Routledge and Kegan Paul, 1964), 5:292.

2. Ibid., 5:127.

3. Ibid., 5:319.

4. Quotations from Shakespeare are taken from William Shakespeare, *The Riverside Shakespeare*, ed. G. Blakemore Evans et al. (Boston: Houghton Mifflin, 1974). Each quotation will be followed by a parenthetical indication of the act, scene, and lines.

5. Janet Adelman, *The Common Liar* (New Haven: Yale University Press, 1973), 31. I wish to acknowledge my general indebtedness to Adelman's book.

6. The statement sometimes made that Enobarbus is not to be found in Plutarch's *Life* is incorrect, although his role there is circumscribed: "But though he [Antonius] had an excellent tongue at will, and very gallant to entertain his soldiers and men of war that he could passingly well do it, as well or better than any captain in his time, yet, being ashamed for respects, he would not speak unto them at his removing, but willed Domitius Aenobarbus to do it." T. B. J. Spencer, ed. *Shakespeare's Plutarch* (Harmondsworth, Middlesex: Penguin, 1964), 228. Consider also: "Furthermore, he [Antonius] dealt very friendly and courteously with Domitius, and against Cleopatra's mind. For, he [Domitius] being sick of an ague when he went and took a little boat to go unto Caesar's camp, Antonius was very sorry for it, but yet he sent after him all his carriage, train, and men; and the same Domitius, as though he gave him to understand that he repented his open treason, he died immediately after," 252–53.

7. Jonathan Dollimore writes perceptively that "the contradiction which constitutes Antony's identity can be seen as a consequence of a wider conflict between the residual/dominant and the emergent power relations," *Radical Tragedy: Religion, Ideology and Power in the Drama of Shakespeare and His Contemporaries* (New York: Harvester Wheatsheaf, 1984), 213. Dollimore's insight is useful even if one is reluctant to see this conflict as the *only* cause of the contradiction. Regrettably, Dollimore tends elsewhere in his chapter on *Antony and Cleopatra* to neglect the historical specificity of Antony's historical moment, using the term "power structure" as a blanket term for any set of political hierarchies anywhere. This leads him to draw anachronistic parallels between Coriolanus's moment and Antony's, while passing over the precariousness of power in Rome during the first century B.C.E. Dollimore's insecure grasp of a particular historical crisis, with the particular effects of power on a particular individual, will give comfort to those who doubt the adequacy of any literary interpretation based on a preexisting political doctrine.

PATRICIA PARKER

Barbers, Infidels, and Renegades: Antony and Cleopatra

Our courteous Antony . . .
Being barber'd ten times o'er . . .

—*Antony and Cleopatra*

One of the most memorable of Shakespearean speeches describes Antony's first meeting with Cleopatra on the Cydnus, in Cilicia in Asia Minor or early modern Turkey. In a speech famous for its "Asiatic" excess as well as the more detached perspective of its speaker Enobarbus, Roman Antony is described as "barber'd ten times o'er":

The barge she sat in, like a burnished throne,
Burned on the water; the poop was beaten gold;
Purple the sails, and so perfumed that
The winds were love-sick with them.
. . . .
Upon her landing, Antony sent to her;
Invited her to supper. She replied
It should be better he became her guest,
Which she entreated. Our courteous Antony,
Whom ne'er the word of "No" woman heard speak,
Being barber'd ten times o'er, goes to the feast . . . (2.2.196–238)[1]

From *Center or Margin: Revisions of the English Renaissance in Honor of Leeds Barroll,* edited by Lena Cowen Orlin, pp. 54–87.

"Barber'd" here is an apparently minor or marginal detail in this famous speech, often forgotten in commentaries on this memorable passage. Its resonances, however, are central to the multiple implications of barbering it manages to suggest, across both Roman and early modern registers.

"Barber'd" here is an extraordinary compound term, compressing into a single word so much of what Egypt and the East are assumed to represent. As coiffed and groomed, it anticipates the reprise of this first meeting on the Cydnus in Cleopatra's elaborate preparations to meet her "curled Antony" (5.2.30) in death, lines whose "curled" summons one of the principal Roman indices of Eastern effeminacy and decadence. As evocation of Roman Antony's enchantment by a "barbarian" queen, it recalls the Battle of Actium that provided the historical climax of this first encounter, where (in Virgil's Augustan rendering) Antony's Egyptian forces include barbarian races and "barbaric" wealth. As a term suggestive of eunuchry and castration, it evokes the Barbary or *Barbaria* associated in the period with cutting and shaving of all kinds, including in contemporary narratives preoccupied with renegades and the "infidel" Turk.

Enobarbus's "barber'd" Antony is also part of the emphasis on beards as indices of masculinity, both within and beyond this play. The scene of the set speech itself begins with Enobarbus's pointed reference to the shaving of Antony's own "beard," in the exchange with Lepidus in Rome, before the meeting between Antony and Octavius Caesar, the figure who would rule as the Emperor Augustus after Antony's Actium defeat:

> I shall entreat him
> To answer like himself. If Caesar move him,
> Let Antony look over Caesar's head
> And speak as loud as Mars. By Jupiter,
> Were I the wearer of Antonio's beard,
> I would not shav't today!
> (2.2.4–8)

Here, the invocation of Mars and the traditionally bearded "Jupiter" identified with an older Roman *virilitas* is combined with the early modern "Antonio" by which Roman Antony in this play is alternately known, counterpart to the anachronistic identification of Virgil and Plutarch's Egyptian queen with a more contemporary "gypsy."

What I want to explore, in beginning from these marginal lines, is not only their centrality in relation to such outward signs but their importance in relation to both of this play's historical registers, ancient Roman and early modern at once.

* * *

> barbers who pluck out the hair of these effeminate creatures. . . .
>
> —Clement of Alexandria

> barberous barbers . . . alongst these shores of Barbaria
>
> —Dekker, *The Gull's Hornbook*

The Roman significance of barbering and of beards was familiar from texts well known to early modern writers. As classicist Maud W. Gleason observes, "hairiness in general" in these texts is one of the visual signs that "announce from afar, 'I am a man'"; and "chief of these signs is the beard."[2] Since the seductive attractiveness of the "boy" was "conventionally held to fade with the arrival of body hair and the beard," shaving, cutting, or depilating—multiple Roman forms of barbering—were associated with attempts to return to the smoothness of the catamite or Ganymede. Ovid in *The Art of Love* counsels men against depilatories as well as curling. The elder Seneca condemns curling, depilation, and shaving, contrasting such practices with the virility of Cato and an older Rome. Seneca the Younger condemns "those who pluck out, or thin out, their beards," declaring of such "effeminate" practices: "How incensed they become if the barber gets careless, as if he were trimming a real man!" *Glaber* ("hairless") was the term used to describe "young men, usually slaves, who were considered sexually attractive because of their smoothness, whether natural or artificially attained." Pliny writes that "dealers in slave-boys, in order to keep their merchandise as marketable as possible, used blood from the testicles of castrated lambs to delay the growth of the beard." Plautus features the depilated player and transvestite male dancer or *saltator*, the well-known Latin word for "leaper" or "dancer" echoed in the condemnation of "wanton" dancing in Stubbes's *Anatomy of Abuses* and other early modern texts, a possible resonance within the "Salt Cleopatra" of Shakespeare's play, as both female seductress and transvestite "boy."[3]

Roman texts associate effeminate barbering with the East in particular. Juvenal's Second Satire aligns the supposed pathic sexuality of the depilated *cinaedus* with the *gallus* or Eastern eunuch. Martial contrasts his own vaunted manliness to an easterner with curled hair and shaven legs. Part of the tradition surrounding Julius Caesar—which may give a homoerotic inflection to the emphasis on "cuts" in Shakespeare's *Julius Caesar*—was his depilation and overconcern for the grooming of his hair, together with the pathic role he is said to have taken (in the ambiguous transition between boy and man) in the East of Asia Minor, under Nicomedes a foreign king, transforming this famous Roman *vir* (in Suetonius's famous phrase) into "Queen of Bithynia." Antony himself—trained in the "Asiatic" style that was associated with eunuchs and the effeminacy of Alexandria and the East, contrasted with more virile "Attic" style and "hirsute philosophy"—was derided not only as a "*catamitus*" but as a male *sponsa* or "bride" to Curio in Cicero's *Philippics*, the satirical attack that famously led to the latter's death.[4]

In the Roman texts on barbering and beards best known to early modern writers, the "natural" and the "constructed" (as Gleason observes) dizzyingly interact, complicating the opposition of bearded and smooth not only by the practices of such Roman leaders, in a period in which most Romans were shaven (in contrast to the older bearded ideal), but by the way in which the beard functioned as a notoriously deceptive index. Juvenal's Second Satire—directed against effeminate or *mollis* men—opens with those "who ape the Curii" of ancient Rome but "live like Bacchanals," observing that "Men's faces are not to be trusted." Martial's epigrams are filled with examples of hidden or secret *cinaedi* or pathics, concealing their identity under the appearance of "an ascetic bearded philosopher."[5]

Both this Roman tradition and its contradictions were transmitted to early modern Europe and England by other texts that underscored the multiple inferences of barbering, cutting, and shaving. Athenaeus's *Deipnosophists* includes beards and the origins of shaving in a passage on the love of boys, which begins with hypocritical Stoics who have smooth-shaven "favourites" and ends with the connection between "shaven chins and posteriors." Dio Chrysostom (in a discourse directed to the inhabitants of Tarsus in Cilicia) traces a degeneration that begins with trimming or cutting the beard and ends with the production of "epicenes," a combination reflected in the "Barber" named "Cutbeard" in Jonson's *Epicoene*. Clement of Alexandria associates shaving with "unnatural acts," complaining of those who ("although they are men") go to barbers to get "their whole bodies made smooth" and of the "barbers who pluck the hair of these effeminate creatures," removing the "beard" that is "the badge of a man" and "shows him unmistakably to be a man," castrating or cutting the visible sign of manhood itself.[6]

Shakespeare's "Roman" play and the lines on the "barbering" of Antony reflect the influence of this Roman tradition, transmitted both by classical texts and by later writers such as Clement of Alexandria, frequently cited in English antitheatrical treatises. What needs to be added is the "infidel" inflection this classical and Roman representation of alleged Eastern practices was given in early modern texts, where barbering of various kinds was increasingly associated with Barbary and the Ottoman Turk, or the new Islamic rulers of both Egypt and the East. For the description of Antony as "barber'd" by

Cleopatra *not* to have such contemporary overtones would be difficult—given the growing interest in the Turk on the English stage and the publishing of accounts that associated "Barbarie" or the North African coast and the "barbarous Turk" with multiple forms of barbering. By the time of the play (1606–7), Egypt and Alexandria themselves had already been subsumed into the expanding Ottoman Empire for almost a century; and the shaving of Joseph in Egypt (part of the biblical narrative of Egyptian captivity) had its counterpart in illustrations that depicted the Pharaoh of the Exodus as a turbaned Islamic ruler.

As Nabil Matar, Jean Howard, Daniel Vitkus, and others have reminded us, dramatizations of the Turk and the Barbary coast had already become prominent on the English stage. The beardless eunuch associated with Egypt and the East in Roman writing was a staple of early modern accounts of the smooth or gelded eunuchs of Ottoman courts. What was claimed as the Turkish custom of castrating prisoners (as well as the circumcising of renegades, frequently conflated with castration) was detailed in popular dramatic and other accounts of the "great Turke." Mason's *The Turk* (1607–8) features not only Mulleasses, the Turk of its title, but a slave who was "a free borne Christians sonne in Cyprus, / When Famagusta by the Turke was sackt," who when captured was made "an Eunuch, / Disabled of those masculine functions, / Due from our sex." "Muly" (like Mulleasses)—the name identified with Barbary and the Turk through Peele's Muly Hamet and contemporary travel writings—was itself associated with gelding or cutting, conflated with the "mule" that was a sign both of the hybrid mingling of kinds and of barbering in this other sense. Middleton's *Spanish Gipsy* makes the connection explicit ("A beast? is't a mule? send him to Muly Crag-a-whee in Barbary," 4.1.22–23).

The anachronistic combination of Roman texts with early modern representations of the Turk was commonplace in English writing. George Sandys's account of his travels, for example, applies Juvenal's Sixth Satire on the gelded eunuch ("so smooth, / so beardless to kiss . . . What the surgeon chops will hurt nobody's trade but the barber's") to the eunuch of the "Turkes," describing the boys "the *Turkes* do buy" and "castrate, making all smooth," in a passage that cites the lines of Juvenal on the *desperatio barbae*, or "chins that of beards despaire."[7] The insertion of Roman excerpts into contemporary accounts of Barbary and the Turk had its counterpart in the anachronistic incorporation of Ottoman references into plays set in ancient Rome. Marlowe's *Dido Queen of Carthage*, though focused on Dido and Roman Aeneas, resonates with reminders of the Barbary coast. "Moores" suggest both ancient and contemporary resonances in Jonson's *Sejanus* (1603), while plays such as Dekker's *Satiromastix* included anachronistic reference to the Turk in a Roman plot.

The identification of "barbering" with "Barbary" (as well as a "barbarous" nicking or cutting) is a striking feature of other contemporary English texts. In the first part of Heywood's *Fair Maid of the West*—usually dated between 1597 and 1604, though it may be later—the apprentice (Clem) who accompanies Bess to "rich Barbary" (5.1.82) appears there as a cultural transvestite, dressed in the clothing of a "fantastic Moor."[8] Enamored of the wealth of the Barbary coast (one of the motives for turning Turk in the period), this English apprentice, who mishears "geld" for Barbary "gold," initially praises the "barbers" of Barbary ("for your country's sake, which is called Barbary, I will love all barbers and barberies the better," 5.1.125–29). But after he is invited to "taste the rasor" (5.2.103), in order to be raised to favored status as a "eunuch," he protests this "Moorish preferment" that would "rob a man of his best jewels," calling the "barber" of Fez not "Davy" but "shavy" and resisting what he calls the Barbary barbers' "cutting honor" (5.2.126–31).

Dekker's *The Gull's Hornbook* (1609), which features an entire chapter devoted to "Long Hair," similarly rails against "base barberous barbers" in a passage on the importance of "laweful heirs" (or hairs) and a text whose later references to an "abominable shaving" combine ingles or catamites with the theft that Dekker elsewhere identifies with renegade English pirates. Expressing disgust for the contemporary "polling and shaving world," Dekker compares it to the barbering to which Christian captives are subjected by the "Mahommedan cruelty" of the "Turks," who "no sooner lay hold on a Christian, but the first mark they set upon him, to make him know he's a slave, is to shave off all his hair close to the skull." The association of "base barberous barbers" with the barbarous "Turk" is retroactively underscored by the opening sentence of the next chapter, which professes to be "weary with sailing up and down alongst these shores of Barbaria."

The association of barbering, shaving, and cutting with Barbary and the Turk was at the same time part of accounts of English and European renegades and captives on the Barbary coast and in Alexandria itself. Captivity narratives reported the forcible shaving of Christian captives, as well as their "barbering" in other senses, including circumcising, gelding, and sodomizing or pathic subjection. Hakluyt includes a voyage to Tripolis in "Barbarie" in 1583, in "a ship called the Jesus," in which Englishmen were not only taken captive but "forceably and most violently shaven, head and beard" (5:301). The "plagues and punishments" visited on "Barberie" (5:308)—in the redemptive ending given to this narrative—recall the plagues on Egypt prior to the Exodus deliverance. But the texts devoted to this major international incident in the pages of Hakluyt include not only captives, but a willing renegade and a figure who has become a "eunuch" in Barbary, who is challenged by Elizabeth's "Ambassador with the Grand Signor" in Constantinople to be like "Joseph" in "Egypt," keeping his "true christian mind & English heart" free from Turkish "vices," notwithstanding that "your body be subject to Turkish thraldom."

Alexandria—already under Ottoman control from the early sixteenth century—provides the locus of other captivity narratives that conflated the biblical Egypt with the "captivitie of the Turkes," including another account in which Christian captives are forcibly barbered or shaved. In the version printed in the 1589 edition of Hakluyt, entitled "The woorthy enterprise of John Foxe an Englishman in delivering 266. Christians out of the captivitie of the Turkes at Alexandria, the 3. of Januarie 1577" (5:153–64), Englishmen in a ship bound from Portsmouth to Seville in 1563 are "beset round with eight gallies of the Turkes" (5:152). Despite "manfully" resisting (an emphasis on "manhood" the account repeatedly stresses), they are "caried prisoners unto an Haven nere Alexandria" (5:156). Hakluyt's narrative focuses on John Foxe, who was "somewhat skilfull in the craft of a Barbour" (5:156), and on a barbering in reverse, in which this English "Barbour" with "an olde rustie sword blade" (5:158), rescues his fellow captives from "thraldome and bondage" (5:163). When the story is re-told by Anthony Munday, in an account that includes a renegade reluctant to leave Alexandria, explicit attention is called to the barbering of the captives by the Turk. As sign of their subjection as "slaves" to this "barbarous . . . tyrant" (before escape from "so barbarous a thraldome"), the "first villany and indignitie that was done to them" was "the shauing off of all of the hayre both of heade and beard."[9]

Barbering in the sense of cutting or shaving (already associated with Barbary pirates or being shaven by thieves) came simultaneously with multiple sexual overtones in the period, combined with Barbary, "infidels," and Turks. "Barbarie pidgeon" was a well-worn synonym for harlot in early modern English, as was turning "Turk," contemporary slang not only for the cutting of eunuchry or circumcision but for the sexual "turning" evoked in Antony's description of Cleopatra as "a triple-turn'd whore," a turning that suggests both turning Turk and turning whore.[10] The association of harlots with barbering derived from the loss of hair from syphilis—routinely described as a "foreign" disease. Robert Greene's *Disputation* (1592) features a "French Barbar," whose spelling combines barbering by a foreigner with a sexualized Barbary ("hee was strangely washt alate by a French Barbar, and had all the haire of his face miraculously shaued off"). Weever's *Faunus* (1600), translating Persius's Roman satires, pictures the removal of "the beard" from "Philosophers" by "Some shamelesse whore," while Rowlands's *Knaue of Harts* (1612) has jacks complain that because they "haue no beards," they are assumed to be panders "whose naked Chinnes are shauen with the Poxe." Joseph Swetnam, in the *Araignment of Lewd, idle, froward, and unconstant women* (1615), compares a lascivious woman to "a Barbers chaire, that so soone as one knaue is out another is in." "Barbers" in the sexual sense thus caused what the "Barber" was supposed to cure. Florio (1598), defining *Barbiera* as both "sheebarber" and "common harlot," cites under "*Andar in barberia*, to go and be cured or laide of the pocks," one of the contemporary functions of the barber surgeon. A bawd in Marston's *Dutch Courtesan* is described as being the "supportress of barber-surgeons" (1.2). Antony Nixon's *Black Yeare* (1606) warns those "conversant with *Venus*" that "the very haires shal be banished from their heads, and poore Barbers be made beggers for want of work." The name "Shavem" is given to a harlot in Massinger's *City Madam* (1632), while Davies of Hereford exploits the commonplace conflation of "hairs" and "heirs" (or "heires apparant") in warning of the "dry-shauing" to be given by a "Kate."

The barber's pole and barber's balls (evoked in Jonson's "half-witted Barbarism! which no Barber's art, or his balls, will ever expunge or take out") were repeatedly associated with the phallic member and the "balls" that could be barbered or gelded. But barbering (and barbaring)—like Barbary itself—was also inseparable from overtones of pathic subjection, as well as eunuchry or gelding: in English texts where "sodomy" was described as "barbarously diverting Nature," by "metamorphosing humane shape into bestiall forme," in the account (in 1594) of a youth of "rare beauty" captured by pirates and "barbarously handled," or in narratives of enslavement by the Turk that included the threat of sodomizing among "barbarous" practices, like the account in Hakluyt of English captives in "Barbarie" which moves from their forcible shaving to the Islamic ruler who desired them. The sodomy already associated with piracy was also ascribed to renegades who "turned Turk" in Barbary, such as the notorious English pirate Ward. His "Sodomie" is decried in contemporary texts, including Daborne's *A Christian Turn'd Turk* (1612), where the cutting or circumcising that is part of his converting or turning Turk in Tunis on the Barbary coast is represented as his being pathically "handled" by "Mahomet" himself.[11]

* * *

> Thou art a Roman, be not barbarous . . .
>
> —*Titus Andronicus*

Both the Roman and "infidel" associations of barbering are reflected in the "smooth-fac'd catamites" and smooth or beardless chins of early modern writing. In Rabelais, the Asiatic "Bacchus, the god of bibbers, tipplers, and drunkards," is described as "most commonly painted beardless and clad in a woman's habit, as a person altogether effeminate, or like a libbed eunuch." The beardless "Ganymede" and the association of beardlessness with effeminacy are already familiar parts of the Shakespeare corpus: from Francis Flute's "Let me not play a woman, I have a beard coming" and the "green corn" that "hath rotted ere his youth attain'd a beard" (2.1.95) in *A Midsummer Night's Dream* to the "beardless vain comparative" (3.2.67) and shaven "chin" of the messenger ridiculed by Hotspur for his "holiday and lady terms" in *Henry IV, Part 1* (1.3.33–46); from the "smooth-faced gentleman, tickling commodity" (2.1.573) and "beardless boy" called a "cockred-silken wanton" in *King John* (5.1.69) to "the beards of Hercules and frowning Mars" in *The Merchant of Venice* (3.2.85). *As You Like It* and *Much Ado* depend on the external "note" or sign of the beard as the ostensible marker of difference between men and boys, as between men and women. *Bearding* in the sense of braving or challenging appears as a comparative index of virility in *Henry VI, Part 1* (4.1.12: "No man so potent breathes upon the ground, / But I will beard him") and *Coriolanus* ("If e'er again I meet him beard to beard, / He's mine, or I am his," 1.10.11–12). In the famous anachronism of *Henry V*—which assumes an Ottoman conquest that had not yet occurred—Henry's hope for a son who will "go to Constantinople and take the Turk by the beard" (5.2.222) applies this familiar topos to the contest with the Turk, famously bearded as well as associated with barbering renegades, captives, and boys.

The association of the Turk with eunuchry and other forms of barbering likewise appears repeatedly in Shakespeare. In *All's Well That Ends Well* (2.3.94)—which includes a "barber's chair that fits all buttocks" (2.2.17)—youths of "little beard" are said to be fit to send "to the Turk to make eunuchs of" (2.3.87–88). In *Twelfth Night*, Viola's plan to become a "eunuch" in Illyria (1.2.56–63) suggests not just the castrato evoked by the name of "Caesario" (from *caesus*, "cut") but the eunuchry identified with the Turk, whose dominions included Illyria, an "infidel" reference underscored when Malvolio is called a "renegado," after the famous "C-U-T" of the letter scene and his fantastic change of clothes.[12] Even the reference in the early texts of *Hamlet* to something in need of cutting ("It shall to th' Barbars [Q2 barbers] with your beard") may be part of the multiple topical allusions in the play to contemporary as well as ancient empires, to turning Turk, and to the Diet of Worms, which was concerned not only with the Lutheran schism but with the Ottoman threat.[13]

In addition to the associations of the beard with the manliness of the full-grown male, and of eunuchry and cutting with the Turk, the Shakespeare corpus directly conflates barbering with the barbarous, both before and after Enobarbus's description of the barbering of Antony. "Barbary" in the Folio text of *The Two Noble Kinsmen* appears as "Barbery" in the Quarto, in the

Morris dance scene which calls attention to the "coast of Barbary" (3.5.60), to cutting (3.5.61), and to the Morisko or "Moor" (3.5.118). In *Titus Andronicus* (1593–4), the "barbarous Moor" appears as a "barberous" Moor in the Quarto version, which similarly renders Lucius's "O barbarous" as "O barberous," in response to the Moor's narrative of Lavinia's barbaric cutting or trimming. Although the play is set in Rome, the "barbarous" (or "barberous") Moor responsible for so much of its barbering suggests a more contemporary Mediterranean geography, the Barbary of the so-called "infidel" as well as "coal-black" Moor, a more contemporary frame of reference suggested by the Moor's sending of his racially mixed son to "*Muliteus* my Countriman," emended by Steevens to the familiar Islamic "Muly."[14]

* * *

> On th'other part with all *Barbaria* force of diuerse armes
> Anthonius drags his traine of nacions thick. . . .
>
> —*Aeneid*, trans. Thomas Phaer (1573)

> Upon a tawny front . . .
>
> —*Antony and Cleopatra*

An "infidel" overlay on the Roman plot of *Antony and Cleopatra* would not be unexpected in relation to a pair whose well-known Virgilian counterparts, the potential renegade Aeneas and Dido the other African Queen, were already part of an anachronistic early modern overlay with Barbary and the Turk. Jerry Brotton, glossing "This Tunis, sir, was Carthage" in relation to the Mediterranean geographies of *The Tempest*, notes the conflation of ancient Roman imperial struggles with more contemporary references in "Thomas Phaer's highly influential translation of the *Aeneid*" (1573), where Iarbas, Dido's African suitor, is compared to "the Turkes."[15] In Roman writing, Cleopatra is repeatedly represented as "barbarous." In Virgil's Battle of Actium description, the Egyptian queen's "barbaric wealth" (*ope barbarica*), is the counterpart of the earlier description of the "gold on which Dido's Carthage is founded" (*Aeneid* 1.357–60).[16] The "barbaric" wealth of both African queens was updated in the "gold of Barbary" familiar from Peele's *Battle of Alcazar* and the enticement of the barbered renegade of Heywood's *Fair Maid*.

Phaer's influential rendering of Virgil's imperial epic translates it into unmistakable early modern accents, both in its description of Aeneas in Carthage and in its version of the confrontation at Actium.[17] Editors and critics of *Antony and Cleopatra* cite the parallel between Antony's subjection to

Cleopatra and Virgil's Aeneas dressed in the clothing of Dido in Carthage. Phaer's culturally translated *Aeneid* pictures Aeneas in Carthage in terms that unmistakably evoke the Tunis that replaced it: "shining read in roabe of *Moorishe* purple, mantle wise, / Hae stood, and from his shoulders down it hing *Morisco* gise." Here, Aeneas captivated by Dido and become what he soon after calls Dido herself—"a Moore among the Moores" (4.377)—is expressly described in terms that align him with the Moriscos and renegades of the early modern Barbary coast.

In Virgil's description of the Battle of Actium, which provides one of Shakespeare's principal sources, Antony and his "Egyptian wife" are ranged with the "powers of the East." But *Orientis* in Virgil's famous description of Cleopatra's "barbaric wealth" had already—by the time of Shakespeare's play—long been part of the title by which European monarchs addressed the Turkish sultan, as Emperor of the East. In Phaer's version of the clash of West and East at Actium, Virgil's *ops barbarica* and the "nacions" of Africa and the East ranged on the side of Antony and Cleopatra his "*Gyptian* wife," are compounded within what he calls "all *Barbaria*": "On th'other part with all *Barbaria* force of diuerse armes / Anthonius drags his traine of nacions thick." When Phaer's translation renders their ignominious retreat, the territories associated with Antony and this "*Gyptian*" Cleopatra sound in both historical registers at once ("All *AEgypt* than, all *Inde* downe couched lowe, / All nations wilde of South *Arabia* . . . / All *Asia* scattring fled, all *Sabey* kingdoms turnd their backs").

The Battle of Actium itself had already been transplanted to this new early modern context, in the confrontation between the Ottoman power and the new "Roman" Emperor Charles V and his European successors. The Battle of Lepanto (in 1571)—led by Charles's bastard son Don Juan of Austria—was celebrated as another Actium, though its victory over the new forces of the "barbarous" East was shortlived.[18] Even more strikingly, in 1538, the forces of this new Roman emperor engaged the Turkish fleets at Prevesa or the site of Actium itself, in a celebrated battle in which history was reversed, yielding as victor not the "Roman" West (which was hopelessly divided) but the new sea power of the Ottoman Turk, which as a result of this victory at this new Actium became virtual master of the seas, and made the Barbary ports and Alexandria itself attractive magnets for renegades who flocked to North Africa from all over Europe. This new Battle of Actium was described at length in Knolles's *Generall Historie of the Turke* (1603), already acknowledged as an influential source for *Othello* in the following year.

Well before *Antony and Cleopatra*, literary and other accounts had already conflated the confrontation between Octavius and Antony with engagements on two fronts—the New World and the territories of Asia,

Africa, and the Turk. The "barbarian hordes" of the East in Virgil's Actium description found their early modern counterparts in the Saracen army of Tasso's *Jerusalem Delivered*, whose English translation by Fairfax in 1600 may be echoed in Enobarbus's speech on Antony and Cleopatra's first meeting. Cleopatra, the Egyptian enchantress of Roman descriptions, had already been given an "infidel" inflection in the well-known epic-romances of Ariosto, Tasso, and Spenser, whose Acrasia evokes in her very name the mingling or mixture condemned as part of the adulterous Roman-Egyptian union of this famous pair. In Tasso, the infidel enchantress Armida—whose role is to impede the Christian crusade to regain Jerusalem by captivating its forces, as Antony was captivated—is described (like Cleopatra) as a "barbarian queen" ("la barbara reina").

Enobarbus's speech on Cleopatra and the "barber'd" Antony summons reminders of the more contemporary overlay the *Aeneid* had already been given. Editors of the play have remarked that its "burned" and "burnished" ("The barge she sat in, like a burnished throne, / Burned on the water") recall not only the flames of Virgil's Actium but also Tasso's palace of Armida, whose gates are inscribed with the Actium story of Antony and Cleopatra's "barbaric" forces, imitated by Spenser and others in the 1590s even before its English translation by Fairfax in 1600.[19] The passage in Fairfax (after evoking Hercules effeminated by Omphale) describes the Battle of Actium carved into the door of the palace of Armida, the infidel enchantress whose impeding of an earlier Christian crusade to regain Jerusalem reverberated with reminders of the crusading ambitions of the new "Roman" Emperor Charles V and other European rulers.

Cleopatra was thus already assimilated to the "infidel" East, as well as identified with Alexandria, controlled by the Turkish Sultan together with its neighboring Barbary coast. *Antony and Cleopatra* goes out of its way to recall this identification of the "gypsy" Cleopatra with the "spells" of such enchantresses—in Antony's "I must from this enchanting Queen break off" (1.2.132) and allusions to her as a "witch" as well as a "Fairy" Queen (4.8.12–18), whose "spell" and "charm" (4.12.2–13) hold Antony captive in Egypt. The triumph of "will" over "reason" that Enobarbus blames for Antony's Actium retreat (3.13.4–5) is an inversion familiar from contemporary accounts of captivating "infidel" enchantresses, both before 1606–7 and in "Turk" plays that retroactively situate Shakespeare's Cleopatra in relation to the problem of renegades and turning Turk. In Massinger's *Renegado*, the potential infidel enchantress Donusa, niece to the Ottoman Emperor or Great Turk himself, recalls the Cleopatra of the Shakespeare play in which Antony dies a renegado, in a play that rewrites both its plot and that of Daborne's *A Christian Turned Turk* (1612), by its conversions or re-turnings in the opposite direction. The "triple-turn'd whore" of Antony's description is assimilated to the sense of turning as both sexual and religious in the period, just as the designation of Shakespeare's Cleopatra as a "gypsy" aligns her with these early modern counterparts—an association that Jonson makes explicit in *The Gypsies Metamorphosed*, where "Queen *Cleopatra*, / The Gypsies grand-matra" is remembered in the "Turk gypsy" of its compound description.[20]

Enobarbus's description of Antony as "barber'd" by Cleopatra thus invokes the keyword not only of Virgilian and Roman writing but also of accounts of English and European renegades in Barbary and the "witchcraft" and "spells" of "infidel" enchantresses. Even the most familiar speeches and scenes of the play sound in these double registers. The play's own opening lines, which are put into the mouth of "Philo" (an invented character whose name, like that of Eros, suggests the different loves with which Antony and Cleopatra are identified), describe the "dotage" of Antony in terms that not only cast him as the most famous renegade of Roman history but underscore his own turning, toward a more contemporary gypsy:

> *Philo*. Nay, but this dotage of our general's
> O'erflows the measure. Those his goodly eyes,
> That o'er the files and musters of the war
> Have glow'd like plated Mars, now bend, now turn
> The office and devotion of their view
> Upon a tawny front; his captain's heart,
> Which in the scuffles of great fights hath burst
> The buckles on his breast, reneges all temper,
> And is become the bellows and the fan
> To cool a gipsy's lust. . . .
> (1.1.1–10)

"Bend" and "turn" sound in these opening lines the familiar terms in the period for turning renegade or Turk, here associated with a "bending" and "turning" upon a "tawny front." "Tawny front" itself combines in a single phrase both the territorial and the personal—the "tawny" forehead of the "gypsy" Cleopatra whom Shakespeare makes "tawny" and "black" rather than Greek and (through the double meaning of "front" as "forehead" and military "front") the Eastern or Egyptian territory to which Antony has "turned." "Reneages" in the Folio text of these opening lines is usually glossed in the sense of "renounces" or "denies." But from the earliest editions (compounding the *renego* appropriate to a "Roman" play), it has also been identified with Old French *reneyes* and Spanish *renegar*, the root of "renegado" or renegade, familiar in its shifting orthography in the period from descriptions like Nicholas de Nicholay's of Algiers on the Barbary coast, as composed "for the most part of Christians reneid."[21]

Perhaps because of Egypt's identification with the "Orient" or East and because Antony and Cleopatra had already been aligned with the "infidel" Turk and the Virgilian counterparts of Aeneas and Dido in Tunis, the history of editorial commentary on the play has itself been inflected in this direction. Hanmer's reading of "reneages" as a variant of Spanish *renegado* identifies the figure the Folio renders as "Anthonio" with the Italian, English, and other European renegades who were flocking to Alexandria, Algiers, and other Barbary ports. In the eighteenth century, the Folio's puzzling "Arme-gaunt Steede" was read as a textual corruption for "Termagant," the alleged Turk or Saracen deity. Even "ribaudred nag" was read as "renegade" by at least one former editor, while the "Terrene" of Antony's "Terrene Moone" has been glossed as a reminder of the Mediterranean or "Terrene Sea" of Marlowe's *Tamburlaine, Part 2*, from the lines in which Tamburlaine speaks of Christian captives and "the cruel pirates of Argiers."[22] Even the reference to three kings in *Antony and Cleopatra*—usually assumed to be one of the adumbrations in the play of the Christian revelation to come under the *pax Romana* of Augustus—may recall the Battle of Alcazar on that same Barbary coast, familiarly known as the battle of Three Kings.[23]

In the context of this framework, the opening emphasis on turning to a "tawny front" and the anachronistic renaming of this Roman-Egyptian pair as "Anthonio" and his "Gypsy," even the set speech that includes Enobarbus's description of Antony as "barber'd ten times o'er" has been thought to have contemporary overtones. In her study of Shakespearean pirates, Lois Potter observes that the "pursed" of Enobarbus's lines on Cleopatra (who, "when she first met Mark Antony, pursed up his heart upon the River of Cydnus," 2.2.186–87) casts the gypsy queen herself as a pirate, in a play whose maritime marauders inevitably recall their early modern equivalents.[24] "Anthonio" as the name given to Shakespeare's Roman Antony allies him not only with the merchant of *The Merchant of Venice* but with the Antonio who is called a "salt-water thief" in *Twelfth Night*.

In Phaer's culturally translated *Aeneid*, Aeneas in the "Moorishe purple" of Dido Queen of Carthage is not only effeminized but dressed as a contemporary "Morisko," as we have seen.[25] In *Antony and Cleopatra*, another change of clothing is described by another North African queen:

> I drunk him to his bed;
> Then put my tires and mantles on him, whilst
> I wore his sword Philippan . . .
> (2.5.21–23)

This famous cross-dressing scene in *Antony and Cleopatra* is usually treated in relation to the play's inversions of gender or the exchange of male and female sexual roles. But it is also a dramatic scene of cultural transvestism, in which "tires" simultaneously evokes both "attire" and the Turkish and Eastern "tires" familiar in early modern writing. "Tires" in the sense of headdresses appear not only in Dekker's *Honest Whore, Part 2* ("The soldier has his morion, women ha' tires, / Beasts have their head-pieces, and men ha' theirs") but earlier in the Shakespeare canon itself, in the lines of *Merry Wives* that contrast exotic foreign tires (including "any tire of Venetian admittance," 3.3) with plainer English head coverings. Minsheu's *Guide unto the Tongues* (1617) observes that "The word *Attire* in English commeth from the Latine word *Tiara*, which is an ornament of the heads of the Persian Kings, Priests, and Women," a headdress which his Spanish *Dictionarie* describes as "a round rolle of linnen which Princes, Priests, &c. did weare in Persia, such as the Turkes weare at this day." Florio (1598) has for "Tiara, a turbant, or round wreath of linen for the head such as the Turks vse to weare." Cotgrave (1611) defines "Tiare" as "A round and wreathed Ornament for the head (somewhat resembling the Turkish Turbant) worne, in old time, by the Princes, Priests, and women of Persia." "Tire" in this early modern sense appears both long before and after the date of *Antony and Cleopatra*. Hall's *Chronicle* (1548) has "ladyes" with "marueylous ryche & straunge tiers on their heades." The Geneva Bible (1560) describes "round tyres" or "tyres of the head" as part of the dress of Babylonian harlots. The Great Bible (1539) portrays Jezebel (another foreign queen) as having "starched her face, and tired her head." Joseph Hall's *Paradoxes* (1653) asks "What Towers doe the Turkish Tires weare upon their womens heads?"[26]

The sense of Antony as barbared as well as "barber'd" or emasculated by Cleopatra is thus strengthened by the dressing of Antony in Cleopatra's "tires and mantles" (2.5.22), making this scene of cross dressing the counterpart not only of the classical emblem of Hercules' effeminization by the Amazon Omphale but also of the dressing of Aeneas as a "Morisko" in Phaer's description of the cultural transvestite at the court of another African queen. In a play whose Egypt summons simultaneously the ancient Egypt of the Ptolemies and Plutarch's *Life of Antony*, the biblical locus of captivity recalled in the description of Cleopatra as the "serpent of old Nile" (1.5.552), and the contemporary Alexandria familiar from accounts of renegades and captives, even the territories named in Antony's notorious "donations" of territory to his gypsy queen contribute to the layering of ancient and early modern within the play. The description by Octavius Caesar in Act 3—of Cleopatra and Antony "publicly enthroned" in "chairs of gold"—recounts Antony's giving to Cleopatra (in the passage from Plutarch) "the stablishment of Egypt," and "absolute" authority over "lower Syria, Cyprus, Lydia" (3.6.4–11), territories associated with the "barbarous" East in the Roman time of the plot and with the dominions of the Turk at the time of the play itself. The play's still-unexplained neologisms "candy" and "discandy" (3.3.162–67; 4.12.20) may also summon the "Candy" or Crete familiar from contemporary accounts of the "infidel" East, as well as the melting or excess associated with Cleopatra's Egypt.

The play in which Antony or "Anthonio" is both "barber'd" on the Cydnus and turned infidel in his clothing is at the same time part of a contemporary context in which a so-called "Asiatic" rhetoric (familiar from Roman writing and the description of Antony's own training in Plutarch) had similarly been given an early modern inflection. Charles Sedley's *Antony and Cleopatra* (1677) would later present Antony as "a mere soft Purple Asian Prince," a description that combines the "purple" of assumed Asiatic decadence with the "purple" passages of "Asiatic" rhetoric condemned by Quintilian and others. What the most recent Arden editor of *Antony and Cleopatra* calls Shakespeare's Antony's "Asiatic" style, is termed a "rodomontade" by one eighteenth-century editor, a term that identifies the "Asiatic" rhetoric of speeches such as Antony's "Let Rome in Tyber melt" with the Saracen opposed to the representative of Rome in Ariosto's rewriting of the *Aeneid*. In the period of the play itself, excessive rhetoric or speaking "large" was identified with the Turk. Dekker's *Satiromastix* (1.2.379), for example, has Tucca say to Horace (or Jonson): "thy title's longer a reading than the style a the Big Turkes."[27]

The barbering or unmanning associated with Barbary—in the conflation of "Muly" as the familiar name of Islamic rulers with the gelded "mule" (reflected in Middleton's "mule" and "Muly Crag-a-whee in Barbary")—may itself be iterated in *Antony and Cleopatra*, in a passage that simultaneously describes Antony's forces at Actium as "unmann'd." "Muly"—the name shared by Peele's "Muly Hamet" (the "barbarous Moore" of Peele's *Battle of Alcazar*), as well as the Mulleasses of Mason's *The Turk* and the Mullisheg of Heywood's *Fair Maid*—may already be evoked in *Titus Andronicus* when Aaron (its "barberous" or "barbarous Moor") sends his racially mixed son to "*Muliteus* my Countriman," the name emended by Steevens to the Islamic "Muly."[28] In the years before *Antony and Cleopatra*, the association of mules with Turks is evoked in the allusion in *All's Well* (1602–3) to "Bajazeth's mule" (4.1.42), in a scene where Parolles contemplates the shaving of his own "beard" (4.1.49) and the play where "boys" of "little beard" are thought fit to be sent to the "Turk" to "make eunuchs of" (1.3.62, 88). *All's Well* itself not only invokes a "barber's chair" (2.2.17) but famously goes out of its way to make reference to the shrine in northwestern Spain identified with St.

James, the Sant'Iago whose association with driving the Moors out of Spain provided the name for the nemesis of the Moor in *Othello*.

"Mules" in *Antony and Cleopatra* are explicitly evoked in the scene in which Enobarbus warns Antony that his ships are not "well-manned":

> *Enobarbus*. Your ships are not well mann'd,
> Your mariners are [muleteers], reapers, people
> Ingross'd by swift impress. . . .
> (3.7.34–36)

Enobarbus's warning here to Egyptianized Antony, of the weakness of his forces, is drawn from the passage of Plutarch's *Life of Antony* which stresses the relation of Antony's fatal decision to engage Octavius by "sea" to his being "subject to a woman's will," in the sentence that goes on to record that his captains "prest by force all sorts of men out of Greece that they could take up in the field, as travellers, muleteers, reapers, harvest men, and yong boys, and yet could they not sufficiently furnish his galleys." The juxtaposition of "not well mann'd" with "muleteers" changes the order of Plutarch's description, aligning the latter with the poorly "manned" that elsewhere in the play is suggestive of eunuchry or gelding. It is to this implication of the "barber'd" Antony that I now turn.

* * *

> I'll spurn thine eyes
> Like balls before me! I'll unhair thy head!
>
> —*Antony and Cleopatra*

Read against the different historical moments its striking anachronisms align, not only Enobarbus's set speech but other familiar speeches in the play resonate in these multiple registers. *Antony and Cleopatra* repeatedly foregrounds beards, barbering, shaving and cutting, as the currency both of its internal or civil division (marked by the older Antony's contemptuous references to the "boy" Caesar) and of reversals within the familiar binary opposition between Egypt and Rome, starting from Cleopatra's own contemptuous reference to the "scarce-bearded Caesar" (1.1.22).

Both beards and hair as the traditional indices of generative virility—together with the sense of diverted patrimony that sounds in Antony's accusation against Cleopatra for preventing the "getting of a lawful race"—become associated with barbering, through the Folio text's sustained conflation of "heires" and "haires." Even Cleopatra's attack on the messenger come from

Rome to announce that Antony is married to Octavia—"I'll spurn thine eyes / Like balls before me! I'll unhair thy head!" (2.5.63–64)—underscores (in ways abetted by the familiar bawdy senses of these terms) the unheiring as well as unhairing or barbering associated with the Egypt in which Antony himself is symbolically castrated or gelded. Shamed, at the Battle of Actium, by a "coward's" flight with the woman he later calls by the generic name of "Egypt," this Roman renegade laments "I followed that I blush to look upon. / My very hairs do mutiny, for the white / Reprove the brown for rashness, and they them / For fear and doting" (3.11.12–15), lines that conflate the cultural semantics of barbering and "hair" with the racialized metaphorics of a mingled "white" and "brown," lawful and unlawful "heirs."

The imputation not only of unhairing (or unheiring) but of "cutting" in its multiple senses, compounded in the description of Antony as "barber'd ten times o'er," connects *Antony and Cleopatra* with other Shakespearean combinations of barbering and cuts. Enobarbus's speech on Antony's "barbering" by Cleopatra in Act 2 prompts Agrippa's response "She made great Caesar lay his sword to bed. / He ploughed her, and she cropped." "Cropped" here may seem at first simply to complete the implication of generative or agricultural fertility in "ploughed." But—in its other sense of cropping or cutting—it simultaneously presents this famous moment, of the laying of a "sword" to "bed," as the unmanning of another Roman leader. "Caesarion"—issue of this earlier Roman encounter with Egypt's barbarous queen—shares with Julius "Caesar" the root of "cutting" itself, the *caedo/caeso* stressed in Varro, in Camden's *Remains*, and in Shakespeare's own *Julius Caesar*, by cuts that include "the most unkindest cut of all." In Suetonius's *Life of Octavius Caesar* and Samuel Daniel's *Cleopatra* (1594)—both important influences on *Antony and Cleopatra*—the name of "Caesarion" is alternately spelled "Cesario," the name Viola chooses in *Twelfth Night* (1601–2), when she announces her intention to become a "eunuch" in Illyria, in a play where the "C-U-T" of the letter read by Malvolio repeats the figure of castration or nicking invoked by the otherwise unrealized "eunuch" at its beginning, in the lines whose "mute" simultaneously evokes Illyria's Turkish connections.[29]

The familiar gender reversals of *Antony and Cleopatra* have been repeatedly rehearsed. But what has been less closely examined, both in general and in relation to the lines on the barbering of Antony with which we began, is the extraordinary emphasis on cutting that pervades this play. In the scene in which Antony announces Fulvia's death to Enobarbus, the latter offers consolation in the following terms: "Why, sir, give the gods a thankful sacrifice. When it pleaseth their deities to take the wife of a man from him, it shows to man the tailors of the earth; comforting therein, that when old robes are worn out, there are members to make new. If there were no more women but Fulvia, then had you indeed a cut, and a case to be lamented" (1.2.168–76). The sexual figure of the "cut" (and "case") as well as "members" is continued in the lines that follow, which turn on the sexual (and territorial) senses of broaching or breaching as well as of occupation or abode: "*Antony*. The business she hath broached in the state / Cannot endure my absence. / *Enobarbus*. And the business you have broached here cannot be without you, especially that of Cleopatra's, which wholly depends on your abode" (1.2.178–82). "Tailors of the earth"—a phrase that may appear to be only about attire or clothing—simultaneously sounds in its familiar early modern and Shakespearean resonance of "tailleur" or "cutter" as well as of a potentially castrated "tail."

The cutting of the phallic "member" is underscored in the emphasis on eunuchry throughout, beginning with the eunuchs in the Egyptian train of Antony and Cleopatra in the opening scene. The Cleopatra who (as both female monarch and boy player) says to Antony "I would I had thy inches!" (1.3.41) famously engages her own eunuch Mardian later in this opening act:

> *Cleopatra*. Thou, eunuch, Mardian!
> *Mardian*. What's your highness' pleasure?
> *Cleopatra*. Not now to hear thee sing. I take no pleasure
> In aught an eunuch has. 'Tis well for thee
> That, being unseminared, thy freer thoughts
> May not fly forth of Egypt. Hast thou affections?
> *Mardian*. Yes, gracious madam.
> *Cleopatra*. Indeed?
> *Mardian*. Not in deed, madam, for I can do nothing
> But what indeed is honest to be done.
> Yet have I fierce affections, and think
> What Venus did with Mars. . . .
> (1.5.8–19)

Like the Caesario of *Twelfth Night* who seeks to become a "eunuch" or *castrato* in Illyria, the "unseminared" Egyptian eunuch here associated with an emasculating lack provides a figure for the sense of barbering or gelding identified with Egypt and the East in the familiar binaries of both Roman and early modern writing.

The sense of cutting or coming "too short," as well as of "balls" evoked in contemporary reminders of the castration associated with the "barber" (as in Jonson's equivocal reference to an incising "barbarism" and a punning "barber's balls" or the phallic overtones of the barber's pole) returns in Cleopatra's exchange with Charmian in Act 2:

Cleopatra. Let's to billiards. Come, Charmian.
Charmian. My arm is sore. Best play with Mardian.
Cleopatra. As well a woman with an eunuch played
As with a woman. Come, you'll play with me, sir?
Mardian. As well as I can, madam.
Cleopatra. And when good will is showed, thou't come too short,
The actor may plead pardon . . .
(2.5.3–9)

"Come too short" here—in the context of a "will" that is repeatedly sexualized in Shakespeare—suggests not only the familiar assumption of the eunuch's deficiency or lack but its extension to Antony "barber'd" in Egypt.

Reminders of cutting or clipping (another of the overdetermined senses of barbering) are foregrounded throughout this play, even in descriptions that could employ other terms. Octavia reminds Antony of the "division" with her brother Octavius ("Wars 'twixt you twain would be / As if the world should cleave, and that slain men / Should solder up the rift," 3.4.30–32), in lines whose cleaving evokes the cutting or severing of Roman unity. The cutting of the cable proposed by the pirate Menas in the scene on the galley of Sextus Pompeius, pirate-son of Pompey the Great, metonymically juxtaposes cutting this cable with another kind of cutting ("cut the cable, / And when we are put off, fall to their throats," 2.7.72–73). In the charged phallic language of *Antony and Cleopatra*, "cut" is suggestively juxtaposed with "slackness," in reports of the Egyptianized Antony's war with Octavius, in the exchange in which Enobarbus warns Antony that "your mariners are [muleters]" (3.7.35). Antony's "Is it not strange, Canidius, / That from Tarentum and Brundusium / He [Octavius Caesar] could so quickly cut the Ionian sea / And take in Toryne?" (3.7.20–23) is followed by Cleopatra's "Celerity is never more admired / Than by the negligent" (3.7.24–25) and his "A good rebuke, / Which might have well becom'd the best of men, / To taunt at slackness" (3.7.25–28). "Cut" here (in "cut the Ionian sea") corresponds to the description in North's translation of Plutarch, of Octavius's quick passage. But the choice of "cut" and "slackness" draws the geopolitical contrast between the two in bodily as well as nautical terms.

Cutting—with the implication of castrating—is part not only of the eunuchry associated with Egypt and Barbary but also of the decapitation familiar from Shakespeare's Roman sources—including the severed head of Pompey presented to Julius Caesar in Egypt, recalled by Shakespeare in *Cymbeline*. Decapitation or cutting off a head is foregrounded in the allusion to the death of "Marcus Crassus" in Act 3 (3.1.2), as well as in earlier echoes of this well-known story. The sense of decapitation similarly surrounds the lines in which the defeated Antony says "To the boy Caesar send this grizzled head, / And he will fill thy wishes to the brim / With principalities" (3.13.18–20), lines whose ambiguity is underscored by Cleopatra's immediately following question: "That head, my lord?" (3.13.20). Cleopatra's promise to have a "Herod's head" (3.3.4) summons not only one of the play's reminders of the Christian dispensation that followed the triumph of Octavius at Actium, but also the severed head of John the Baptist, adding the Levantine Salome or Herodias to the barbering of Antony by this Egyptian queen.

Antony is himself described as "plucked" (3.12.3), in the post-Actium scene in which his schoolmaster-ambassador arrives to parley with the triumphant Octavius ("Caesar, 'tis his schoolmaster; / An argument that he is plucked, when hither / He sends so poor a pinion of his wing," 3.12.3–5). The language of cutting, nicking, or emasculating continues in the scene that immediately follows in Egypt, when Enobarbus responds to the defeated Cleopatra's "Is Antony or we in fault for this?" (3.13.3):

> Antony only, that he would make his will
> Lord of his reason. What though you fled
> From that great face of war, whose several ranges
> Frighted each other? Why should he follow?
> The itch of his affection should not then
> Have nick'd his captainship, at such a point,
> When half to half the world oppos'd. . . .
> (3.13.4–9)

"Nick'd" here implies that Antony's "captainship" is conceived as "the blade of a sword, which Cleopatra has damaged and made useless,"[30] in lines that go out of their way to invoke the phallic idiom of "such a point." *OED* cites this passage for the sense of "nick" as "To cut into or through" as well as "cut short." That Antony is "nick'd" at such a "point" by "the itch of his affection" simultaneously recalls the syphilis identified with the unheiring strumpet—the *Barbiera* Florio reminds his readers could be both a "sheebarber" and "common harlot"—here attached to the "gypsy" denounced as a "triple-turn'd whore" by Antony himself. "Make his will / Lord of his reason" summons not only gender inversion in general but familiar contemporary accounts of enthrallment to "infidel" enchantresses, including those already identified with this Egyptian queen.

Editors have frequently related Enobarbus's description of Antony's "nick'd" captainship to the description of the Roman triumvirate and its civil war as a "three-nook'd world" (4.6.6), a "nook'd" whose homophonic-semantic link with the indented or "nick'd" had already been exploited in the description of England as a "nook-shotten isle" in *Henry V*. In the English context of civil war, nicking as indenting in the root sense of incising or cutting is exploited in *Henry IV, Part 1*, in the scene of "indentures tripartite" (3.1.79) dividing territory among the three rebel leaders that calls attention to territorial broaching not only as a "deep indent" (3.1.103) but as "Gelding the opposed continent" (108), in a play of infidels within (2.3.29) that itself opens with the "knife" of "civil butchery" (1.1.13) and includes an extended exchange on a "gelding" named "Cut" (1.3.5–98). In the context of the Roman triumvirate, Antony's "nick'd" captainship at Actium is the fulfillment of this later play's opening lines on the "triple pillar of the world transform'd / Into a strumpet's fool" (1.1.11–12), which transfer to this phallic Roman "pillar" the figure of the nicked or gelded "fool" familiar from *The Comedy of Errors* (5.1.175). The nicking of Antony's captainship, in the lines that follow Enobarbus's description of the overmastering of his "reason" by his "will," at the same time recalls the nicking or cutting identified with the contemporary threat from the Turk and the North African coast. The Variorum glosses Caesar's "three nook'd world" by reference to Europe, Asia, and Africa as the "three Angles" of the Globe, and the three races emanating from Japheth, Shem, and Ham, a division capable of Roman and early modern reference at once. *Nick* was itself a keyword of contemporary dramatic plots of barbering in Barbary—from the "Nick" Bottom of *A Midsummer Night's Dream*, who remarks that he must to the "barbers" in the scene of his own enthrallment to an exoticized Fairy Queen, to the juxtaposition of "nick" and "Turk" in *The Knight of Malta*, to the transformation of "Nicke the Barbor" into a threatening "Barberoso" in *The Knight of the Burning Pestle*.[31]

But Why Enobarbus?

Both the lines on Antony as "barber'd" by Cleopatra and those on the shaving of "Antonio's beard" in Rome are, finally, put into the mouth of Enobarbus, whose own name and its link with beards or "barbes" the play goes out of its way to underscore, in its shortened form of "Enobarbe" (2.7.144). Even to call him "Enobarbus" (or "Red-beard") rather than "Domitius" (as Antony's lieutenant was also known) calls attention to the "barbe" or "beard" on which so much stress is laid, in Roman as well as early modern culture, as well as to the red beard he may have worn on stage. The association of Enobarbus or "Enobarbe" with shaving, barbering, and beards within the play is entirely Shakespearean, since this figure does not appear in earlier English or continental theatrical representations of this story.[32]

The influential brief note by Dawson in 1987—whose answer to the question "But Why Enobarbus?" has become a standard reference for editors and critics of this play—argued that Shakespeare's "Enobarbe" would have worn on stage the red beard associated with Jews and the defector Judas, thus announcing from his first appearance the betrayal of Antony that would be his "place in the story."[33] I want, however, to suggest a historically more inclusive answer to this famous question, in relation to Barbary and infidels of all kinds, as well as the Roman significance of this Shakespearean figure. Critics and editors of *Antony and Cleopatra* have tended to depend primarily on Plutarch's *Life of Mark Antony* for details about Enobarbus, sometimes even assuming that Shakespeare constructed this memorable dramatic character out of two different historical figures briefly cited in this particular source.[34] But in fact there were numerous other accounts well known to Shakespeare and his contemporaries, which not only detailed the pivotal role and family history of this "Red-beard" or "Aheno-barbus" but repeatedly drew attention to beards, barbering, and shaving in ways that made clear his "place" in the "story" and called into question the binary opposition of civil West to barbarous East that *Antony and Cleopatra* famously both evokes and undoes.

Antony's Enobarbus (or "Domitius Enobarbus," to use both names by which he is called in the play) appears several times in Plutarch's *Life of Antony*—as the lieutenant of Antony who participates in the Parthian campaign, argues against Cleopatra's participation in the war, and finally deserts Antony in Egypt for Rome, though he repents his defection and dies soon after. Plutarch's striking ending then describes the ultimate Roman story in which Antony's Enobarbus was a pivotal figure: the marriage of his son to the daughter of Antony and Octavia and the combination of the families of Antony, Enobarbus, and Octavius or Augustus that produced the ultimate "Domitius Enobarbus," the emperor whose adopted name was Nero. The larger "story" of Enobarbus, which Plutarch goes out of his way to underscore, is thus one in which Actium itself was ultimately reversed by the imperial "Enobarbus" (product of Antony's "lawful race") who brought Alexandrian revels—and the theatricality condemned in both ancient and early modern antitheatrical treatises—into Rome itself.[35]

Enobarbus—and the history of the "Ahenobarbi" in which he is a pivotal figure—is also part of a larger Roman as well as early modern "story" of barbering and beards. Suetonius's *Life of Nero*, which Shakespeare had already recalled in the Claudius and matricidal "Nero" of *Hamlet*, begins with the entire history of the Ahenobarbus line, from the Red-beard origin of the name to the culminating Domitius Enobarbus renamed Nero when he was adopted as Claudius's stepson and heir. In the Latin text used by Shakespeare and others before Holland's English translation in 1606, "Ahenobarbi" appears as "Ahenobarborum," with other case endings that underscore the associations of barbering and "barbarian" that Enobarbus's famous speech exploits.[36]

Suetonius describes each generation of Ahenobarbi in turn, starting with Enobarbus's grandfather, Cnaeus Domitius Ahenobarbus, of whom it was said that "It was no mervaile he had a brasen beard whose face was made of Iron, and heart of lead."[37] This Enobarbus is described elsewhere as a defender of the *virilitas* of ancient Rome, opposing the introduction of Eastern practices, including the rhetoric associated with the "shaven" or smooth. His son (father of Antony's Enobarbus) is likewise aligned with the older republican Rome of Cato and opposition to the rise of Caesar. When Suetonius comes to the Enobarbus who was Antony's lieutenant ("worthy without question, to be preferred before all others of his name and linage"), he stresses not only his alternation between warring sides in Rome's civil wars before his final desertion of Antony for Octavius but (along with Tacitus and other sources known to Shakespeare) his command of a fleet and his crucial involvement in battles by sea.

Like Plutarch, Suetonius then fills in the history between Antony's Domitius Enobarbus and Nero as the culminating "Domitius Aenobarbus," starting with the son of Antony's lieutenant who, having married into the imperial line of Augustus, "produced upon the stage to acte a comicall and wanton Enterlude," anticipating the outrageous "theatricals" of Nero himself. That this subsequent history of Antony's Enobarbus was known well before the date of *Antony and Cleopatra* is underscored not only by its appearance in Suetonius and Tacitus (the latter the source of the more skeptical view of Augustus in Shakespeare's play) but also by the reference to this theatrical Enobarbus in the "villanous out-of-tune fiddler AENOBARBVS" of Jonson's *Poetaster* in 1601, a "fiddler" (in both musical and sexual senses) who proleptically evokes the Nero who fiddled while Rome burned. Suetonius then describes the Enobarbus of Tiberius's reign who was "father to Nero" himself, a riotous reveller, drinker, and lascivious adulterer, fitting progenitor (with the sexually transgressive Agrippina) to the climactic "Domitius Ahenobarbus" of the entire line.[38]

This larger place in the "story" of Shakespeare's Enobarbus calls repeated attention to the Roman significance of barbering, shaving, and beards. When Suetonius describes the Enobarbus whose name was changed to Nero, he records that his "Paedagogues" were a transvestite dancer (*saltator*) and a barber.[39] The link in sound between barber and Enobarbus does not work in Latin (where "barber" is *tonsor*, source of slurs against tonsured priests as "shavelings" in Protestant English polemics). But it does resonate with the "barbus" of "AEnobarbus" in Holland's 1606 translation, which recounts the slur of Nero's stepbrother Britannicus, who continues to call Nero, after his adoption, by the name "AEnobarbus," an origin that haunted the adopted emperor throughout his history. This same section records not only Nero's castrating or gelding of

"Sporus" as his male bride but this emperor's "prostituting" his "owne body" to "bee abused" in turn, being "by Doriphorus his freed-man . . . wedded like as Sporus unto him" (Holland, *Suetonius*, 2:123). The description of the "gelding" of Sporus goes out of its way to call attention to Nero's "AEnobarbus" lineage—remarking of his castration of this boy "whose Genitories he cut out" (assaying thereby to "transforme him into the nature of a woman") that it was joked that "it might have beene wel and happie with the World, if his father Domitius had wedded such a wife," preventing the begetting of the heir who would become the imperial Enobarbus, or Nero.

Suetonius repeatedly connects barbering of different kinds with this imperial Enobarbus, who "cut off the first beard that he had (*barbam primam*) and laid it in a golden box and consecrat[ed] it in the Capitol." His narrative of Nero's matricide (Holland, *Suetonius*, 2:130) is followed by yet another barbering, which relates the cutting of his first beard to the death of the aunt (Domitia) in whose household he was tutored by a "dauncer" and "Barber": when, after "handling the tender downe of his beard new budding forth," she remarks "Might I but live to take up this soft haire when it fals, I would be willing to dye," he responds by promising to "streight wayes . . . cut it of(f)." The association of this ultimate "Domitius AEnobarbus" with shaving, beards, and hair continues in different forms, as the insult levelled at him by Britannicus's "Ahenobarbus" (ch. 7) is repeated in taunts by his Roman subjects. Suetonius proceeds from "this name appropriate to his house and family, wherewith he was thus in contumelious manner twitted" to call equivocal attention to the long "hair" of a "Gallus," the term that could mean both "Gaul" (origin of the red-bearded Ahenobarbi) and "castrate," as in the eunuch "Galli" associated with the castrated Attis. The Nero whose real name was "AEnobarbus" is taunted with this double-meaning "Gallus" (ch. 43), when Romans objecting to his bringing Eastern entertainers from Alexandria, place a "curl" on his statue in Rome, with a Greek inscription alluding to the long hair worn by this new "Ahenobarbus" on his trip to the East. Suetonius's description (ch. 12) of Nero's presiding over Eastern entertainments from his *cubiculum* or "his owne Bed-chamber" (Holland)—the same Latin term used for the "Bedchamber" of England's King James—provides an account of the pyrrhic "daunces" of "ephebes" or young Greek males, who simply for dancing were accorded Roman citizenship by an emperor who frequented "Actours and players." At these games, Nero takes the prize for rhetoric and lays the "harp" presented to him for his lyre playing at "the Statue of Augustus" (Holland, *Suetonius*, 2:108)—implicating the line of Octavius in this Easternizing of Rome's imperial seat.

Beards and hair continue to be foregrounded in Suetonius's description of this imperial Roman "AEnobarbus," including in the chapters on his bringing of Alexandrian revels into Rome itself, which picture him in his "wastfull riotousnesse" wearing what Holland glosses (out of Dio Cassius) as a "peruke and cap of counterfeit hair" (Holland, *Suetonius*, 2:272), immediately before the famous description of his "unnaturall abusing of boyes freeborne" (2:122) and his cutting of the "Genitories" of the boy Sporus, in the passage where taunting reference is once again made of his "Ahenobarbus" origins. When Tacitus records the "Juvenalia" in celebration of this first shaving of Nero's beard (*Annals* 14.15), he accompanies it with a passage on the obscene gestures or "postures" this imperial Enobarbus encouraged Roman actors to assume, described as "never meant for the male sex" (*ad gestus modosque haud virilis*). The passage—along with the hetero- and homoerotic *modi* or postures of Ovid and Martial—is famously recalled in Aretino and Giulio Romano, early modernizers of the "modi" or "I modi" that were the Italian counterpart of this Roman "*modus*." In relation to the final English translation of this "story" in Shakespeare's own simultaneously Roman and early modern play, we might see the extension of such postures in the lines of *Antony and Cleopatra* on the boying on the English stage of the greatness of Antony's Egyptian queen, by "some squeaking Cleopatra" in "the posture of a whore," in a play whose "Salt Cleopatra" may evoke not only the "salt" of female sexuality or a "gypsy's lust" but also the figure of the *saltator, salter*, or transvestite dancer familiar from Plautus and other Roman writers and from the condemnation of such spectacles in contemporary antitheatrical literature.[40]

The subsequent history of Antony's Enobarbus—familiar from Plutarch's *Life* as from Suetonius and Tacitus, already well-known Shakespearean sources—thus stresses the "story" of an imperial history in which the binaries opposing Rome (or its later emulators) to Egypt or a more contemporary "Turk Gypsy" are brought into "Rome" itself, including the theatricality that Shakespeare's Octavius emulates as well as ostensibly condemns.[41] In relation to barbering and beards, and the topos of decline from the *virilitas* of an old "bearded" Rome evoked in Enobarbus's "By Jupiter, / Were I the wearer of Antonio's beard, / I would not shave it today," Antony's Enobarbus occupies a pivotal position within a larger history that charts the breakdown of this very binary opposition—from the stern consul Enobarbus identified with resisting the importing of rhetoric and other Eastern practices into Rome to the ultimate Enobarbus or Nero, who brought Alexandrian revels into Rome's own imperial center. Shakespeare's Enobarbus thus has a pivotal "place" in the "story" of Rome as well as the Ahenobarbus line and of the Roman history of barbering and beards, between the past of a bearded older Rome (signalled by the *barbus* of his own name) and the barbaring of Rome by the ultimate imperial "Domitius Enobarbus," heir not of a "barbarous" Egyptian but of the intermarriage or mingling of the "lawful race" of Antony, Enobarbus, and Octavius or Augustus himself.

* * *

> Barbaroxa, a famous pyrate among the Moores which had a red beard . . .
> —Minsheu (1599)

> a eunuch of Solymans court, sent by him as Barbarussa his companion. . . .
> —Knolles, *Generall Historie of the Turke* (1603)

The Enobarbus or "Enobarbe" of Shakespeare's play who delivers the lines on the danger of shaving "Antonio's beard" in Rome has both a name and a history that resonate with the supposedly natural Roman index of virility, even as his simultaneous reference to the "wearer" of that beard calls attention to the prosthetic stage beard that complicated the very categories of natural and constructed.[42] In the network of Latin and translated sources whose metamorphoric *Ahenobarbi* and *Ahenobarborum* resonate not only with *barbus* or beard but with the *barbarus* or barbaric, the fact that it is likewise Enobarbus who speaks the lines on Antony as "barber'd" on the Cydnus, in Cilicia or early modern Turkey, may connect this Roman defector and renegade Red-beard, finally, with two historical registers at once: not just the Roman history in which he is first a renegade with Antony and then defects back to Rome but also the more proximate history of renegades and defectors, and the Barbary and Egypt that were so central to early modern representations of barbering and beards. Suetonius, Tacitus, and others, like Plutarch, emphasize that Antony's Enobarbus was an experienced sea commander during the civil wars, who "commanded a fleet in the Adriatic against the triumvirs" before joining the side of Antony, the reason why he is the one who counsels Antony on his weakness by "sea." In relation to the Enobarbus of *Antony and Cleopatra*, who engages in the major exchange with the pirates of Sextus Pompeius and begs Antony not to give in to Cleopatra's desire to fight with Octavius by sea, where the Egyptian forces are not well "manned," it is important, then, to record that Enobarbus is not only a "master leaver" or deserter (after his sojourn with Antony, in Egypt, as a fellow renegade) but master of a "fleet" at sea.[43]

In his *Remains Concerning Britain* (1605), William Camden explicitly connects Roman "Aenobarbus" with his early modern counterpart "Barbarossa," as "red-beards" from both ancient and early modern worlds, commenting on what he calls "*Aenobarbus* of the Latines, or *Barbarossa* of the Italians," as simply different versions of the same name.[44] In relation to the preoccupation of *Antony and Cleopatra* not only with piracy and battles by "land" and "sea" but also with barbering, barbaring, and beards, and the description of the "barber'd" Antony that Shakespeare chooses to put into the mouth of Enobarbus in Rome, it would not be inappropriate to end with the most famous Red-beard defector of early modern memory. The story of this Red-beard renegade was detailed at length, only a few years before, in Knolles's *Generall Historie of the Turke* (1603), already an acknowledged influence on *Othello* (1604). From his origins in a renegade family, he spread the power of the new Emperor of the East from Alexandria and Egypt across the entire North African coast, literally creating the Barbary ports associated with the taking of captives and with renegades who flocked from all over Europe, including to Tunis and Algiers, the Barbary ports that would figure so prominently in the Mediterranean geographies of *The Tempest*.

This renegade Barbarossa—whose name was rendered in one English account as *Barbarus*—was none other than the naval commander who led the forces of the East at the new Battle of Actium fought at Prevesa in 1538, establishing Ottoman mastery and reversing the story of the ancient battle by defeating the forces of the new Roman Emperor Charles V. Knolles's *Historie* recounts at length this reversal of East and West at this early modern "ACTIVM" (687)—describing the Antony-like retreat of Andrea Doria, leader of the Western forces, as done "in such hast" that "it seemed rather a shamefull flight than an orderly retreat" (689–90). Knolles goes on to record the scorn of the triumphant renegade "Barbarussa" at this western commander's loss of "honour" in so "shamefull a flight." And he then proceeds to recount the story of a "sonne" taken captive with his father at this new Actium battle, a "young gentleman . . . beautifull with all the good gifts of nature, who afterwards presented to *Solyman*, turned Turke; and growing in credit in *Solymans* chamber, after three yeares miserable imprisonment, obtained his poore fathers libertie, and sent him well rewarded home againe into SPAINE" (689), a Joseph-in-Egypt story in which the Egyptianized son gains redemption for his family but does not himself return home.[45]

By the time of *Antony and Cleopatra*, this renegade Barbarossa or Red-beard was an established part of the network linking barbering, Barbary, and beards—appearing in Minsheu's 1599 dictionary as "Barbaroxa, a famous pyrate among the Moores which had a red beard," as the Red-beard "Barbaroja" in the Captive's Tale of *Don Quixote* (published in 1605, and circulating in English by 1607) recalling the red beard or *barba roja* of the earlier "barber" named Nicolas or Nick, as "Barbarussa" in Knolles's Turkish *Historie*, which remarks of the Battle of Lepanto in 1571 that it was only a temporary shaving of the Sultan's beard, and as the assumed name of "Nicke the Barbor" in Beaumont's *Knight of the Burning Pestle*, a "Barbarossa"/"Barberoso" who keeps captives in his cave.[46] In a play in which Roman Antony is called alternately "Antonio" (the name of the Merchant of Venice and in *Twelfth Night* of an alleged pirate or "salt-water thief") and in which (as Leeds Barroll has demonstrated) the exchange between Enobarbus and the pirates casts empire itself as a form of piracy,[47] it is not at all impossible that (as in Camden only a few years before) the Red-beard Enobarbus who so pointedly evokes this network of barbering may have recalled not only Judas or the stage beard of the Jew but the most memorable Red-beard from what *The Jew of Malta* calls the other "circumcised nation"—the Barbarossa who reversed not only Actium but the very direction of Enobarbus's defection and was a renegade who, like Antony, chose never to return.

Notes

1. All quotations from Shakespeare are taken from *The Riverside Shakespeare*, ed. G. Blakemore Evans et al. (Boston: Houghton Mifflin, 1974).

2. Maud W. Gleason, *Making Men: Sophists and Self-Presentation in Ancient Rome* (Princeton, NJ: Princeton University Press, 1995), 68–69. For recent studies of the importance of the beard in early modern writing, see Will Fisher, "The Renaissance Beard: Masculinity in Early Modern England and Europe," *Renaissance Quarterly* 54, no. 1 (Spring 2001): 155–187, and Elliott Horowitz, "The New World and the Changing Face of Europe," *The Sixteenth Century Journal* 28, no. 4 (Winter 1997): 1181–1201.

3. See Gleason, *Making Men*, 113; on Pliny and the *glaber*, Craig A. Williams, *Roman Homosexuality* (Oxford: Oxford University Press, 1999), 26, 73; Plautus, *Men.* 513–14; *Asin.* 402; Bruce R. Smith, *Homosexual Desire in Shakespeare's England* (Chicago: University of Chicago Press, 1991), 169.

4. See Arthur L. Little, Jr., *Shakespeare Jungle Fever* (Stanford: Stanford University Press, 2000) (for the *Philippics* charge); Amy Richlin, "Not Before Homosexuality: The Materiality of the *Cinaedus* and the Roman Law against Love between Men," *Journal of the History of Sexuality* 3, no. 4 (1993): 523–73; Gleason, *Making Men*, 72–73; William J. Dominik, ed., *Roman Eloquence* (New York: Routledge, 1993), e.g. 41–46, 84–87, 91–107.

5. Gleason, *Making Men*, 73.

6. See Discourse 33 (to Tarsus) para. 62–64 (pp. 331–33 of vol. 3 of the Loeb *Dio Chrysostom*, trans. J. W. Cohoon and H. Lamar Crosby, 5 vols. (Cambridge, MA: Harvard University Press, 1940; reprinted in 1951); Clement of Alexandria, *Paidagogus*, book 3, chapter 3, trans. Simon P. Wood, *Clement of Alexandria: Christ the Educator* (New York: Fathers of the Church, 1954), 212–14, with the rest of chapters 3 and 4 (e.g. p. 221) on eunuchs and youths; chap. 11 (esp. pp. 246–48, 256, 258, on beards, hair, and barbers).

7. Cited from George Sandys, *A Relation of a Journey Begun An: Dom: 1610: Foure bookes* (London, 1615), 70.

8. On *Fair Maid*, see Jean E. Howard, "An English Lass Amid the Moors: Gender, Race, Sexuality, and National Identity in Heywood's *The Fair Maid of the West*," in *Women, "Race," and Writing in the Early Modern Period*, ed. Margo

Hendricks and Patrick Parker (London: Routledge, 1994), 101–17; Barbara Fuchs, *Mimesis and Empire: The New World, Islam, and European Identities* (Cambridge: Cambridge University Press, 2001), 129–34; and Jonathan Burton, "English Anxiety and the Muslim Power of Conversion: Five Perspectives on 'Turning Turk' in Early Modern Texts," *Journal for Early Modern Cultural Studies*, 2, no. 1 (Spring/ Summer 2002): 35–67, esp. 53–59.

9. See *The Admirable Deliverance of 266. Christians by Iohn Reynard Englishman from the captiuitie of the Turkes, who had been Gally slaues many yeares in Alexandria* (London, 1608), attributed to Anthony Munday, which describes the shaving of the captives' heads and beards on sig. B2r. Vitkus in *Piracy, Slavery, and Redemption: Barbary Captivity Narratives from Early Modern England*, ed. Daniel J. Vitkus (New York: Columbia University Press, 2000), 55–70, mentions (57) this different account, though it prints only the version from the 1589 edition of Hakluyt's *Principal Navigations.*

10. See Daniel J. Vitkus, "Turning Turk in *Othello*: The Conversion and Damnation of the Moor," *Shakespeare Quarterly* 48, no. 2 (1997): 145–76, esp. 154, 157–58.

11. See respectively I. H., *This World's Folly, or a Warning-Peece Discharged upon the Wickednesse thereof* (1615); John Dickenson, *Arisbas, Euphues Amidst his Slumbers; Or, Cupid's Iourney to Hell* (London, 1594), sig. D2; Robert Daborne, *A Christian Turn'd Turk* (1612), 13.52–55, in *Three Turk Plays from Early Modern England*, ed. Daniel J. Vitkus (New York: Columbia University Press, 2000), which includes "a barber" (13.60–72) and multiple references to the barbarous. In relation to wordplay on barbers, balls, and barbarisms, see Jonson's *Magnetic Lady* (2.7.51–52) and Dekker, *Noble Spanish Soldier* (c. 1626) 5.4.143 ("Shee loves no Barbars washing . . . My Balls are sav'd then"); with other examples in Williams, *Dictionary*, 1:62–63.

12. See *Twelfth Night* 3.2.7 ("a very renegado"), and 2.5.86–88, 130–38. On Illyria and the Turk, see Samuel Chew, *The Crescent and Rose* (1937 rprt; New York: Octagon Books, 1965), 132, citing John Foxe, *A Sermon of Christ Crucified, preached at Paules Crosse the Friday before Easter commonly called Goodfryday* (London, 1570), on the growing empire of the Turk, including "the Empire of Constantinople, Greece, Illyria, with almost all Hungary and much of Austria"; and the Second Part of *Tamburlaine* (3.1.1–4), where the territories of "Callapinus, Emperor of Turkey" include Illyria, here cited from Christopher Marlowe, *Tamburlaine the Great, Parts 1 and 2*, ed. J. W. Harper (New York: Hill and Wang, 1973), 122. On *caesus*/cut, *castrati*, and eunuchry in *Twelfth Night*, see Keir Elam, "The Fertile Eunuch: *Twelfth Night*, Early Modern Intercourse, and the Fruits of Castration," *Shakespeare Quarterly* 47, no. 1 (Spring 1996): 1–36; Stephen Orgel, *Impersonations* (Cambridge: Cambridge University Press, 1996), 53–57. See also my forthcoming Norton Critical Edition of *Twelfth Night* on the "eunuch" as a musical instrument, with no sound of its own.

13. On this aspect of the Diet of Worms, see Dorothy M. Vaughan, *Europe and the Turk: A Pattern of Alliances 1350–1700* (New York: AMS Press, 1976), 108.

14. On Steevens's emendation of "Muliteus" to "Muly" (familiar from Peele's *Battle of Alcazar*), see Bate, *Titus*, 222, with Jack D'Amico, *The Moor in English Renaissance Drama* (Tampa, FL: University of South Florida Press, 1991), 141. On "Mulatto" and mule, below, see Margo Hendricks, "'Obscured by dreams': Race, Empire, and Shakespeare's *A Midsummer Night's Dream*," *Shakespeare Quarterly* 47 (1996): 37–60, esp. 56–60. For the variant spellings in *Titus Andronicus* and *Two*

Noble Kinsmen, see the corresponding passages in the Arden 3 editions of those plays by Jonathan Bate and Lois Potter respectively.

15. Jerry Brotton, "'This Tunis, sir, was Carthage': Contesting Colonialism in *The Tempest*," in *Post-colonial Shakespeares*, ed. Ania Loomba and Martin Orkin (London: Routledge, 1998) 23–42, 41.

16. David Quint, *Epic and Empire* (Princeton, NJ: Princeton University Press, 1993), 24.

17. See 4.377 (p. 80) and 4.377 (p. 82) of *The Aeneid of Thomas Phaer and Thomas Twyne*, ed. Steven Lally (New York: Garland Publishing, 1987).

18. See both here and in relation to what follows, the discussion of echoes of the *Aeneid* and of Cleopatra's Islamic counterparts in Quint, *Epic and Empire*, 21ff., 49, 157–58.

19. Both Arden editions of the play and David Bevington's New Cambridge edition (124) note the echoes of Edward Fairfax's translation of Tasso's *Jerusalem Delivered*, under the English title *Godfrey of Bulloigne* (1600), 16.4 ("The waters burnt about their vessels good, / Such flames the god therein enchased threw").

20. See Jonson's *The Gypsies Metamorphosed*; and the texts of Daborne and Massinger in Vitkus, *Three Turk Plays*.

21. See the commentary in the New Variorum edition of the play (which cites among other glosses Hanmer's 1744 derivation of "reneages" here from Spanish *renegar*) and Nicholas de Nicholay, in *Navigations, Peregrinations and Voyages Made into Turkie*, trans. T. Washington (London, 1585), book 1, 8.

22. See the New Variorum edition commentary on each of these passages.

23. See *The Battell of Alcazar, Fought in Barbarie, betweene Sebastian king of Portugall, and Abdelmelec king of Marocco. With the death of Captaine Stukeley* (1594), which begins with the summary title "The Tragical battell of Alcazar in Barbarie. with the death of three Kings, and Captaine Stukley an Englishman."

24. Lois Potter, "Pirates and 'turning Turk' in Renaissance drama," in *Travel and Drama in Shakespeare's Time*, ed. Jean-Pierre Maquerlot and Michele Willems (Cambridge: Cambridge University Press, 1996), 125–140.

25. See 4.377 (p. 80) and 4.377 (p. 82) of the *Aeneid*, trans. Phaer and Twyne.

26. See *OED*, "tire" and "attire" (noun and verb); the Globe Quartos edition of *Honest Whore*, Part 2, p. 129; and Spenser, *Faerie Queene* (1590) 1.10.31.

27. See John Wilders's Arden 3 edition of *Antony and Cleopatra* (London: Routledge, 1995); the New Variorum glosses on 1.1.22ff for Upton (1748, p. 89) on Antony's "Asiatic manner of speaking" as "a very rodomontade." See Mary Nyquist, "'Profuse, Proud Cleopatra': 'Barbarism' and Female Rule in Early Modern English Republicanism," in *The Representation of Gender in the English Revolution, 1640–1660*, ed. Sharon Achinstein, *Women's Studies* 24 (1994), 85–130, who cites "motifs from the discourse of barbarism that are frequently voiced by Roman characters" including Caesar, who refers to Antony as "a mere soft Purple Asian Prince (4.1.51), from *The Poetical and Dramatic Works of Sir Charles Sedley*, ed. V. de Sola Pinto (London: Constable, 1928), 1:105.

28. See Bate, *Titus*, 226, with D'Amico, *Moor in English Renaissance Drama*, 141, on "Muly" and Muliteus.

29. For "Caesario" as spelling of Caesarion, see Suetonius, *History of Twelve Caesars*, trans. Philemon Holland (1606), ed. Charles Whibley, 2 vols. (London: David Nutt, 1899), vol. 1 (*Life of Octavius Caesar Augustus*), 94; and the 1594 play *Cleopatra* by Samuel Daniel, long acknowledged as an influence on *Antony and*

Cleopatra (where Caesarion appears as "Caesario," for example, throughout Act 4, Scene 1).

30. See Maurice Charney, *Shakespeare's Roman Plays* (Cambridge, MA: Harvard University Press, 1961), 131.

31. See the New Variorum glosses on "nickt" (3.13.1–8), including for the nicking of "the hair of Fools" and Theobald (ed. 1733) on "three-nook'd world" as "Europe, Asia, and Africk making . . . the three Angles of the Globe . . . the American Parts not being then discover'd"; for contemporary Jacobean resonances for this division, H. Neville Davies, "Jacobean Antony and Cleopatra" (pp. 126–65), 133–34, in John Drakakis, ed., New Casebooks volume on *Antony and Cleopatra*; *Henry IV, Part 1*, 2.4.69–119; *Henry V*, 3.5.14; *Comedy of Errors*, 5.1.175, cited in David Bevington's New Cambridge edition; Michael Neill's Oxford edition, which observes (of "nicked") that "Various senses of the verb are possible: (1) cut, damage, cut short; (2) catch, take unawares; (3) to win against a competitor (as in the game of hazard); (4) cheat, defraud"; Wilders's Arden 3 gloss (212); Barbara Fuchs, *Passing for Spain* (Urbana: University of Illinois Press, 2003), 2–30, on the importance of Cervantes' barber named Nicolas, with *Don Quijote*, part 1, esp. chapters 21–22, 27, 29, 32, 39–43; *The Knight of the Burning Pestle*, ed. Andrew Gurr (Berkeley and Los Angeles: University of California Press, 1968), 3.2.78 ("Nick the Barbor") and 1.192 (on a "double gelding" Barbary horse).

32. See Elkin Calhoun Wilson, "Shakespeare's Enobarbus," in *Joseph Quincy Adams: Memorial Studies*, ed. James G. McManaway, Giles E. Dawson, and Edwin E. Willoughby (Washington, DC: Folger Shakespeare Library, 1948), 391–408, 391: "There is no trace of Enobarbus in any of the French, Italian, German, and English plays about Antony and Cleopatra—Estienne Jodelle's *Cléopatre Captive* (1552), Robert Garnier's *Marc-Antoine* (1578), Nicolas de Montreux's *Tragédie de Cléopatre* (1595), Alessandro Spinello's *Cleopatra* (1540), Cesare De' Cesari's *Cleopatra* (1552), Celso Pistorelli's *Marc'Antonio e Cleopatra* (1576), Battista Giraldi Cinthio's *Cleopatra* (1583), Hans Sach's *Tragedi* (1560), the Countess of Pembroke's *Antoine* (1592), Samuel Daniel's *Cleopatra* (1594), and Samuel Brandon's *The Vertuous Octavia* (1598)."

33. R. MacG. Dawson, "But Why Enobarbus?," *Notes and Queries* (June 1987): 216–17, which also points out the stress on the beard through the shortened "Enobarbe" and the fact that Shakespeare uses Enobarbus more often than "Domitius." The association of red beards with Judas and Jews has been well documented. See, for example, Ruth Mellinkoff, *Outcasts* (Berkeley and Los Angeles: University of California Press, 1993).

34. Arthur M. Z. Norman, "Source Material in *Antony and Cleopatra*," *Notes and Queries* 201 (1956): 59–61, introduced several such confusions into criticism of the play, which continue to be repeated in Wilders's 1995 Arden 3 edition (e.g. p. 87).

35. See *Plutarch's Lives, Englished by Sir Thomas North in Ten Volumes* (London: J. M. Dent, 1899), 56; 77–78; 86–87; 117–18; the entry on "Domitius Ahenobarbus, Gnaeus," in the *Oxford Classical Dictionary*; and for glosses on the appearances of Domitius Enobarbus in this source for the play, Plutarch, *Life of Antony*, ed. C. B. R. Pelling (Cambridge: Cambridge University Press, 1988), which also comments on its striking ending, which goes out of its way to connect Antony, Enobarbus, and the line of Octavius to the ultimate Domitius Enobarbus, Nero (323–27). Pelling (325) points out that this concluding connection with Nero suggests that Octavius's defeat of Antony was "not total," since Antony's descendants became Octavius's

"successors" as emperors of Rome; that it links Antony with Nero via two family lines; and that it implicates Octavius himself in the ancestry of Nero, through the marriage of the only son of Antony's Enobarbus to the daughter of Antony and Octavia. It is ironically thus the lawful race of Antony (not the unlawful relationship with Cleopatra) that produces the ultimate Domitius Enobarbus, Nero, who brought Alexandrian revels into the imperial seat of Rome itself. I am grateful for these references, as well as information on other textual sources for Enobarbus, to classicists Anthony Corbeill and Brendon Reay.

36. See the Loeb edition of *Suetonius*, trans. J. C. Rolfe, 2 vols. (London: William Heinemann, 1914), 2:86. Suetonius also provides other details about Antony's Enobarbus and his line—beyond the *Life of Nero*—including in texts consulted by Shakespeare, before *Antony and Cleopatra*. Most important, in relation to Antony's Enobarbus, Suetonius's *Life of Octavius Caesar Augustus* (a more negative view of Octavius than Virgil or his encomiasts) provides a much fuller account than Plutarch's of the return of Enobarbus (here "T. Domitius") with Sosia from Rome to Antony in Egypt, as the triumvirate disintegrates and the collision course is set for Actium. Here it is made very clear that this "Domitius" is very close to Antony, of "his neerest acquaintance and inward friendes." Even before Holland's English translation of Suetonius in 1606, Matthew Gwynne's Latin play *Nero* (1603)—whose preface acknowledges Suetonius, Tacitus, Dio Cassius, and Seneca among its sources—made clear Nero's Ahenobarbus family origins, while Jonson's *Sejanus* (in that same year), in which not only Burbage but Shakespeare played a role (possibly Tiberius), focused on the Roman history known from Suetonius and other classical writings. Thomas May—whose 1626 *Cleopatra* is frequently cited in relation to *Antony and Cleopatra*—signalled precisely such an awareness of the "Enobarbus" connection in his later play on Nero's mother (*Julia Agrippina* of 1639), which cites Dio Cassius as well as Plutarch among its authorities and echoes Suetonius's *Nero* directly in the scene in Act 1 in which the adopted Nero is taunted by his new "brother" Britannicus (as "Domitius Aenobarbus").

37. On the red-beard Enobarbus name, see also Thomas Cooper, *Thesaurus linguae Romanae & Britannicae* (London, 1565), cited in *A New Variorum Edition of Shakespeare, Antony and Cleopatra*, ed. Marvin Spevack (New York: The Modern Language Association of America, 1990). For speculations on the name (Ahenobarbus) as also combining the attributes of Bacchus and Hercules, wine-bibbing (*oeno-*) and manly valor (*-barbus*), see Donald Cheney, "'A very Antony': Patterns of Antonomasia in Shakespeare," *Connotations* 4, no. 1–2 (1994/5): 8–24.

38. See Holland trans. *Suetonius*, 2:101–2; Jonson, *Poetaster* (1601), 3.4.283, on p. 254 of the Herford and Simpson edition.

39. For this "dauncer" (*saltator*) and "Barber," see Holland, *Suetonius*, 2:103.

40. *Saltator* (related to "leap," hence also French "sault") was—with its vernacular variants—well known as the term for dancer, in sixteenth-century manuals on dancing, as well as from condemnations of dancing, including Philip Stubbes. In addition to the possible resonances of the Roman *saltator* or wanton transvestite dancer (known from Plautus and other sources) in "Salt Cleopatra" (the queen who in Shakespeare's play famously reveals herself to be a transvestite English boy player), see also in the Shakespeare canon the dancing "Saltiers" of *The Winter's Tale*, 4.4.327.

41. On the complication of these binaries in the play, see inter alia Jonathan Gil Harris, "'Narcissus in thy face': Roman Desire and the Difference It Fakes in *Antony and Cleopatra*," *Shakespeare Quarterly* 45 (1994): 408–25.

42. On the prosthetic as opposed to the allegedly "natural" beard as masculine index, see Fisher, "Renaissance Beard," *Renaissance Quarterly* 54, no. 1 (2001), 155–87; and "'His Majesty the Beard': Facial Hair and Masculinity on the Early Modern Stage," in *Staged Properties*, ed. Natasha Korda and Jonathan Gil Harris (Cambridge: Cambridge University Press, 2002); and Gleason, *Making Men*, 73, for the complication of this binary in Roman and classical texts.

43. It is difficult to read the accounts (in Florus, Appian, and other well-known histories) of Roman pirates on the Mediterranean, Adriatic, and Ionian seas without thinking of the "Barbary" pirates on those same seas. In Plutarch's *Life of Antony*, the very passage that inspired the scene of *Antony and Cleopatra* where Menas offers to "cut" the "cable" (and the throats of their guests) registers in both temporal frames, evoking the early modern threat of pirates to European fortunes on the "seas": "Sextus Pompeius at that time kept in Sicily, and so made many an inroad into Italy with a great number of pinnaces and other pirates' ships, of the which were captains two notable pirates, Menas and Menecrates, who so scoured all the sea thereabouts, that none durst peep out with a sail." Menas (like Antony and the "master-leaver" Enobarbus) was not only a pirate, but a renegade, who repeatedly changed sides, capturing Sardinia for Sextus Pompeius (son of Pompey the Great), then turning it over to Octavius, and finally returning to the service of Pompey.

44. See Camden, *Remains Concerning Britain* (1605). Perhaps thinking in the same associational fashion, Barnabe Barnes, in *The Devil's Charter* (1607)—the play used to date *Antony and Cleopatra* because it echoes Cleopatra's asps—used "Barbarossa" for the first time, as the name of an actual character in early modern English drama.

45. On Barbarossa and the new Battle of Actium at Prevesa, see Fernand Braudel, *The Mediterranean and the Mediterranean World in the Age of Philip II* (New York: Harper and Row, 1972), 1:116; 2:884–85, 1242 (on "the age of Barbarossa, the golden age of the Turkish armadas"); S. Soucek, "The Rise of the Barbarossas in North Africa," *Archivum Ottomanicum* 3 (1971), 238–50; John F. Guilmartin, Jr., *Gunpower and Galleys* (Cambridge: Cambridge University Press, 1974), esp. 20–26, 42–56; Palmira Brummett, *Ottoman Seapower and Levantine Diplomacy in the Age of Discovery* (Albany: State University of New York Press, 1994); *The copye of the goyng away of the chefe Captayne of the Turke called Barbarossa, oute of Fraunce* (London, ca. 1545), where he is alternately called *Barbarus*; the account in Richard Knolles, *The Generall Historie of the Turkes* (London, 1603), 686–92, which, as Guilmartin notes (47), was written "almost within living memory of Prevesa." For Minsheu, see *A Dictionarie in Spanish and English, first published into the English tongue by R. Perciuale Gent. . . . Now enlarged and amplified . . . by Iohn Minsheu Professor of Languages in London* (London, 1599).

46. The Folio and all three Quartos of *The Knight of the Burning Pestle* have "Barbarossa" (rather than the "Barberoso" it is sometimes editorially emended to) for the lines on "Barbarossa's cell, / Where no man comes but leaves his fleece behind" (3.3.28). For the reprise of the barber's "barba roja" in the allusion to the renegade corsair Barbaroja in the Captive's Tale, in relation to Cervantes' exploitation of the discursive nexus that includes barbers and beards, see Fuchs, *Passing for Spain*, 23–30.

47. See the masterful discussion of the echoes in *Antony and Cleopatra* of the tradition of Alexander and the pirate and its critique of empire itself as a form of pillaging or theft, in J. Leeds Barroll's book-length study of this play.

ALAN STEWART

Lives and Letters in Antony and Cleopatra

When Octavius Caesar receives the news of Antony's suicide, at the end of Act 5, Scene 1 of *Antony and Cleopatra*, he invites his Council of War to

> Go with me to my Tent, where you shall see
> How hardly I was drawne into this Warre,
> How calme and gentle I proceeded still
> In all my Writings. Go with me, and see
> What I can shew in this.
> (5.1.73–77)[1]

Octavius is anxious to furnish textual evidence that will support his account of his "calme and gentle" actions toward Antony and his reluctant entry into war against him. He is not alone in valuing how he will be viewed by posterity. Antony applauds the "Noblenesse in Record" (4.14.100) that suicide brings, and Cleopatra famously frets lest Rome's "quicke Comedians / Extemporally will stage vs," and, while still alive, she will be forced to witness "Some squeaking *Cleopatra* Boy my greatnesse / I'th' posture of a Whore" (5.2.215–16, 219–20). W. B. Worthen notes that "*Antony and Cleopatra* is, of course, centrally concerned with how events are written into narrative, transformed into history, literature, and myth";[2] C. C. Barfoot

From *Shakespeare Studies* 35 (2007): 77–104.

has suggested that "the chief protagonists in *Antony and Cleopatra* are above all committed to fulfilling the destiny of their names," acutely aware "of how the future will regard them when they are entirely in the past";[3] indeed, as Garrett Sullivan sums up, *Antony and Cleopatra* is "a play dominated by the retrospective characterization of people and events."[4]

In an important essay, Linda Charnes has demonstrated how, despite their shared concern for posterity, the characters' approaches to posthumous reputation—and their success in achieving it—vary widely. While noting that "all the 'actors' in this play are obsessed with playing to reviewers near and far," she argues that "they are not equally in control of the effects of their performances" since Rome is "the play's 'original' center of the narrative imperative, of the incitement to discourse that drives imperialist historiography." In her reading the play "represents the ultimate triumph of Octavius, who will later sculpt himself into the Augustus of Virgil, Horace, and Ovid," writers who had a profound influence on Renaissance readers such as Shakespeare. Not only did he have "a monumental machinery of language at his disposal," but "[a]s Augustus Caesar, Octavius was to become chief executive of a massive discursive empire, the productions of which would be referred to again and again, from Dante to Pope, as models of literary, moral, and historical 'authority.'"[5]

The historical Octavius certainly provided for posterity, not only through his patronage of great writers, but also by leaving to the safekeeping of the Vestal Virgins "a catalogue of his achievements which he wished to be inscribed on bronze tablets and set up in front of his mausoleum"; in the sixteenth century, a copy of this text was found inscribed in the temple of Rome and Augustus in Ancyra in Galatia (modern Ankara), and fragments of the text were later found in Apollonia and Antioch in Pisidia, testifying to the emperor's success in disseminating his version of his life.[6] This emphasis on documentary culture chimes with the portrait of Octavius given in one of Shakespeare's sources, Sir Thomas North's Englishing of "The Life of Octavius Caesar Augustus" by the French Calvinist Simon Goulart (included in the 1603 edition of Plutarch's *Lives*). Goulart depicts Octavius as "learned in the liberall sciences, very eloquent, and desirous to learne," a bookworm for whom reading is a favorite and enthralling pursuit. Delighting in the great authors, he would plunder their works for "sentences teaching good maners," and "hauing written them out word by word, he gaue out a copy of them to his familiars: and sent them about to the gouernours of prouinces, and to the magistrates of ROME and of other cities." He was, Goulart reveals, "not curious to set himselfe out, as litle caring to be shauen, as to weare long haire: and in stead of a looking-glasse, reading in his booke, or writing, euen whilest the Barber was trimming of him." Even "in the middest of all his infinite affairs" while at war, "he did reade, he wrote, and made orations amongst his familiars." This was no *sprezzatura* performance, but a painstakingly careful and prepared campaign. Although he "had speech at commaundement, to propound or aunswer to any thing in the field," Octavius "neuer spake vnto the Senate nor people, nor to his souldiers, but he had first written and premeditated that he would say vnto them." In order not to "deceiue his memory, or lose time in superfluous speech," the emperor "determined euer to write all that he would say" (Goulart claims he was "the first inuenter" of this habit). No matter to whom he was talking—even his wife—"he would put that downe in his writing tables, because he would speake neither more nor lesse."[7]

For Shakespeare's Octavius similarly, the image he will present to posterity lies in "all my Writings." Charnes's account assumes a triumphalist narrative not only of Octavius's imperialism, but of the Renaissance humanist claims for the continuing dominance of Roman textual achievements. But, as I shall argue, the play's attitude to such a narrative is by no means secure:[8] while Charnes's argument may be a valid claim for the lasting success of Octavius's version of historiography into the Renaissance, it fails to address the complexities of the characters' multifarious bids for posterity in *Antony and Cleopatra*. To return to the specific incident of inviting his officers into his tent to view his writings: this moment, surely a crucial point in Octavius's propaganda campaign,[9] is taken directly from Plutarch's life of Antony:

> *Caesar* [i.e., Octavius] hearing these newes [of Antony's death], straight withdrewe himselfe into a secret place of his tent, and there burst out with teares, lamenting his hard and miserable fortune, that had bene his friend and brother in law, his equall in the Empire, and companion with him in sundry great exploits and battels. Then he called for all his friends, and shewed them the letters *Antonius* had written to him, and his answers also sent him againe, during their quarrell and strife: and how fiercely and proudly the other answered him, to all iust and reasonable matters he wrote vnto him.[10]

But the play's adaptation of this passage seriously weakens the force of Octavius's appeal to his writings. Plutarch tells how Octavius produces "the letters *Antonius* had written to him," as well as "his answers also sent him againe," and depicts an ongoing, responsible epistolary exchange, as Antonius "fiercely and proudly . . . answered . . . all iust and reasonable matters [Octavius] wrote vnto him." In the play, however, we are promised only "all my Writings," only one side of a supposed correspondence. Moreover, on hearing the news, Shakespeare's Octavius does not retire to his tent to weep, but instead launches into his eulogy for Antony, only to interrupt himself:

> Heare me good Friends,
> But I will tell you at some meeter Season,
> The businesse of this man lookes out of him,
> Wee'l heare him what he sayes.
> (5.1.48–51)

The interruption, "this man," turns out to be an "*Aegyptian*," his "businesse," a message from Cleopatra. Octavius sends the man back with assurances that he will not be "vngentle" to his prisoner (5.1.60), but is struck with the idea that Cleopatra might kill herself and sends Proculeius, Gallus, and Dolabella to prevent it;[11] only then does he issue his invitation to view his "Writings." The effect of this interruption is twofold: first, it hints at the likelihood of Cleopatra's suicide in the following scene; and second, it ensures—as Octavius dispatches his men on various missions—that the writings are presented to a sadly depleted Council, probably only numbering two, Agrippa and Maecenas. It betrays the fact that Octavius's letters are going to mean little to posterity compared with the iconic act of Cleopatra's suicide.

As I shall argue, this incident is just one of a series of moments when Octavius's textual bid for history is pitted against a nontextual bid by Cleopatra. Far from leading to Octavius's posthumous dominance, *Antony and Cleopatra* consistently challenges the grounds on which Roman historiography is to be built—Octavius's "Writings," his letters—and, in so doing, offers a different, and determinedly theatrical, challenge to the sway of Roman epistolary historiography.

It is, of course, a commonplace to read *Antony and Cleopatra* as a confrontation between two civilizations, West and East, Rome and Egypt, Caesar and Cleopatra.[12] In the words of John F. Danby, Shakespeare is writing "the vast containing opposites of Rome and Egypt, the World and the Flesh,"[13] or as Maurice Charney puts it, "Rome and Egypt represent crucial moral choices, and they function as symbolic locales in a manner not unlike Henry James's Europe and America."[14] The play's imagery pits Rome against Egypt relentlessly: cold versus hot, rigour versus luxury, scarcity versus bounty, masculine versus feminine, political versus domestic, rational versus irrational, Attic versus Asiatic, *virtus* versus *voluptas*.[15] Rome takes a passive role in this battle of binaries, often suggested as the negative of Egypt, rather than being fully portrayed in its own right: Rome is not, simply because Egypt is, a place of pleasure, sensuality, sex, appetite, shifting moods, sudden violence, infinite—and destabilizing—variety. In these readings, Antony is torn between the two: though Roman-born, he is easily swayed by Egyptian pleasures—Danby memorably summarizes his choice as between "soldiering for a cynical Rome or whoring on furlough in reckless Egypt."[16] Recent criticism has successfully complicated this binary model, while still preserving its basic terms: we now see the Rome in Egypt and the Egypt in Rome, their complementarity, the specularity of the two cultures, the complex ways in which we are led to see one through the eyes of the other.[17] But an examination of the modes of communication used by the two cultures—letters, messages, messengers, the kinds of communication that by their very nature have to work *across* those cultures—provides us with a way of understanding not only the differences between Egypt and Rome, but also their points of contact, practical and ideological.[18] *Antony and Cleopatra* is a play overrun with messages and messengers,[19] and necessarily so. With its action spread across two continents, disparate events have to be reported, verbally or by letter, in order to provoke a response; its characters spend much of the play recounting, hearing of, and commenting on what has happened elsewhere. While scholars have commented on this abundance and the effect of reportage they produce,[20] the play's various letters—the letters that Octavius evokes to prove his historiographic case—have yet to be scrutinized in any detail.

Rome's power is built on its use of letters, its geographically vast empire controlled by an epistolary network.[21] Messages from Rome arrive in letter form. In Alexandria, Antony receives letters containing the details of Fulvia's death in Sicyon (1.2.123–28); he is petitioned by "the Letters too / Of many our contriuing Friends in Rome" (1.2.188–90). Silius asks Ventidius if "thou wilt write to *Anthony*" (3.1.30). Rather than mere verbal agreements, Rome insists on written, sealed contracts: we see Pompey asking that "our composi[ti]on may be written / And seal'd betweene vs" (2.6.58–59), and Enobarbus reports of Pompey's collaborators that "The other three are Sealing" (3.2.3). This Roman empire is epitomized by Octavius Caesar, significantly first encountered by the audience in the act of "*reading a Letter*" from Alexandria (1.4.0, SD), an entrance motif that is repeated later (4.1.0, SD). He sees letters as documentary evidence, orally paraphrasing to Lepidus "the newes . . . From Alexandria" (1.4.3–4) but then offering the letter containing the news in support of what he says: "You / Shall finde there a man, who is th' abstracts of all faults, / That all men follow" (1.4.8–10).[22] He uses letters to control: in planning the sea battle, he commands Taurus with written instructions: "Do not exceede / The Prescript of this Scroule" (3.8.4–5). He has respect for petitions submitted in letter form: in temporarily holding back an assault against Antony, he tells his sister Octavia that it was "your Letters did with-holde our breaking forth" (3.6.81). And, as befits a man with such investment in letters, he shows himself to be hyperefficient in matters epistolary. When he recites to Agrippa Antony's charges against him, Agrippa urges "Sir, this should be answer'd," but Octavius is a step ahead: "'Tis done already, and the Messenger gone" (3.6.31–32). He sees letters as evidence: when he turns on Lepidus, after their joint victory against Pompey, he "accuses him of Letters he had formerly wrote to *Pompey*" (3.5.9).[23] Material gains from war can be "Put . . . i'th'roll of Conquest" (5.2.180); even physical injuries take on a textual form, as he reassures his prisoner Cleopatra that "The Record of what iniuries you did vs, / Though written in our flesh, we shall remember / As things but done by chance" (5.2.117–19).

Against Rome's literate culture, Egypt is presented as predominantly oral—a choice that seems to be the playwright's, rather than an effect of dominant opinion. Indeed, discourses about Egypt circulating in the early modern period, recently surveyed by John Michael Archer, point to the respect paid to Egypt as an early, if not originary, civilization in the development of writing.[24] Philemon Holland, writing in 1603, provides a typical summation: "The wisdome and learning of the Aegyptians hath bene much recommended unto us by ancient writers, and not without good cause: considering that *Aegypt* hath bene the source and fountaine from whence have flowed into the world arts and liberall sciences, as a man may gather by the testimony of the first Poets and philosophers that ever were."[25]

Shakespeare's Cleopatra, however, is seen to prefer spoken messages to letters. For the queen, news arrives in bodily form, moving violently from the throat to the ear: "Ramme thou thy fruitefull tidings in mine eares" (2.5.24); "Powre out the packe of matter to mine eare" (2.5.54). She refuses to *hear* that Antony is dead: "If thou say so Villaine, thou kil'st thy Mistris" (2.5.26–27), "The Gold I giue thee, will I melt and powr / Downe thy ill vttering throate" (2.5.34–35). The messenger pleads to be *heard*: "Good Madam heare me . . . Wilt please you heare me?" (2.5.35, 41). By contrast to the Roman emphasis on written and sealed contracts, for Cleopatra (as Antony acknowledges) a "Kingly Seale, / And plighter of high hearts" is not made of wax and affixed to a letter, but "My play-fellow, your hand" (3.13.130–31).

Cleopatra's understanding of news in bodily terms renders her incapable of distinguishing the message from its physical vessel, the messenger. When news arrives of Antony's marriage to Octavia, she lectures the messenger:

> Though it be honest, it is neuer good
> To bring bad newes: giue to a gratious Message
> An host of tongues, but let ill tydings tell
> Themselues, when they be felt.
> (2.5.85–88)

Her analysis is borne out by her behavior, as the messenger bears the brunt of her anger at the message he bears. Even before he makes the announcement, Cleopatra has said that his reward will depend on the news he brings:

> I haue a mind to strike thee ere thou speak'st:
> Yet if thou say *Anthony* liues, 'tis well,
> Or friends with *Caesar*, or not Captiue to him,
> Ile set thee in a shower of Gold, and haile
> Rich Pearles vpon thee.
> (2.5.42–46)

Ultimately, of course, she "*Strikes him downe*" (2.5.61, SD) calling down "The most infectious Pestilence vpon thee" (2.5.61); she "*Strikes him*" (2.5.62, SD) again, and "*hales him vp and downe*" (2.5.64, SD), claiming she'll "spurne thine eyes / Like balls before me: Ile vnhaire thy head, / Thou shalt be whipt with Wyer, and stew'd in brine, / Smarting in lingring pickle" (2.5.63–66). Finally she "*Draw[s] a knife*" (2.5.73, SD) and the messenger flees. "Gratious Madam," he claims, "I that do bring the newes, made not the match. / . . . What meane you Madam, I haue made no fault" (2.5.66–67, 74). But for Cleopatra, there is no distinction: he is not merely the carrier of written news, but the embodiment of the news itself.

Although this binary of literate, letter-bound Rome versus oral, physical Egypt is attractive, strictly dichotomous models of message-bearing are, perforce, impossible to sustain, since the carrying of messages is by its nature transactive, moving not only within a single culture, but *across* the play's two cultures. So Cleopatra is shown as literate: when Antony leaves her, she proves her love by twice calling for her writing implements: "Inke and paper *Charmian*. . . . Get me Inke and Paper, / he shall haue euery day a seuerall greeting, or Ile vnpeople Egypt" (1.5.68, 79–81). Once separated geographically, Egypt seems to engage in "Roman" letter writing. But, despite her intentions, there is nothing in the text to suggest that Cleopatra ever does write a letter. She certainly sends an army of messengers to her beloved, asking Alexas "Met'st thou my Posts?" "I Madam," he answers, "twenty seuerall Messengers. / Why do you send so thicke?" (1.5.64–6).[26] The queen replies portentously, "Who's borne that day, when I forget to send to *Anthonie*, shall dye a Begger" (1.5.66–68). Later, having beaten Antony's messenger, Cleopatra again appears to resort to letter writing. Plying the hapless messenger with gold, she informs him that

> I will employ thee backe againe: I finde thee
> Most fit for businesse. Go, make thee ready,
> Our Letters are prepar'd.
> (3.3.35–37)

But it turns out that in fact the letters are not prepared—or at least that Cleopatra is not finished with them. Within ten lines, she announces that she has "one thing more to aske him yet good *Charmian*: but 'tis no matter, thou shalt bring him to me where I will write; all may be well enough" (3.3.44–46). Even in her final moments, when she produces for Caesar "the breefe: of Money, Plate, & Iewels / I am possest of," assuring him "'tis exactly valewed, / Not petty things admitted" (5.2.137–39), it turns out to be incomplete, and even her treasurer will not endorse it. These incidents show Cleopatra equipped with the understanding and skills to enter into the Roman epistolary world, but temperamentally unsuited to it, refusing to respect its rules.

Antony, as one might expect, is depicted as torn between these two cultures. In Plutarch's account, Antony, in common with every other major political player of his day, is involved in extensive epistolary correspondence, and his affair with Cleopatra is kept afloat during lengthy periods of separation through letters, sometimes to his detriment: Antony is specifically charged "That diuerse times sitting in his tribunall and chaire of state, giuing audience to all Kings and Princes: he had receiued loue letters from *Cleopatra*, written in tables of Onyx or Christall, & that he had red them, sitting in his Imperiall seat."[27] It's a great image, but one that Shakespeare chooses not to use: his Antony does not read love letters. In other early modern accounts, by contrast, Antony makes good use of letters. Samuel Brandon's dramatization of his relationship with Octavia hinges on the fact that Antony halts Octavia's journey to him at Athens by sending her letters; Brandon even composed a fictional pair of letters between husband and wife on this emotionally fraught occasion, while Samuel Daniel similarly confected "A Letter sent from Octauia to her husband Marcus Antonius into Egypt."[28]

In the play, however, when in Cleopatra's company, Antony is seen to opt out of, if not refuse completely, his native Roman letter-writing culture. Octavius complains to Antony that "I wrote to you, when rioting in Alexandria you / Did pocket vp my Letters: and with taunts / Did gibe my Misiue out of audience" (2.2.76–79). Although Antony weakly objects that Octavius's messenger had violated protocol by entering without being properly admitted,[29] Octavius's anger is warranted: Antony publicly humiliated his messenger (and therefore Octavius himself), and was seen to "pocket vp" the letters instead of affording them his attention. Antony's decline from Roman etiquette is measured by his performance in diplomatic relations with Caesar. He decides to send "our Schoolemaster" (3.11.72) as an ambassador, a choice that Dolabella correctly interprets as "An argument that he is pluckt, when hither / He sends so poore a Pinnion of his Wing, / Which had superfluous Kings for Messengers, / Not many Moones gone by" (3.12.3–6). The schoolmaster-ambassador himself expresses amazement and shame at his appointment: "Such as I am, I come from *Anthony*: / I was of late as petty to his ends, / As is the Morne-dew on the Mertle leafe / To his grand Sea" (3.12.7–10). As an ambassador, he is shockingly incompetent, presenting a verbal petition and then immediately, in the same sentence, assuming it will not be granted: Antony "Requires to liue in Egypt, which not granted / He Lessons his Requests" (3.12.12–13). It is only when the schoolmaster has returned with Caesar's denials that Antony returns to writing letters, as he challenges Caesar (for the second time) to single combat:

> I dare him therefore
> To lay his gay Comparisons a-part,
> And answer me declin'd, Sword against Sword,
> Our selues alone: Ile write it:
> (3.13.25–28)

Presumably this is the letter that Caesar is shown reading at the beginning of act 4 ("*Enter Caesar, Agrippa, & Mecenas with his Army, Caesar reading a Letter*" [4.1.0, SD]), as he complains

> He calles me Boy, and chides as he had power
> To beate me out of Egypt. My Messenger
> He hath whipt with Rods, dares me to personal Combat.
> *Caesar* to *Anthony*.
> (4.1.1–4)

Antony has by this point fallen away from epistolary protocols, allowing his prejudice against Octavius's youth to find its way into a letter (which Octavius characteristically sees as evidence), as well as physically abusing his letter-bearer.

But this anti-Roman attitude is by no means consistent. Although enthralled by Cleopatra, Antony necessarily remains part of the Roman epistolary world. As we have seen, he receives news of his wife Fulvia's death by letter, and petitions from his friends in Rome to return home. After his defeat at sea, Antony dismisses his attendants, but uses letters to recommend them to posts elsewhere:

> Friends be gone, you shall
> Haue Letters from me to some Friends, that will
> Sweepe your way for you.
> (3.11.15–17)

It is revealed in passing that Antony is in correspondence with Octavius: when challenged that he was complicit with attacks against Octavius by his brother and wife, Antony points out that "Of this, my Letters / Before did satisfie you" (2.2.56–57).

Rome and Egypt, then, can be seen to have different attitudes to the bearing of messages, Rome fixating on written epistolary documentation, Egypt preferring the personally conveyed oral message, although both civilizations are capable—perhaps through necessity—of drawing on the other's techniques. In terms of the posterity of historiography, Rome might seem to have the upper hand here, its messages preservable in written form while Egypt's are by their nature transient. But this notion is not allowed to pass unchallenged. In the figure of Antony—the Roman in Egypt, ostensibly rejecting but often complicit in the culture of Roman letters—we are presented with an uncertain resistance to Roman historiography, focused on his claim to be a Roman, at the moment of his death.

* * *

In Antony's final words he paints a self-portrait of how he should be remembered:

> The miserable change now at my end,
> Lament nor sorrow at: but please your thoughts
> In feeding them with those my former Fortunes
> Wherein I liued. The greatest Prince o'th' world,
> The Noblest: and do now not basely dye,
> Not Cowardly put off my Helmet to
> My Countreyman. A Roman, by a Roman
> Valiantly vanquish'd. Now my Spirit is going,
> I can no more.
> (4.15.53–61)

According to Antony, he did not submit to a fellow "Countreyman," but was "Valiantly vanquished," in the only way a Roman should be, by an equal, a Roman. The "Countreyman" must be Octavius Caesar, whose control he has escaped, since the two Romans are both Antony, vanquisher and vanquished—he has already claimed that "Not *Caesars* Valour hath o'rethrowne *Anthony*, / But *Anthonie*'s hath Triumpht on it selfe," and Cleopatra has confirmed approvingly that "none but *Anthony* should conquer *Anthony*" (4.15.15–18). Self-killing is, of course, understood by the Renaissance as the classic Roman gesture of courage,[30] and as he contemplates the act in a rare soliloquy, Antony is drawn, uncharacteristically, to a Roman image of contract: "Seale then, and all is done" (4.14.50). Yet this confident assertion is belied by what the audience has seen—Antony first asking his servant to kill him, then witnessing that servant bravely kill himself rather than execute his master, then botching his own suicide, before vainly pleading with his guards to finish the job, and finally being hauled up to his deathbed by (foreign) women. And there is something very wrong with this sentence: who is Antony's "Countreyman" if not a Roman? If the countryman is not a Roman, then what is Antony?

The first official report of Antony's demise, given by Decretas to Octavius explains that he died,

> Not by a publike minister of Iustice,
> Nor by a hyred Knife, but that selfe-hand
> Which writ his Honor in the Acts it did,
> Hath with the Courage which the heart did lend it,
> Splitted the heart.
> (5.1.20–24)

The awkward reference to Antony's "selfe-hand" might alert us to a problem. Hands are prominently portrayed throughout the play, shaken, kissed, read by a soothsayer.[31] But the lovers show a surprising lack of control over their own hands. When Antony exclaims, "[Cleopatra] hath betraid me, And shall dye the death," Mardian replies, "Death of one person, can be paide but once, / And that she ha's discharg'd. What thou would'st do / Is done vnto thy hand" (4.14.26–29). The phrasing here is odd, but telling: Mardian means that the action Antony would do (raise his hand to kill Cleopatra) has already been done; but in so doing, the act has been done "vnto thy hand," almost as if an attack *on* his hand. When Cleopatra goes to stab herself, she exclaims, "Quicke, quicke, good hands" (5.2.38), but Caesar's man Proculeius is too fast, and disarms her. And, in this case too, the hand is not under Antony's control: although Decretas talks of "that selfe-hand / Which writ his Honor," the audience already knows that Antony's first impulse is to use someone else's hand to do the deed: the hand of Eros.

Antony's confident assertion that he is "A Roman, by a Roman / Valiantly vanquish'd," and Decretas's report that he was killed by "that selfe-hand / Which writ his Honor in the Acts it did," need to be tempered by the knowledge of his call on Eros: to what extent is Antony really vanquished by a Roman, or by his self-hand? Significantly, even before his suicide, Antony's sense of a discrete self is already shaken: indeed, the scene opens with him asking his servant Eros the bewildering question "*Eros*, thou yet behold'st me?" (4.14.1). Although Eros answers in the affirmative, Antony objects that, as when we see clouds that bear a certain shape, "now thy Captaine is / Euen such a body: Heere I am *Antony*, / Yet cannot hold this visible shape (my Knaue)" (4.14.12–14) as a result of Cleopatra's betrayal. In his mind, Antony cannot be seen, yet Eros assures him that *he* can see Antony: Eros's sight is required in order for Antony to be visible. Antony has some comfort for his servant:

> Nay, weepe not gentle *Eros*, there is left vs
> Our selues to end our selues.
> (4.14.21–22)

Antony's meaning, as will soon become explicit, is that he will end his own life. But his phrasing, using the plural form "Our," suggests something else: that it will take both of them to kill themselves. Antony's death then is not at the hand of Antony, but at the combined hand of Antony and Eros; his "selfe-hand" is not his own, but theirs jointly.

If Antony's "selfe-hand" is not his own, to what extent is he killed by a Roman? There is another element to Eros that urges us to question this. The incident appears, at first sight, to be taken directly from Plutarch:

> Now he had a man of his called *Eros*, whom he loued and trusted much, and whom he had long before caused to sweare vnto him, that he should kill him when he did command him: and then he willed him to keepe his promise. His man drawing his sword, lift it vp as though he had meant to haue striken his master: but turning his head at one side, he thrust his sword into himself, and fell downe dead at his maisters foote. Then said *Antonius*: o noble *Eros*, I thanke thee for this, and it is valiantly done of thee, to shew me what I should do to my selfe, which thou couldest not do for me. Therewithall he tooke his sword, and thrust it into his belly, and so fell downe vpon a litle bed.[32]

However, as Leeds Barroll has demonstrated so convincingly,[33] in creating the man whom Antony asks to kill him, Shakespeare goes beyond Plutarch's account. Rather than the vagueness of the "long before . . . promise," whereby Eros inexplicably agreed to kill Antony if required, Shakespeare has Antony recalling a specific moment—"When I did make thee free, swor'st thou not then / To do this when I bad thee?" (4.14.82–83)—that makes Eros a freedman, an enfranchised slave.

Where does this notion of Eros as a freedman come from? Thomas North's translation describes him merely as "a man of his," while Jacques Amyot's French makes him "vn sien seruiteur."[34] In other late Elizabethan adaptations of the moment, Mary, Countess of Pembroke seems to follow North in referring to "*Eros* his man" in her closet verse drama *Tragedie of Anthonie* (1592);[35] the original of her translation, Robert Garnier's *M. Antoine, Tragedie* (1578), follows Amyot in using "Eros son seruiteur."[36] These epithets—"his man" and "his servant" (serviteur)—certainly seem to be standard for Eros: we might add contemporary allusions by Sir Richard Barckley in his 1598 *A Discovrse of the Felicitie of Man* to "his man *Eros*";[37] and Robert Allott, in his 1599 *Wits Theater of the little World*, where Eros is described as "the seruant of Antonius."[38] (Another variant from the Herbert circle, Samuel Brandon's 1598 *The Tragicomoedi of the vertuous Octauia* omits Eros.)[39] Plutarch's Greek, however, has something very different: Eros as "αυτον πιοτς"—a trusted household slave of his, and emphatically not an απελεντηεον, one of his "infranchised bondmen." Shakespeare's Eros is thus notably different from other contemporary versions of the story—but why? Barroll's inquiry is undertaken in the cause of dating the play, largely in relation to the 1607 revision of Samuel Daniel's closet drama *Cleopatra*—Daniel also makes Eros "his late infranchis'd seruant," suggesting he may have seen or read Shakespeare's play.[40] But what does it mean that Eros should be an enfranchised slave? A freedman was never fully free, but bound to the conditions of the freedman's oath (*iusirandum liberti*), by which the freedman might perform certain *operae* or services, perhaps a weekly ration of domestic or skilled labor, or working as a generalized procurator, managing the master's affairs.[41] But beyond this, the *operae* might include certain specific tasks—and it is this arrangement to which Antony refers.

In rendering Eros a freedman, Shakespeare draws (as Barroll suggests) not only on Plutarch's Eros but also on other characters in Plutarch's *Lives*. The first is Rhamnus, another servant to whom Antony turned in a low moment during the Parthian campaign: "*Antonius* called for one *Rhamnus*, one of his slaues infranchised that was of his guard, and made him giue him his faith that he would thrust his sword through him when he would bid him, and cut off his head, because he might not be taken aliue of his enemies, nor knowne when he were dead."[42] This identification of Rhamnus with Eros is strengthened by the fact that Antony urges Eros to "Draw that thy honest Sword, which thou hast worne / Most vsefull for thy Country" (4.14.80–81), implying that Eros has been a soldier, and that Eros himself alludes to the Parthian campaign in this final scene: "Shall I do that which all the Parthian Darts, / (Though Enemy) lost ayme, and could not" (4.14.71–72).[43] In

Barroll's argument, Shakespeare's Eros "has in effect taken on the characteristics of Plutarch's suicide helper *B*—Rhamnus from the Plutarchan Parthian expedition . . . And the manumission (from Plutarch's Rhamnus) has become so significant in Shakespeare that it is part of the structure of Antony's effort to persuade Eros—a persuasion, indeed, telling enough to force Eros either to honor Antony's plea or to kill himself to avoid the debt."[44]

Second, Eros recalls the man who slays Cassius "at his earnest request . . . a faithfull seruant of his owne called *Pindarus*, whom he had infranchised."[45] Elsewhere, Plutarch elaborates that Pindarus was "one of his freed bondmen, whom he reserued euer for such a pinch, since the cursed battell of the PARTHIANS"; Pindarus decapitates Cassius as ordered, "but after that time *Pindarus* was neuer seene more. Whereupon, some tooke occasion to say that he had slaine his maister without his commaundement."[46] In dramatizing this incident in *Julius Caesar*, as Barroll notes "Shakespeare altered this sequence,"[47] making the enfranchisement a delayed reward contingent on the killing:

> In Parthia did I take thee Prisoner,
> And then I swore thee, sauing of thy life,
> That whatsoeuer I did bid thee do,
> Thou should'st attempt it. Come now, keepe thine oath,
> Now be a Free-man, and with this good Sword
> That ran through *Caesars* bowels, search this bosome.
> (5.3.37–42)

Having performed the act, Pindarus meditates on his fate: "So, I am free, / Yet would not so haue beene / Durst I haue done my will," and decides to go into exile "Where neuer Roman shall take note of him" (5.3.47–50). The Cassius-Pindarus narrative, with its coercive promises and its shameful outcome, makes clear the dangerous bargain that is involved in this claim on the freedman, a bargain repeated in the Antony-Eros encounter. As Antony notes,

> When I did make thee free, swor'st thou not then
> To do this when I bad thee? Do it at once,
> Or thy precedent Seruices are all
> But accidents vnpurpos'd.
> (4.14.82–85)

Antony claims that unless Eros obeys, his previous *operae* are rendered redundant, the terms of his freedom violated.

In both cases, the bargaining of Cassius and Antony belies the supposed freedom of their erstwhile slaves as, despite their enfranchisement, Pindarus and Rhamnus—and, it follows, therefore Eros—are shown to be still committed to certain formidable duties for their masters. Elsewhere, Antony has invoked another freedman over whom he exerts control. After beating him, he tells Caesar's messenger Thidias to

> Get thee backe to *Caesar*,
> Tell him thy entertainment: looke thou say
> He makes me angry with him. For he seemes
> Proud and disdainfull, harping on what I am,
> Not what he knew I was. . . .
> . . . .
> If he mislike.
> My speech, and what is done, tell him he has
> *Hiparchus*, my enfranched Bondman, whom
> He may at pleasure whip, or hang, or torture,
> As he shall like to quit me.[48]
> (3.13.144–48, 152–56)

This Hipparchus is introduced by Plutarch as "the first of all his infranchised bondmen that reuolted from him, and yeelded vnto *Caesar*, and afterwards went and dwelt at CORINTH."[49] It is clear from Antony's speech, however, that he still recognizes Hipparchus as his own to punish, despite his doubly removed status—freed from bondage and then revolted from Antony's mastery. This notion, thus insistently made, that manumission does not fully free an ex-slave, is betrayed in Samuel Daniel's 1607 revision of his *Cleopatra*, which critics have seen as drawing on Shakespeare's play. Following Eros's suicide, Daniel's Antony exclaims

> O *Eros*, . . . and hath fortune quite
> Forsaken me? must I b'outgone in all?
> What? can I not by loosing get a right?
> Shall I not haue the vpper hand to fall
> In death? must both a woman, and a slaue
> The start before me of this glory haue?[50]

Antony objects to the fact that two lesser beings, two non-Roman citizens in the form of a foreign woman (Cleopatra) and a slave (Eros), have beaten him to the virtuous Roman act of self-killing. As Eros has just been introduced by Daniel as "his late infranchis'd seruant,"[51] this seems inconsistent, but the implication here must be that Daniel's Antony is registering the notion that a slave is never fully manumitted—and equally that a freedman is never considered fully a Roman citizen.

But there is another aspect to Antony's relationship to Eros, and it takes us back directly to Antony's relationship to Roman letters. Whereas in Plutarch's *Lives* we are introduced to Eros only at the moment of Antony's attempted suicide, in *Antony and Cleopatra* he has made a series of important entries.[52] Eros first appears on stage in 3.5 in a brief encounter with Enobarbus, where, although his social function is not clear, he is seen to be in possession of "strange Newes come" (3.5.2), knowledge of Antony's whereabouts and action, and the detail that Octavius has accused Lepidus "of Letters he had formerly wrote to *Pompey*" (3.5.9–10). His second appearance is in 3.11, immediately following Antony's ignominious defeat at sea. In Plutarch's account, it is "*Cleopatraes* women," sometime afterward, who "first brought *Antonius* and *Cleopatra* to speake together, and afterwards to sup and lie together."[53] In the play, the scene occurs immediately after Antony has dismissed his attendants, and it is not solely Cleopatra's women who bring about the reconciliation. Eros enters alongside Charmian and Iras, leading Cleopatra; it is here his role to bring the two together, encouraging first the queen ("Nay gentle Madam, to him, comfort him," [3.11.25]) then the despondent general ("See you heere, Sir? . . . Sir, sir . . . The Queene my Lord, the Queene . . . Most Noble Sir arise, the Queene approaches . . . Sir, the Queene" [3.11.30, 42, 46, 50]). It is still not specified who Eros is, but unlike Cleopatra's women, he seems to be able to talk to both parties. His next appearance is in 4.4, as Antony calls for his servant to prepare him for battle: "*Eros*, mine Armour *Eros* . . . *Eros*, come mine Armour *Eros* . . . Come good Fellow, put thine Iron on" (4.4.1, 2, 3). This scene places Eros in competition with Cleopatra: Antony's calls for Eros are at first interrupted by Cleopatra's pleas for him to "Sleepe a little" (4.4.1) and then by her offers to help him arm. Although at first her attempts seem misplaced, soon Antony is impressed: "Thou fumblest *Eros*, and my Queenes a Squire / More tight at this, then thou: Dispatch" (4.4.14–15). Eros is here portrayed as the devoted servant, intent on arming his master before thinking of himself: when Antony orders him to "Go, put on thy defences," Eros puts him off with a "Briefely Sir" (4.4.10).

The servant's name, of course, is serendipitous,[54] and it is not left unexploited throughout these scenes. Antony constantly *names* Eros, often calling for him urgently—five times as Eros arms him (4.4), no fewer than fifteen times in the suicide scene (4.14). If Eros equals Love, however, there is no single way of reading that love. In bringing together Antony and Cleopatra following the sea disaster, Eros may be seen as pandering their affair, assuring heterosexual love; but it could equally be argued that Eros is in competition with Cleopatra for Antony's love, as they squabble over who should arm him. Both readings are possible in Antony's distracted speech, as his thoughts of the dead Cleopatra are interrupted by his calls for Eros:

> *Eros*? I come my Queene. *Eros*? Stay for me,
> Where Soules do couch on Flowers, wee'l hand in hand,
> And with our sprightly Port make the Ghostes gaze:
> *Dido*, and her *Æneas* shall want Troopes,
> And all the haunt be ours. Come *Eros*, *Eros*.
> (4.14.51–55)

But perhaps the most telling scene of their relationship arrives when Antony realizes that Enobarbus has gone, and he orders Eros to "send his Treasure after" him (4.5.12):

> write to him,
> (I will subscribe) gentle adieu's, and greetings;
> Say, that I wish he neuer finde more cause
> To change a Master. Oh my Fortunes haue
> Corrupted honest men. Dispatch *Enobarbus* [or *Eros*?][55]
> (4.5.13–17)

Antony expects Eros to draft the letter, according to his general instructions ("Say, that I wish . . ."), and he will provide the subscription and salutation. Clearly Eros is here functioning as Antony's secretary, a position in which many freedmen continued to serve their erstwhile masters: the most famous is probably Cicero's Tiro, who dealt with his master's finances, appeased his creditors, revised his accounts, supervised his gardens and building operations, and acted as his confidant, secretary, and literary collaborator.[56] To early modern readers, the secretary suggested a role of unparalleled intimacy based not only on physical proximity (although Eros's duties in arming and disarming Antony also testify to such a relationship) but on the sharing of intellectual knowledge and secrets. In his 1592 discourse "Of the Partes, Place and Office of a Secretorie," Angel Day insists that the secretary is not made merely by "the praisable endeuour or abilitie of well writing or ordering the pen," but rather by his relationship with his master: his position thus "containeth the chiefest title of credite, and place of greatest assurance, in respect of the neerenesse and affinitie they haue of *Trust, Regard*, & *Fidelitie*, each with the other, by great conceyte and discretion."[57] Beyond this, and worryingly, the secretary writes both for and—as in this case—*as* his master, as he composes his words. As Richard Rambuss has shown, "Secretaryship . . . does not simply mean transcribing, copying down the words of the master; rather it entails becoming the simulacrum of the master himself."[58] We see this phenomenon at work in Timon of Athens' steward Flavius, who preempts an order by Timon to go to the Senate and drum up cash by asserting,

> I haue beene bold
> (For that I knew it the most generall way)
> To them, to vse your Signet, and your Name,
> But they do shake their heads, and I am heere
> No richer in returne.
> (2.2.204–8)

It is not clear from Flavius's statement whether he has written a letter from Timon, signing it as his master ("your Name") and sealing it with his master's seal ring ("your Signet"), or whether he has merely spoken to the senators in his master's name, producing the signet ring as proof that he was speaking with Timon's authority. But whatever the case, it is beyond doubt that Flavius is comfortable and probably accustomed to speaking, writing and sealing as his master.

The letter-writing scene is unique to Shakespeare's play, without parallel in any of the possible sources. So why does Shakespeare make Eros a letter-writing secretary? I suggest that the scene is a deliberate foreshadowing of the moment when Antony will demand Eros's hand to perform another task on his behalf—his suicide. The link between these two secretarial, manual functions, writing and self-killing, is made explicit in Decretas's report: Antony is killed, he claims, by "that selfe-hand / Which writ his Honor in the Acts it did." By turning to the trope of a handwritten honor, Decretas unconsciously draws attention to the fact that Antony does not do his own writing, and perhaps he did not write his own honor. Antony's hand is shown not to be his own. Here, the contrast with Caesar is vivid: Octavius's focus on writing is entirely personal—he reads, gathers "sentences" from the great authors, writes on tables to prepare his speeches, and writes his own letters. Antony's writing, his very hand, conversely, is the joint work of himself and Eros, and therefore his self-killing cannot be the work of his hand alone. He knows this, and so he calls on his secretary to kill him; but ultimately, the true secretary—the man whose hand is his master's—cannot be his master's hand in this task. Eros thus refuses to do the ultimate secretarial act: to use his (self-)hand against his master's body.

In building the servant Eros into both a freedman and a secretary, the play deliberately complicates Antony's actions to the point that they no longer mean what he claims they do. The impossible dual place of the secretary—the servant who is also "the simulacrum of the master"—is imposed on the impossible dual place of the freedman, slave and Roman. Antony's "selfe-hand" is no longer his, and his position as a Roman, so much a part of his self-vision, is ultimately not assured.

* * *

If Octavius's Roman historiography fails, and even Antony's very status within Roman historiography is compromised, then how does Cleopatra fare? At the climax of *Antony and Cleopatra*, there is a missing letter. Plutarch relates how after a countryman had delivered a basket and figs, and Cleopatra had dined,

> she sent a certaine table written and sealed vnto *Caesar*, and commaunded them all to go out of the tombes where she was, but the two women, then she shut the doores to her. *Caesar* when he receiued this table, and began to reade her lamentation and petition, requesting him that he would let her be buried with *Antonius*, found straight what she meant, and thought to haue gone thither himselfe: howbeit, he sent one before in all hast that might be, to see what it was.

However, by that time, it was too late: despite running "in all hast possible," Caesar's messengers "found *Cleopatra* starke dead."[59] The play dispenses with Cleopatra's sealed letter to Caesar. Instead, "*an Ægyptian*" (5.1.48, SD) is sent with a verbal message from Cleopatra asking for Caesar's "instruction, / That she preparedly may frame her selfe / To'th' way shee's forc'd too" (5.2.54–56). The omission of this letter runs true to form with the play's depiction of Cleopatra as preferring verbal to epistolary communication, and, in that way, it might be said to support the notion that oral Egypt is presented in opposition to literate Rome. But the omission of the letter—or more precisely, the introduction of the Egyptian messenger—can be seen to challenge the efficacy of Rome's documentary culture.

In Shakespeare's treatment, it is this Egyptian's oral message that serves to interrupt Octavius's invitation to his men to view his writings. As noted earlier, the message alerts Octavius that Cleopatra may harm herself, and he gives orders for his men to prevent her doing so, not out of humane compassion, but, once again, with an eye to posterity:

giue her what comforts
The quality of her passion shall require;
Least in her greatnesse, by some mortall stroke
She do defeate vs. For her life in Rome,
Would be eternall in our Triumph.
(5.1.62–66)

If a living, captured Cleopatra in Rome will be eternal in Caesar's triumph (as Cleopatra also imagines), then it follows that her death in Egypt will be eternal in Caesar's defeat. This defeat is enacted when Dolabella reaches Cleopatra's monument, and a guard enters, noisily "*rustling in*" (5.2.318, SD) to announce that "*Caesar* hath sent—" The sentence is unfinished, and in the First Folio unpunctuated (modern editors tend to add a dash), and Charmian finishes the sentence with the sardonic "Too slow a Messenger" (5.2.320). Here, the limitations of Caesar's network of messengers are revealed. While Caesar hoped to clinch the narrative by showing his letter-book to his Council of War, instead the Romans march into the monument to examine the corpses, hoping to understand the cause of death, while Caesar pays tribute to the future longevity of this couple's memory:

No Graue vpon the earth shall clip in it
A payre so famous: high euents as these
Strike those that make them: and their Story is
No lesse in pitty, then his Glory which
Brought them to be lamented.
(5.2.358–62)

Linda Charnes reads this as the crowning glory of the Roman success in historiography: "Upon learning of Cleopatra's suicide, Octavius understands immediately the political uses to which he can put a mythologized 'Antony and Cleopatra' . . . He swiftly translates them from rebellious figures who escaped his control and punishment into legendary lovers. . . . Antony and Cleopatra can become epic lovers in the world's report only once Octavius has full control of the machinery of reproduction. Only then can they be put to historiographic use."[60] But to what extent is this myth of Antony and Cleopatra as eternally embracing "legendary lovers" truly Octavius's impulse? The notion that the queen "shall be buried by her *Anthony*" (5.2.357) is the request contained in her sealed letter; Antony explicitly determined to "bee / A Bride-groome in my death, and run intoo't / As to a Louers bed" (4.14.100–102). The historical Octavius ignored Antony and Cleopatra in his autobiography: the queen disappears altogether, and

Antony is evoked only obliquely as "the tyranny of a faction" that Octavius suppressed in his youth.[61] But Shakespeare's Octavius, far from having "full control of the machinery of reproduction" as he hoped to have with the letters in his tent, is forced to take Cleopatra and Antony's version of events; his only power is to enshrine it in Roman historiography.

In the play's final two scenes, then, we see competing memorializing impulses played out, in ways that insist again on opposing values of Rome and Egypt, as Shakespeare depicts them. For Octavius Caesar, the history of Antony and Cleopatra will be written from the epistolary evidence of his correspondence with Mark Antony. For Cleopatra, the history will be inspired by the physical tableau of the almost perfect female corpses, and the oral testimonies of the man who last saw her alive, her guard. And, as Rosalie Colie observes, Cleopatra gets the last laugh: while Rome may seem to dominate the play—a play that "begins and ends with expressions of the Roman point of view," nevertheless, "seen from another angle, Egypt commands the play, where the action begins and ends and where all the major episodes take place."[62] Colie's formulation implicitly contrasts Roman "expressions" versus Egyptian "action," Octavius's words versus Cleopatra's gestures. In this, Colie subscribes tacitly to the oft-asserted association between Cleopatra and the theater, in which commonplace antitheatrical prejudice is deployed against the exotic, foreign, stagy queen.[63] Here, however, that same Egyptian theatricality becomes an effective challenge to Roman historiography and, within the terms of the play, may be said to defeat it.[64] For the showing of these "Writings" is superseded by the call to see the queen: the play ends not in Octavius's tent, with the viewing of his letters, but—through heeding the oral message of her Egyptian servant—inside Cleopatra's monument. In allowing that image to occupy the final moments of the play, Shakespeare—or perhaps theater itself—comes down on the side of Egyptian spectacle, and against Roman letters.

Notes

I am grateful to James Shapiro and Garrett Sullivan for their comments on an earlier version of this article.

1. Unless otherwise noted, quotations of Shakespeare's plays follow the text *The First Folio of Shakespeare*, prep. Charlton Hinman (New York: W. W. Norton, 1968), a facsimile edition of *Mr. William Shakespeares Comedies, Histories & Tragedies* (London, 1623). They are cross-referenced to act, scene, line numbers keyed to *Antony and Cleopatra*, ed. John Wilders (New York: Routledge, Arden Shakespeare, 3rd series, 1998); *Julius Caesar*, ed. David Daniell (New York: Thomson, Arden Shakespeare, 3rd series, 1998); and *Timon of Athens*, ed. H. J. Oliver (New York: Methuen, Arden Shakespeare, 2nd series, 1969).

2. W. B. Worthen, "The Weight of Antony: Staging 'Character' in *Antony and Cleopatra*," *Studies in English Literature, 1500–1900* 26 (1986): 297.

3. C. C. Barfoot, "News from the Roman Empire: Hearsay, Soothsay, Myth and History in *Antony and Cleopatra*," in *Reclamations of Shakespeare*, ed. A. J. Hoenselaars (Atlanta, GA: Rodopi, 1994), 113. I am grateful to Garrett Sullivan for bringing Professor Barfoot's useful essay to my attention.

4. Garrett A. Sullivan, "'My oblivion is a very Antony'," in *Memory and Forgetting in English Renaissance Drama* (Cambridge: Cambridge University Press, 2005), 89.

5. Linda Charnes, "Spies and Whispers: Exceeding Reputation in *Antony and Cleopatra*," in *Notorious Identity: Materializing the Subject in Shakespeare* (Cambridge, MA: Harvard University Press, 1993), 106, 107.

6. P. A. Brunt and J. M. Moore, eds., introduction to *Res gestae divi Augusti: The Achievements of the Divine Augustus* (Oxford: Oxford University Press, 1967), 1–16.

7. Simon Goulart, "The Life of Octaius Caesar Augustus," in *The Lives of Epaminondas, of Philip of Macedon, of Dionysivs the Elder, and of Octavivs Caesar Avgvstvs: collected out of good Authors; Also the liues of nine excellent Chieftaines of warre, taken out of Latine from Emylivs Probvs*, trans. Thomas North (London: Richard Field, 1603), e4r–g4r (51–75) at e4v–e5r (52–53).

8. Here I share common ground with Ronald Macdonald, who argues that Shakespeare indulged in "an historical questioning of classicism in general, the peculiar prestige accorded it in learned Renaissance circles, and its centrality for European culture. He came to see that the centrality of classicism was not a 'natural' phenomenon at all, but a cultural and historical construct, and one, like all constructs, embodied assumptions of an ideological kind, about what we know and how, about the nature of history, about stability and order, and perhaps most of all, assumptions about language and its role in shaping the very assumptions we so often take for fact." Ronald R. Macdonald, "Playing Till Doomsday: Interpreting *Antony and Cleopatra*," *English Literary Renaissance* 15 (1985): 79.

9. Worthen, one of the few critics to comment on these letters, argues similarly: "Throughout the play, Caesar relies on narrative—the 'news' of Alexandria, Antony's 'reported' (I.iv.67) exploits in the Alps, perhaps even in the 'writings' he offers in his defense after Antony's death (V.i.76)—to characterize his general, means which enable Caesar more easily to assimilate Antony's actions to an interpretive text: Antony becomes the 'abstract of all faults / That men follow' (I.iv.9–10). Caesar's characterization of Antony consistently privileges the absent 'character' of history over the present 'character' of performance." "The Weight of Antony," 299.

10. Plutarch, *The Lives of the Noble Grecians and Romaines, compared together . . . Hereunto are affixed the liues of Epaminados . . . etc* [by Simon Goulart], trans. Thomas North (London: Richard Field for Thomas Wight, 1603), Llll 5v (946).

11. He later remembers that he has already sent Dolabella, too late, to implore Antony to yield.

12. For a recent analysis of this notion, see James Hirsh, "Rome and Egypt in *Antony and Cleopatra* and in Criticism of the Play," in *Antony and Cleopatra: New Critical Essays*, ed. Sara Munson Deats, 175–91 (New York: Routledge, 2005).

13. John F. Danby, *Poets on Fortune's Hill: Studies in Sidney, Shakespeare, Beaumont and Fletcher* (London: Faber & Faber, 1952), 140.

14. Maurice Charney, *Shakespeare's Roman Plays: The Function of Imagery in the Drama* (Cambridge, MA: Harvard University Press, 1961), 93.

15. See, for example, Charney, *Shakespeare's Roman Plays*, 93–112; Rosalie L. Colie, "*Antony and Cleopatra*: The Significance of Style," in *Shakespeare's Living*

Art (Princeton: Princeton University Press, 1974), 168, 177, 179. The most recent Arden edition attests to the tenacity of this reading: "For the Romans the ideal is measured in masculine, political, pragmatic, military terms, the subservience of the individual to the common good of the state, of personal pleasure to public duty, of private, domestic loyalties to the demands of empire. Alexandria, on the other hand, is a predominantly female society for which the ideal is measured in terms of the intensity of emotion, of physical sensation, the subservience of social responsibility to the demands of feeling." Wilders, *Antony and Cleopatra*, 28.

16. Danby, *Poets on Fortune's Hill*, 151.

17. Jonathan Gil Harris, "'Narcissus in thy face': Roman Desire and the Difference it Fakes in *Antony and Cleopatra*," *Shakespeare Quarterly* 45 (1994): 408–25; Carol Cook, "The Fatal Cleopatra," in *Shakespearean Tragedy and Gender*, ed. Shirley Nelson Garner and Madelon Sprengnether, 241–67 (Bloomington: Indiana University Press, 1996); Hirsh, "Rome and Egypt."

18. In 1958, Benjamin Spencer argued that the play "shows . . . an as yet undefined synthesis lying beyond both Rome and Egypt but partaking of the values of both." Spencer, "*Antony and Cleopatra* and the Paradoxical Metaphor," *Shakespeare Quarterly* 9 (1958): 373–78.

19. "No one gets far into *Antony and Cleopatra* without discovering that it is a play swarming with messengers": Macdonald, "Playing Till Doomsday," 85.

20. Janet Adelman, *The Common Liar: An Essay on Antony and Cleopatra* (New Haven: Yale University Press, 1973), esp. 34–39; Charnes, "Spies and Whispers"; Barfoot, "News from the Roman Empire."

21. Barfoot has commented similarly that "Verbally, orally, the Roman Empire is observed articulating itself, giving conscious expression to itself through word of mouth, and through deliberate acts of writing; and defining itself spatially, geographically, through the need to conduct business by letter and messenger, and historically by the provision of documents and of witnesses (since presumably what we see in the play, on and across the stage, is a mere fraction of all the messages that are being dispatched about the Empire)." However, Barfoot does not make a distinction, as I shall attempt, between Roman and Egyptian modes of communication. Barfoot, "News from the Roman Empire," 108.

22. F1 reads "abstracts"; F2 and all subsequent editions read "abstract." Wilders glosses "there" as "i.e., in the letter"; *Antony and Cleopatra*, ed. Wilders, 114, note on 1.4.8.

23. Barfoot notes, "Significantly, the main charge levelled against Lepidus when he is deposed is that he wrote letters to Pompey (3.5.8–10): clearly letter writing can be a contentious and dangerous occupation in the Roman Empire, and may be used in evidence against you." "News from the Roman Empire," 108–9.

24. John Michael Archer, *Old Worlds: Egypt, Southwest Asia, India, and Russia in Early Modern English Writing* (Stanford, CA: Stanford University Press, 2001), 23–62. Archer discusses Book 2 of Herodotus' *Histories*, trans. B.R. as *The Famous Hystory of Herodotus* (London: Thomas Marshe, 1584); Diodorus Siculus's *Library of History; Ethiopica*, trans. Thomas Underdowne in 1587.

25. Philemon Holland "The Summarie" to his trans., Plutarch, "Of Isis and Osiris," in *The Philosophie, commonlie called the Morals* (London: Arnold Hatfield, 1603), Qqqqqv–Qqqqq2r (1286–87).

26. Wilders sees this as a symptom of Alexandria's female/Egyptian emotionalism: "Hence Cleopatra must send to Antony every day a several greeting or she'll

unpeople Egypt"; *Antony and Cleopatra*, 28. Barfoot would counter: "At first we may suspect that Cleopatra's tally of 'twenty several messengers' is a characteristic piece of self-indulgent hyperbole; but we have no reason for believing that it is, and if what we as the audience see in the three hours' traffic on the stage is anything to go by, for all we know there are twenty thousand envoys currently employed at any single moment through the length and breadth of the Empire." "News from the Roman Empire," 108–9.

27. Plutarch, *Lives*, Llllv (938).

28. Samuel Brandon, *The Tragicomoedi of the virtuous Octauia* (London: William Ponsonby, 1598), B3r; for the letters see F8r (argument), F8v–H2r (Octavia to Antony), and H2r–H7v (Antony to Octavia); Samuel Daniel, "A Letter sent from Octauia to her husband Marcus Antonius into Egypt," in *Certaine Small Workes heretofore Divulged . . . & now againe by him corrected and augmented* (London: I.W. for Simon Waterson, 1607), F2r–7G2v.

29. "Sir, he fell vpon me, ere admitted, then: / Three Kings I had newly feasted, and did want / Of what I was i'th' morning: but next day / I told him of my selfe, which was as much / As to haue askt him pardon" (2.2.79–84).

30. See Anton J. L. van Hooff, *From Autothanasia to Suicide: Self-killing in Classical Antiquity* (New York: Routledge, 1990); Timothy D. Hill, *Ambitiosa Mors: Suicide and Self in Roman Thought and Literature* (New York: Routledge, 2004).

31. For important considerations of hands in the early modern period, see Jonathan Goldberg, "Hamlet's Hand," *Shakespeare Quarterly* 39 (1988): 307–27; Goldberg, *Writing Matter: From the Hands of the English Renaissance* (Stanford, CA: Stanford University Press, 1990); Katherine Rowe, *Dead Hands: Fictions of Agency, Renaissance to Modern* (Stanford, CA: Stanford University Press, 1999).

32. Plutarch, *Lives*, Llll 5r–v (945–6).

33. Leeds Barroll, *Politics, Plague, and Shakespeare's Theater: The Stuart Years* (Ithaca: Cornell University Press, 1991), 160–65.

34. Plutarch, *Les vies des hommes illvstres grecs et romains, compares l'vne avec l'avtre,* trans. Jacques Amyot with additions by Charles de l'Écluse (Paris: Pierre Cheuillot, 1579), EEE. iijr.

35. Mary [Sidney Herbert], Countess of Pembroke, *The Tragedie of Antonie, Doone into English* (London: William Ponsonby, 1595), F5r.

36. Robert Garnier, *M. Antoine, Tragedie* (Paris: Mamert Patisson, 1578), I.jr.

37. Richard Barckley, *A Discovrse of the Felicitie of Man, or His Summum bonum* (London: William Ponsonby, 1598), D6v–D7r: "*Antonius* turning to his man *Eros* whom he had prouided before to kill him if neede were, required him to performe his promise. *Eros* taking his sword in his hand, & making as though he would strike his master, suddenly turned the point to his own bodie, and thrust him selfe through, and fell downe dead at his maisters feet. Which when *Antonius* saw; well done *Eros* (quoth he) thou hast aptly taught me by thine owne example, that thou couldest not finde in thy heart to do it, and therewith he thrust the sword into his owne belly, & cast him selfe vpon his bed."

38. Robert Allott, *Wits Theater of the little World* (London: I.R. for N.L., 1599), K6v–K7r: "Eros, the seruant of Antonius, hauing promised to kill his Maister when hee requested him, drew his sword, and holding it as if hee would haue killed him, turned his Maisters head aside, and thrust the sword into his own body. *Plutarch*."

39. Brandon, *Tragicomoedi of the virtuous Octauia*, F4v.

40. Daniel, "The Tragedie of Cleopatra," in *Certaine Small Workes*, G3r–Lr, at G8r. The scene (Dircetus's account to Caesar of Antony's demise) is not in earlier editions of the play.

41. There is evidence that freedmen filled the posts of *procurator* (general manager, often involving several other functions), *lorarius* (overseer), *cocus* (cook), *structor* (headwaiter or meat-carver), *cubicularius* (keeper of the bedchamber), *nomenclator* (who reminded the master of his social duties), *pedisequi* (footmen), *pedagogi* and *grammatici*, doctors, clerical staff, including private secretary—(*a manu* or *amanuensis*), *anagostae* (readers), *librarii* (copyists), *librarioli* (bookmakers), *glutinatores* (roll-makers)—and, notably, letter carriers. A number of high-grade bureaucrats were also freedmen. See A. M. Duff, *Freedmen in the Early Roman Empire* (Oxford: Clarendon Press, 1928), 90–91; Susan Treggiari, *Roman Freedmen during the Late Republic* (1969; repr., Oxford: Clarendon Press, 2000), 68–81, 145–49; Aaron Kirschenbaum, *Sons, Slaves and Freedmen in Roman Commerce* (Jerusalem: Magnes Press/Washington, DC: Catholic University of America Press, 1987), 98, 127–40.

42. Plutarch, *Lives*, Kkkk 5r (933).

43. The Rhamnus moment had earlier been dramatized by Samuel Brandon:

> That *Antony*, with feare of treason mooued,
> Made *Ramnus* humbly sweare vpon his knee,
> To strike that head, that head so much beloued,
> From of his shoulders, when he once should see
> Vneuitable danger, to lay holde,
> Vpon himselfe . . .

Brandon does not, however, confer any status on Rhamnus. *Tragicomoedi of the virtuous Octauia*, B6r.

44. Barroll, *Politics, Plague, and Shakespeare's Theater*, 163.

45. Plutarch, *Lives*, Iiii 5r (921).

46. Ibid., Rrrrv (1010).

47. Barroll, *Politics, Plague, and Shakespeare's Theater*, 163n14.

48. Again, the passage is taken from North's Plutarch: "Whereupon *Antonius* caused him to be taken and well fauouredly whipped, and so sent him vnto *Caesar*: and bad him tell him that he made him angrie with him, because he shewed himselfe proud and disdainefull towards him, and now specially, when he was easie to be angred, by reason of his present miserie. To be short, if this mislike thee (said he) thou hast *Hipparchus* one of my infranchised bondmen with thee: hang him if thou wilt, or whippe him at thy pleasure, that we may crie quittance." Plutarch, *Lives*, Llll 4v (944). The character is named Thyrsus in North's Plutarch.

49. Plutarch, *Lives*, Llll 3v (942).

50. Daniel, "Tragedie of Cleopatra," G8v.

51. Ibid., G8r.

52. Wilders makes the general point, but somehow misses the earliest introduction of the character: "This is Plutarch's first reference to Eros, but Shakespeare introduces him as early as 3.11.24 [*sic*—it's in 3.5] and gives his name repeatedly in 4.4." On 258, note on 4.14.63–68.

53. Plutarch, *Lives*, Llll 3v (942).

54. In Edward Phillips's *The New World of English Words, or, A General Dictionary* (London: E. Tyler for Nath. Brooke, 1658), Antony's Eros is the definition of the word: "*Eros*, the servant of *Mark Antony*, who killed himself, because he would not see his master fall" (O2v). Only in the third edition of 1671 is the usual definition also given: "*Eros*, according to the *Ethnic* Poets the God of love, who in Latin is commonly called *Cupido*, also the name of *Mark Anthony's* servant who killed himself, because he would not see his Master fall, the word in Greek signifying love." *The New World of Words, or a General English Dictionary . . . the third Edition* (London: Nath. Brook, 1671), R2r.

55. F1 reads *Enobarbus*, while F2 gives *Eros*; editors often now follow F1, but separate "*Enobarbus*" from the imperative "Dispatch," turning it into a reflective sigh.

56. Kirschenbaum, *Sons, Slaves and Freedmen*, 135–38.

57. Angel Day, *The English Secretorie* (London: Richard Jones, 1592), P4v. On the figure of the secretary, see Jonathan Goldberg, *Writing Matter: From the Hands of the English Renaissance* (Stanford, CA: Stanford University Press, 1990), 231–78; Richard Rambuss, *Spenser's Secret Career* (Cambridge: Cambridge University Press, 1993), 30–48; Alan Stewart, "The Early Modern Closet Discovered," *Representations* 50 (1995): 76–100.

58. Rambuss, *Spenser's Secret Career*, 43. Rambuss cites a passage from Day's *English Secretorie*, whose elusive and fraught syntax betrays the concerns about the master–secretary relationship:

> Much is the felicity that the Master or Lord receaueth euermore of such a seruant, in the charie affection and regard of whome affying himselfe assuredly, hee findeth he is not alone a commaunder of his outward actions, but the disposer of his very thoughtes, yea hee is the *Soueraigne* of all his desires, in whose bosome hee holdeth the respose of his safety to be far more precious, then either estate, liuing, or aduauncement, whereof men earthly minded are for the most part desirous.

As Rambuss comments of the line "yea hee is the *Soueraigne* of all his desires," "Is the antecedent of 'he' the master, making the antecedent of 'his' the secretary? Or is it just the opposite?" The effect is that "Day does not allow the possibility of grammatically distinguishing between the master and the secretary, thus undoing the familiar and socially grounding distinctions between commander and commanded, disposer and disposed, sovereign and servant." Day, *English Secretorie*, R4v; Rambuss, *Spenser's Secret Career*, 46.

59. Plutarch, *Lives*, Mmmmr (949).

60. Charnes, 144–45.

61. "Annos undeviginiti natus exercitum privato consilio et privata impensa comparavi, per quem rem publicam a dominatione factionis oppressam in libertatem vindicavi" ["At the age of nineteen on my own responsibility and at my own expense I raised an army, with which I successfully championed the liberty of the republic when it was oppressed by the tyranny of a faction"]. *Res gestae divi Augusti*, ed. Brunt and Moore, 18, 19.

62. Colie, "*Antony and Cleopatra*: The Significance of Style," 180.

63. See, for example, Phyllis Rackin, "Shakespeare's Boy Cleopatra, the Decorum of Nature, and the Golden World of Poetry," *PMLA* 87 (1972): 201–12; Jyotsna Singh, "Renaissance Antitheatricality, Antifeminism, and Shakespeare's *Antony and Cleopatra*," *Renaissance Drama* n.s., 20 (1990): 99–121.

64. Phyllis Rackin makes a similar argument for Cleopatra's supremacy: "By admitting the reality of Rome, Shakespeare is able to celebrate the power of Egypt: by acknowledging the validity of the threat, he can demonstrate the special power that shows have to overcome the limitations of a reality that threatens to refute them." Rackin, "Shakespeare's Boy Cleopatra," 207.

Chronology

1564	William Shakespeare christened at Stratford-on-Avon April 26.
1582	Marries Anne Hathaway in November.
1583	Daughter Susanna born, baptized on May 26.
1585	Twins Hamnet and Judith born, baptized on February 2.
1587	Shakespeare goes to London, without family.
1589–90	*Henry VI, Part 1* written.
1590–91	*Henry VI, Part 2* and *Henry VI, Part 3* written.
1592–93	*Richard III* and *The Two Gentlemen of Verona* written.
1593	Publication of *Venus and Adonis*, dedicated to the Earl of Southampton; the *Sonnets* probably begun.
1593	*The Comedy of Errors* written.
1593–94	Publication of *The Rape of Lucrece*, also dedicated to the Earl of Southampton. *Titus Andronicus* and *The Taming of the Shrew* written.
1594–95	*Love's Labour's Lost, King John*, and *Richard II* written.
1595–96	*Romeo and Juliet* and *A Midsummer Night's Dream* written.
1596	Son Hamnet dies.

1596–97	*The Merchant of Venice* and *Henry IV, Part 1* written; purchases New Place in Stratford.
1597–98	*The Merry Wives of Windsor* and *Henry IV, Part 2* written.
1598–99	*Much Ado about Nothing* written.
1599	*Henry V*, *Julius Caesar*, and *As You Like It* written.
1600–01	*Hamlet* written.
1601	*The Phoenix and the Turtle* written; father dies.
1601–02	*Twelfth Night* and *Troilus and Cressida* written.
1602–03	*All's Well That Ends Well* written.
1603	Shakespeare's company becomes the King's Men.
1604	*Measure for Measure* and *Othello* written.
1605	*King Lear* written.
1606	*Macbeth* and *Antony and Cleopatra* written.
1607	Marriage of daughter Susanna on June 5.
1607–08	*Coriolanus*, *Timon of Athens*, and *Pericles* written.
1608	Mother dies.
1609	Publication, probably unauthorized, of the quarto edition of the *Sonnets*.
1609–10	*Cymbeline* written.
1610–11	*The Winter's Tale* written.
1611	*The Tempest* written. Shakespeare returns to Stratford, where he will live until his death.
1612	*A Funeral Elegy* written.
1612–13	*Henry VIII* written; The Globe Theatre destroyed by fire.
1613	*The Two Noble Kinsmen* written (with John Fletcher).
1616	Daughter Judith marries on February 10; Shakespeare dies April 23.
1623	Publication of the First Folio edition of Shakespeare's plays.

Contributors

HAROLD BLOOM is Sterling Professor of the Humanities at Yale University. Educated at Cornell and Yale universities, he is the author of more than 30 books, including *Shelley's Mythmaking* (1959), *The Visionary Company* (1961), *Blake's Apocalypse* (1963), *Yeats* (1970), *The Anxiety of Influence* (1973), *A Map of Misreading* (1975), *Kabbalah and Criticism* (1975), *Agon: Toward a Theory of Revisionism* (1982), *The American Religion* (1992), *The Western Canon* (1994), *Omens of Millennium: The Gnosis of Angels, Dreams, and Resurrection* (1996), *Shakespeare: The Invention of the Human* (1998), *How to Read and Why* (2000), *Genius: A Mosaic of One Hundred Exemplary Creative Minds* (2002), *Hamlet: Poem Unlimited* (2003), *Where Shall Wisdom Be Found?* (2004), and *Jesus and Yahweh: The Names Divine* (2005). In addition, he is the author of hundreds of articles, reviews, and editorial introductions. In 1999, Professor Bloom received the American Academy of Arts and Letters' Gold Medal for Criticism. He has also received the International Prize of Catalonia, the Alfonso Reyes Prize of Mexico, and the Hans Christian Andersen Bicentennial Prize of Denmark.

J. LEEDS BARROLL is professor emeritus at the University of Maryland Baltimore County and has been a scholar-in-residence at the Folger Shakespeare Library. He is the founder of the Shakespeare Association of America. His many publications include *Artificial Persons: The Formation of Character in the Tragedies of Shakespeare* and *Politics, Plague, and Shakespeare's Theater: The Stuart Years.*

MICHAEL GOLDMAN is an emeritus professor at Princeton University. His work includes *Shakespeare and the Energies of the Drama* and *The Actor's Freedom: Toward a Theory of Drama.*

NORTHROP FRYE was University Professor at the University of Toronto and also a professor of English at Victoria College at the University of Toronto for many years. He wrote numerous books, including the seminal work *Anatomy of Criticism.*

JONATHAN GIL HARRIS is a professor at George Washington University. He is the associate editor of *Shakespeare Quarterly.* He is the author of *Shakespeare and Literary Theory, Untimely Matter in the Time of Shakespeare* and other work.

SUSAN SNYDER is a professor emerita at Swarthmore College. She is the author of *The Comic Matrix of Shakespeare's Tragedies* and other work and the editor of Oxford's critical edition of *All's Well That Ends Well.* She has been a scholar-in-residence at the Folger Shakespeare Library.

THOMAS M. GREENE was an emeritus professor at Yale University. His work includes *The Light in Troy: Imitation and Discovery in Renaissance Poetry* and *The Vulnerable Text: Essays on Renaissance Literature.* He served as president of the Renaissance Society of America and was a recipient of their lifetime achievement award.

PATRICIA PARKER is a professor at Stanford University. She is the author of *Shakespeare from the Margins.* She is coeditor of *Shakespeare and the Question of Theory* and the editor of Norton and Arden editions of Shakespeare plays.

ALAN STEWART is a professor at Columbia University and International Director of the Centre for Editing Lives and Letters in London. His publications include *Shakespeare's Letters*, and he is editor of the *Henry VI* plays in the Barnes and Noble Shakespeare series.

Bibliography

Adelman, Janet. *Suffocating Mothers: Fantasies of Maternal Origin in Shakespeare's Plays,* Hamlet *to* The Tempest. New York: Routledge, 1992.

Anderson, Judith H. *Reading the Allegorical Intertext: Chaucer, Spenser, Shakespeare, Milton*. New York: Fordham University Press, 2008.

Berger, Harry, Jr. *Making Trifles of Terrors: Redistributing Complicities in Shakespeare*. Stanford, Calif.: Stanford University Press, 1997.

Bielmeier, Michael G. *Shakespeare, Kierkegaard, and Existential Tragedy*. Lewiston, N.Y.: Edwin Mellon Press, 2000.

Blanc, Pauline. "'All Joy of the Worm': Tragi-Comic Tempering in Shakespeare's *Antony and Cleopatra*." *Q/W/E/R/T/Y: Arts, Litteratures & Civilisations du Monde Anglophone* 10 (October 2000): 5–18.

Blits, Jan H. "*New Heaven, New Earth: Shakespeare's* Antony and Cleopatra." Lanham, Md.: Lexington, 2009.

Bloom, Allan. *Shakespeare on Love and Friendship*. Chicago: University of Chicago Press, 2000.

Brown, John Russell. *Shakespeare Dancing: A Theatrical Study of the Plays*. Basingstoke, England: Palgrave Macmillan, 2005.

Charnes, Linda. *Notorious Identity: Materializing the Subject in Shakespeare*. Cambridge, Mass.: Harvard University Press, 1993.

Charney, Maurice. *Wrinkled Deep in Time: Aging in Shakespeare*. New York: Columbia University Press, 2009.

Colie, Rosalie L. *Shakespeare's Living Art*. Princeton, N.J.: Princeton University Press, 1974.

Deats, Sara Munson, ed. Antony and Cleopatra: *New Critical Essays*. New York: Routledge, 2005.

Del Sapio Garbero, Maria, ed. *Identity, Otherness and Empire in Shakespeare's Rome*. Aldershot; Burlington, Vt.: Ashgate, 2009.

Dillon, Janette. *The Cambridge Introduction to Shakespeare's Tragedies*. Cambridge, UK; New York: Cambridge University Press, 2007.

Dollimore, Jonathan. *Radical Tragedy: Religion, Ideology and Power in the Drama of Shakespeare and His Contemporaries*. Basingstoke, England: Palgrave Macmillan, 2004.

Grene, Nicholas. *Shakespeare's Tragic Imagination*. New York, N.Y.: St. Martin's Press, 1992.

Halio, Jay L., and Hugh Richmond, ed. *Shakespearean Illuminations: Essays in Honor of Marvin Rosenberg*. Newark: University of Delaware Press, 1998.

Hall, Joan Lord. Antony and Cleopatra: *A Guide to the Play*. Westport, Conn.; London: Greenwood Press, 2002.

Holbrook, Peter. *Shakespeare's Individualism*. Cambridge, England: Cambridge University Press, 2010.

Kirsch, Arthur, ed. *W. H. Auden: Lectures on Shakespeare*. Princeton, N.J.: Princeton University Press, 2000.

Knight, George Wilson. *The Imperial Theme: Further Interpretations of Shakespeare's Tragedies Including the Roman Plays*. London; New York: Routledge, 2002.

Knowles, Ronald. *Shakespeare's Arguments with History*. Houndmills, Basingstoke, Hampshire; New York: Palgrave, 2002.

Ko, Yu Jin. *Mutability and Division on Shakespeare's Stage*. Newark: University of Delaware Press, 2004.

Kujawinska-Courtney, Krystyna. *Th' Interpretation of the Time: The Dramaturgy of Shakespeare's Roman Plays*. Victoria, B.C.: English Literary Studies, University of Victoria, 1993.

Langis, Unhae. *Shakespeare's Cleopatra as Virtuous Virago. Genre: An International Journal of Literature and the Arts* 28 (2008): 215–229.

Langley, Eric. *Narcissism and Suicide in Shakespeare and His Contemporaries*. Oxford; New York: Oxford University Press, 2009.

Levin, Harry. *Scenes from Shakespeare*, edited by Gwynne B. Evans. New York: Garland, 2000.

Lewis, Cynthia. *Particular Saints: Shakespeare's Four Antonios, Their Contexts, and Their Plays*. Newark: University of Delaware Press; London; Cranbury, N.J.: Associated University Presses, 1997.

Lindley, Arthur. *Hyperion and the Hobbyhorse: Studies in Carnivalesque Subversion*. Newark: University of Delaware Press; London; Cranbury, N.J.: Associated University Presses, 1996.

Logan, Robert. *Shakespeare's Marlowe*. Aldershot, Hants, England; Burlington, Vt.: Ashgate, 2006.

Madelaine, Richard. "'What are you?': The Staging of Messenger-Function in *Antony and Cleopatra*." *Parergon* 25, no. 1 (2008): 149–70.

Moncrief, Kathryn M., and Kathryn R. McPherson, ed. *Performing Maternity in Early Modern England*. Aldershot, England; Burlington, Vt.: Ashgate, 2007.

Miles, Geoffrey. *Shakespeare and the Constant Romans*. Oxford; New York: Clarendon Press, 1996.

Miller, Anthony. "*Varieties of Power* in Antony and Cleopatra." *Sydney Studies in English* 30 (2004): 42–59.

Paris, Bernard J. *Bargains with Fate: Psychological Crises and Conflicts in Shakespeare and His Plays*. New Brunswick, N.J.: Transaction Publishers, 2009.

Poole, William, and Richard Scholar, ed. *Thinking with Shakespeare: Comparative and Interdisciplinary Essays for A.D. Nuttall*. London: Legenda, 2007.

Riley, Dick. *Shakespeare's Consuls, Cardinals, and Kings: The Real History Behind the Plays*. New York: Continuum, 2008.

Rose, Mark, ed. *Twentieth Century Interpretations of* Antony and Cleopatra: *A Collection of Critical Essays*. Englewood Cliffs, N.J.: Prentice-Hall, 1977.

Rosenberg, Marvin. *The Masks of* Anthony and Cleopatra, edited and completed by Mary Rosenberg. Newark: University of Delaware Press, 2006.

Stone, James W. *Crossing Gender in Shakespeare: Feminist Psychoanalysis and the Difference Within*. New York: Routledge, 2010.

Streete, Adrian. "The Politics of Ethical Presentism: Appropriation, Spirituality and the Case of *Antony and Cleopatra*." *Textual Practice* 22, no. 3 (2008): 405–31.

Thomas, Vivian. *Shakespeare's Roman Worlds*. London; New York: Routledge, 1989.

Tucker, Kenneth. *Shakespeare and Jungian Typology: A Reading of the Plays*. Jefferson, N.C.: McFarland & Co., 2003.

Welsh, Alexander. *What Is Honor?: A Question of Moral Imperatives*. New Haven: Yale University Press, 2008.

Wofford, Susanne L., ed. *Shakespeare's Late Tragedies: A Collection of Critical Essays*. Upper Saddle River, N.J.: Prentice Hall, 1996.

Zender, Karl F. "*Shakespeare, Midlife, and Generativity*." Baton Rouge: Louisiana State University Press, 2008.

Acknowledgments

J. Leeds Barroll, "The View from out of Rome." From *Shakespearean Tragedy: Genre, Tradition and Change in* Antony and Cleopatra, pp. 241–78. Published by Folger Books. Copyright © 1984 Associated University Presses.

Michael Goldman, "*Antony and Cleopatra*: Action as Imaginative Command." From *Acting and Action in Shakespearean Tragedy*, pp. 112–39, 178–79. Copyright © 1985 by Princeton University Press.

Northrop Frye, "*Antony and Cleopatra.*" From *Northrop Frye on Shakespeare*, edited by Robert Sandler. Copyright © 1986 by Fitzhenry and Whiteside.

Jonathan Gil Harris, "'Narcissus in thy face': Roman Desire and the Difference It Fakes in *Antony and Cleopatra.*" From *Shakespeare Quarterly* 45, no. 4 (Winter 1994). Copyright © Folger Shakespeare Library 1994.

Susan Snyder, "Meaning in Motion: *Macbeth* and Especially *Antony and Cleopatra.*" From *Shakespeare: A Wayward Journey*, pp. 62–77. Published by University of Delaware Press. Copyright © 2002 Rosemont Publishing & Printing.

Thomas M. Greene, "Pressures of Context in *Antony and Cleopatra.*" From *Poetry, Signs, and Magic*, pp. 158–76, 298. Published by University of Delaware Press. Copyright © 2005 by Rosemont Publishing & Printing.

Index